BEYOND BASICS

Issues and Research in TESOL

Marianne Celce-Murcia
Editor

NEWBURY HOUSE PUBLISHERS, INC.
ROWLEY, MASSACHUSETTS 01969
ROWLEY • LONDON • TOKYO

1985

Library of Congress Cataloging in Publication Data
Main entry under title:

Beyond basics.

Includes index.
1. English language--Study and teaching--Foreign
speakers--Addresses, essays, lectures.   I. Celce-Murcia,
Marianne.
PE1128.A2B46   1985   428'.007   84-27236
ISBN 0-88377-288-4

NEWBURY HOUSE PUBLISHERS, INC.

Language Science
Language Teaching
Language Learning

ROWLEY, MASSACHUSETTS 01969
ROWLEY • LONDON • TOKYO

First printing: April 1985
5   4   3   2   1

Printed in the U.S.A.

In loving memory of my parents,
Ernest and Caroline Burgbacher

ACKNOWLEDGMENTS

Many people have assisted me in the completion of this anthology. My first and greatest debt is to my contributors. Without their cooperation, hard work, and patience this undertaking would have been impossible.

Special thanks are due Linda Galloway, Evelyn Hatch, Mary McGroarty, Amado Padilla, and Margarita Vincent, who graciously shared their expertise and helped me improve this volume in many ways.

I am also most grateful to Elizabeth Lantz of Newbury House for excellent editorial guidance, to Joan Samara for typing the manuscript with great care, and to Cindi Jenkins for assisting with the index and giving me the benefit of her skill and attention in this task.

Finally, love and thanks to my husband Daniel and my daughter Caroline for their patience and support while I was working on this project.

PREFACE

In 1979, when *Teaching English as a Second or Foreign Language,* which I coedited with Lois McIntosh, was first published by Newbury House, Lois and I promised ESL teachers a sequel that would deal from their perspective with more theoretical topics such as language acquisition, language policy, attitude and motivation, and language testing. This volume represents the long-promised sequel.

Because of the death in 1981 of my friend and colleague Lois McIntosh, I have had to carry out this project without her assistance. However, I have edited this book with fond memories of Lois, who is very much a part of me professionally.

CONTRIBUTORS' BIOGRAPHIES

Kathleen M. Bailey (Ph.D., University of California, Los Angeles, 1982) completed her M.A. in TESL as well as her Ph.D. in Applied Linguistics at UCLA. Her dissertation research dealt with the communication problems of foreign teaching assistants in U.S. universities. She has since coedited a book on this topic, which was published by the National Association for Foreign Student Affairs. *Second Language Acquisition Studies* is an earlier book, coedited with Michael H. Long and Sabrina Peck, and published in 1983 by Newbury House. Dr. Bailey's professional interests include classroom-centered research, language testing, and teacher training. She is currently the chairperson of the Division of American Language and Culture and director of the TESOL M.A. program at the Monterey Institute of International Studies in Monterey, California.

Marianne Celce-Murcia (Ph.D., University of California, Los Angeles, 1972) is a professor of English in the ESL section at UCLA, where since 1972 she has been teaching courses in English grammar and discourse and also courses in language methodology and materials development. Professor Celce-Murcia has worked outside the United States in Nigeria (1964–1966), Egypt (1980), and Canada (1983) and has presented invited papers and workshops in Mexico, Israel, and Brazil. She has served TESOL as associate convention chair (Mexico City, 1978), editorial advisory board member (1983), and executive board member-at-large (1984–1987). Professor Celce-Murcia is coeditor with Lois McIntosh of *Teaching English as a Second or Foreign Language* (Newbury House, 1979) and coauthor with Diane Larsen-Freeman of *The Grammar Book: An ESL/EFL Teacher's Course* (Newbury House, 1983).

Andrew D. Cohen (Ph.D., Stanford University, 1973) is an associate professor of applied linguistics at the School of Education, Hebrew University of Jerusalem, and is director of the Centre for Applied Linguistic Research. Professor Cohen also taught in the ESL section at UCLA (1972–1975, 1980–1981).

He is chair of the Israeli Association for Applied Linguistics and served as member-at-large on the TESOL executive board (1983–1984). Professor Cohen has published in the fields of bilingual education, language testing, and language learning. His major publications include *A Sociolinguistic Approach to Bilingual Education* (Newbury House, 1975) and *Testing Language Ability in the Classroom* (Newbury House, 1980). Cohen has spent at least six years of his life evaluating one or another federally funded bilingual education program in the United States.

Fred Davidson (M.A., University of Illinois, 1980) is a Ph.D. student in Applied Linguistics at the University of California, Los Angeles. He has taught ESL in Illinois, Ohio, and California, and has also taught abroad in Liberia. Currently, he is working as a test developer at National Education Corporation: International Division as well as pursuing his doctoral studies at UCLA. Mr. Davidson has presented papers at both affiliate and international TESOL conferences and has published in the areas of ESL reading syllabus design and language testing. His current interests include language testing, reading, and composition.

José L. Galvan (Ph.D., University of Texas at Austin, 1980) is assistant director of the undergraduate admissions office at UCLA, with direct responsibility over UCLA's educational development programs in the state's public schools. Dr. Galvan came to UCLA in 1976 as an assistant professor of English and taught in the TESL M.A. and Applied Linguistics Ph.D. programs. His articles on accentedness, language acquisition, and cross-cultural training have appeared in several journals and books.

Judy Wagner Gough (M.A., University of California, Los Angeles, 1975) is an instructor of English in the ESL section at Santa Monica College, where she has taught courses in composition, research, grammar, and intercultural communication since 1979. She has taught English in Iran and France and upon completing a master's in TESL at UCLA, she developed and coordinated an intensive ESL program at Marymount Palos Verdes College. She has published articles on second language acquisition in journals and anthologies devoted to second language learning and instruction.

Dayle Davidson Hartnett (Ph.D., University of California, Los Angeles, 1980) is director of the ESL program and a professor of English in the ESL section at Santa Monica College, where she has been teaching courses in English grammar, oral communication, and advanced writing since 1977. Dr. Hartnett has presented papers and workshops at CATESOL, TESOL, AERA, and the UCLA Conference on Human Brain Function. In addition, Dr. Hartnett works as a consultant in the areas of language training and intercultural communication.

Evelyn Hatch (Ph.D., University of California, Los Angeles, 1969) is a professor of English in the ESL section at UCLA. Professor Hatch has taught seminars in Egypt, Hungary, Morocco, and the Philippines as well as having presented invited papers in Mexico, Scotland, Finland, Greece, Canada, Sweden, Germany, and Denmark. She has taught English as a foreign and second language in the United States and abroad, and courses in linguistics, psycholinguistics, discourse analysis, ESL reading, and second language acquisition. Her major publications include *Second Language Acquisition* (1978), *Psycholinguistics: A Second Language Perspective* (1983), and (with H. Farhady) *Research Design and Statistics for Applied Linguistics* (1982). All three of these books are with Newbury House.

Barbara Hawkins (M.A., University of California, Los Angeles, 1982) is a Ph.D. student in Applied Linguistics at UCLA. She has taught ESL in the United States to junior high, senior high and university students for the past five years. She has also taught EFL in Spain for two years (1975–1977). She has presented papers in second language acquisition research at the tenth University of Michigan Conference on Applied Linguistics, 1983, and at TESOL '84 (Houston). Her paper from the tenth Michigan Conference, "Is an Appro-

priate Response Always So Appropriate?" appears in *Input in Second Language Acquisition,* edited by Susan Gass and Carolyn Madden (Newbury House, 1985).

Thom Hudson (M.A., University of California, Los Angeles, 1978), is in the UCLA Ph.D. program in Applied Linguistics and is a test developer at National Education Corporation: International Division. He has taught ESL/EFL in the United States and Egypt. From 1978 to 1980 he worked on a trinational English language curriculum development project in Cairo, Egypt, sponsored through UCLA/USAID, the British Council, and the Egyptian Ministry of Education. He has published and presented papers in the areas of reading, program evaluation, and language testing. His areas of interest are testing, research design, reading, and discourse analysis.

Diane Larsen-Freeman (Ph.D., University of Michigan, 1975) is on the faculty of the MAT program at the School for International Training in Brattleboro, Vermont. At SIT, she teaches courses in English grammar, language teaching methodology, second language acquisition, and testing and evaluation. From 1975 to 1978 she was an assistant professor of English in the ESL section at UCLA. Prior to teaching at UCLA, Dr. Larsen-Freeman taught EFL for two years in Malaysia as a Peace Corps volunteer and then for two years at the University of Michigan's English Language Institute. She has served as a member of the TOEFL research committee, as a consultant for USIS in Indonesia and Italy, and as an instructor in the Fulbright Commission's Italian Teachers of English Program. She is editor of *Discourse Analysis in Second Language Research* (Newbury House, 1980), coauthor (with M. Celce-Murcia) of *The Grammar Book: An ESL/EFL Teacher's Course* (Newbury House, 1983), and author of *Techniques and Principles in Language Teaching* (Oxford University Press, 1985). From 1980 to 1985 Dr. Larsen-Freeman was editor of *Language Learning,* a journal of applied linguistics.

Brian Lynch (M.A., University of California, Los Angeles, 1982) is a student in the Ph.D. program in Applied Linguistics at UCLA, where he has been a teaching associate in the ESL section for the past two years. He has also taught EFL in the Peoples Republic of China (1980–1981) at the Guangzhou English Language Center and worked as the assistant coordinator of UCLA TESL Programs in China (1981–1982). At present he is working as a test developer at National Education Corporation: International Division while pursuing his doctoral studies. His current research interests are language testing and program evaluation.

Mary McGroarty (Ph.D., Stanford University, 1982) is assistant professor in the ESL section at UCLA, where she teaches courses for ESL teachers in bilingual education, language policy with emphasis on minority language issues, and intercultural communication. Professor McGroarty has worked with English teachers outside the United States in Peru (1972–1974), where she held a Fulbright lectureship, and in Venezuela (1984). She has also taught ESL in Massachusetts, Minnesota, and California in various settings, including a high school, a vocational training program, and an intensive ESL course for university students. She has served the California TESOL organization as a member of the advisory committee recommending standards for ESL certification and as a member of the steering committee for a conference dealing with partnerships in ESL research between researchers and practitioners.

Elite Olshtain (Ph.D., University of California, 1979) teaches Linguistics, The Structure of English, Second Language Acquisition, Discourse Analysis, TEFL Methodology and Material Development, at the School of Education and the Department of Linguistics at Tel Aviv University in Israel. Since 1979 she has headed an M.A. program in TEFL at TAU. She has coordinated a team of textbook writers producing a series entitled *English for Speakers of Hebrew* and has acted as linguistic advisor for the English programs on instructional television in Israel. Since 1978, Professor Olshtain has been working with an inservice program designed to prepare Italian

teachers of English as teacher trainers. She has published professional articles in journals and anthologies and is coauthor (with Fraida Dubin) of *Facilitating Language Learning* (McGraw-Hill, 1977), *Reading by All Means* (Addison-Wesley, 1981) and *Three Easy Pieces* (Addison-Wesley, 1984).

Sabrina Peck (M.A., University of California, Los Angeles, 1977) is a doctoral candidate in Applied Linguistics at UCLA. She has presented papers at TESOL and at second language research conferences, published articles on child second language acquisition, and coedited with Kathleen Bailey and Michael Long a volume entitled *Second Language Acquisition Studies* (Newbury House, 1983).

Rina G. Shapira (M.A., University of California, Los Angeles, 1976), who returned to Israel in spring, 1984, studied both English as a Second Language and Linguistics while at UCLA. Her research interests included attitude and motivation, second language acquisition, and syntax and semantics. In addition to teaching ESL for the UCLA Extension Division, she also taught Hebrew at several schools in the Los Angeles area.

Marguerite Ann Snow (M.A. in TESL, University of California, Los Angeles, 1979) is a doctoral candidate in Applied Linguistics at UCLA, where she is pursuing her research interests in immersion foreign language education, English grammar, and language methodology. Ms. Snow has worked with both native English-speaking and ESL university students, developing content-based English curricula, and has taught adult ESL in Los Angeles since 1979. She has presented papers at many conferences, including AILA, TESOL, and ACTFL, and she has published her research in *Second Language Acquisition Studies* (Newbury House, 1983), several professional journals, and in reports to the U.S. Department of Education (Grant No. GOO-82-01527) and the National Institute of Education.

INTRODUCTION

The editor of this anthology, *Beyond Basics,* assumes that readers will already have some background in language methodology; that is to say, it is assumed that they know about current methods and approaches to language teaching and that they understand how the four skills (listening, speaking, reading, writing) and the three language areas (pronunciation, grammar, and vocabulary) can be taught effectively. A basic ESL/EFL methodology text such as *Teaching English as a Second or Foreign Language* (eds. Celce-Murcia and McIntosh, 1979, Newbury House) can provide the initial professional orientation that should come prior to the use of this complementary volume.

Moreover, the editor of this anthology also assumes that most readers will have had some prior teaching experience; it is just such a combination of prior basic knowledge and teaching experience that renders pertinent most of the questions addressed in this anthology:

- Why do certain language methods/teachers/environments produce good results with some learners but not with others?

- Why do almost all second language learners tend to make similar errors when learning English?

- Under what conditions is classroom instruction productive, given that many learners acquire a language without any formal instruction?

- What is the best way to develop a language program or a language course?

The chapters in this anthology have been written to help ESL teachers begin to formulate their own answers to questions such as these.

Another more general question that motivated this anthology is:

- What should be the relationship between research and teaching (or researchers and teachers)?

In reality, teachers often feel intimidated by research, and researchers are often condescending when interacting with classroom teachers. Such a situation is counterproductive, since the language classroom is one of the best laboratories for answering research questions. A knowledgeable and cooperative language teacher can be the researcher's best partner and best source of data and ideas. For example, language teachers and students can be observed or interviewed and their interactions both inside and outside the classroom can be recorded, transcribed, and analyzed. The language performance of learners—oral or written—can be elicited in a variety of ways and then analyzed and evaluated. In the long run, therefore, partnerships between teachers and researchers will be more productive than the current trend toward segregation.

For this partnership to take place, teachers must understand what the research process is, namely, (1) posing relevant questions and (2) making appropriate methodological selections—from among many options —for pursuing answers to the questions. It is possible that some research questions pertinent to language teaching can be answered by going to the library, e.g., What has been the official government position in country X regarding the status of English over the past 30 years? Other questions lend themselves to observational research, e.g., What are the various reactions that junior high ESL learners manifest when given overt verbal teacher correction in the classroom? Yet other questions require survey-type research methods such as the use of polls or questionnaires, e.g., How do the residents of community X feel about bilingual education? Do they want this type of education for their children? And many other questions require that experimental, quantitative research be carried out, e.g., Do ESL learners with good listening comprehension skills perform better on integrative language measures such as dictation or cloze tests than do ESL learners of comparable global proficiency but with significantly weaker listening skills?

In language learning and teaching there is thus more than one kind of research and more than one kind of researcher. Teachers should seek out researchers who are working in areas of greatest interest to the teachers themselves: Researchers should seek out teachers whose practical experience will complement the researchers' theoretical concerns. As teachers become better informed about research questions and research options, they can participate as partners with researchers—or become researchers themselves—as an integral part of their professional development.

In the best of all possible worlds, every ESL teacher will be a researcher and every ESL researcher a teacher. In this way we will ultimately arrive at better questions and better answers to our questions. This at least has been part of the philosophy guiding the development of this anthology.

The goal of the anthology therefore is to help ESL teachers go beyond their day-to-day routines and preoccupations. The background in ESL research concerns that this text provides should go a long way toward making ESL teachers aware of questions which are crucial in our field but which have not yet yielded clear-cut answers or solutions. It should also assist interested and motivated ESL teachers in beginning to seek out answers to such questions.

It is believed that this anthology will be useful to ESL teachers who are taking a survey course in second language research. It will also be useful to graduate students in TESL or Applied Linguistics who are looking for a thesis or dissertation topic. Finally, it will be a useful reference for those teachers in the field who have good professional background but who wish to learn more about the research being done in their field with an eye toward becoming involved in the research process.

All ten chapters were written especially for this anthology. As with the previous volume in this set (i.e., *Teaching English as a Second or Foreign Language*), each chapter concludes with a set of discussion questions, a number of related suggested activities—some of which are mini research projects–and some suggestions for further reading to stimulate and guide anyone who gets interested in a given chapter's content and who wants to learn more about the topic. Following the composition of the previous volume, everyone who has contributed to this anthology is (or has been) at UCLA as a professor and/or a graduate student.

A total of seventeen authors have contributed to this anthology. We felt that readers might like to know something about the background and experiences of the contributors; thus a short biographical statement on each of the contributors precedes this introduction.

CONTENTS

PART I
THE LEARNER

INTRODUCTION

In this first section of the anthology we begin by looking at the second language learner as a complex individual with social, psychological, and cognitive attributes, which to a great extent determine the learner's attitudes and aptitudes.

In this first chapter Snow, with Shapira, provides us with an excellent overview of the relevant research that has been done on attitude and motivation over the years, while Hartnett, in the second chapter, introduces us to the elusive domain of cognitive research, which encompasses notions such as hemisphere dominance and cognitive style—and their potential interrelationships.

Together these two chapters provide us with the background we need to begin to be able to answer one of TESOL's most important and persistent questions: why do some people succeed so much more than others at learning a second or foreign language?

THE ROLE OF SOCIAL-PSYCHOLOGICAL FACTORS IN SECOND LANGUAGE LEARNING

Marguerite Ann Snow *with*
Rina G. Shapira

The question of why some second language learners achieve greater proficiency than others under the same conditions has been puzzled over for many years. Numerous explanations have been offered to account for such variation in second language achievement. In this chapter we will consider the role of social-psychological variables and their influence on second language acquisition processes. We will begin with a historical overview of this research area, move on to discuss more recent developments in social-psychological research, and finally show how these notions have been incorporated into current theories of second language acquisition.

As in all areas of research, there exists a wide range of opinion as to the appropriate and acceptable directions that inquiry into social-psychological factors should take. While there is little dispute about the significant role of affective variables in second language acquisition, much debate has centered on the measurement of these variables. Some have argued that serious theoretical and statistical problems weaken the validity of previous research studies (Oller and Perkins, 1978; Oller, 1981); others have countered that validity of research on affective variables is supported by a strong empirical base with large samples, much replication, and diverse research settings (Gardner, 1980; Gardner and Gliksman, 1982). With this in mind, the reader should approach the study of social-psychological factors with a critical eye, looking for both the strengths and the weaknesses of previous research.

BACKGROUND

For many years scholars have tried to find an acceptable explanation for the fact that some people can successfully learn a second or foreign language while others fail. An early attempt to explain this phenomenon was provided by Carroll and Sapon (1959). Following up on traditional folk beliefs which held that some people simply have "a knack for languages" or "an ear for languages," Carroll and Sapon tried to account for individual variation by measuring language learning aptitude. While it is true that some learners more than others have the mental capacity to learn languages, the fact that everyone acquires a first language is proof that we all have language learning aptitude. Moreover, not all learners with high language aptitude are good language learners, and conversely, not all low-aptitude students demonstrate poor language proficiency. Thus, only to a certain extent can language aptitude explain the variance in second language proficiency.

A second approach to the issue of individual differences is the belief that proficiency in the target language is related to methods and techniques of instruction. As a result, there have been many changes in teaching methodologies during past decades. However, the division between students who easily achieve a high level of proficiency and those who make slower progress has still existed within every major method of instruction, whether grammar translation, audio-lingual, audio-visual, cognitive code, or programmed instruction. Even with more recent methods such as Silent Way, Suggestopedia, or the Natural Approach, there are no claims that all students will progress in the same way.

The third approach, the social-psychological perspective, is the main focus of this chapter. Gardner and Lambert (1959) were the first to look at the relationship between attitudes and motivation and achievement in a second language. In their landmark study, they identified two independent factors which were related to achievement in French by English-speaking high school students: language aptitude and an attitudinal/motivational dimension. The attitudinal/motivational dimension was further divided into three variables: attitudes toward French Canadians, learner orientation, and motivational intensity. Their findings indicated that achievement in French was related to attitudes toward French Canadians and an interest in learning French in order to become socially closer to the French-speaking community.

In their 1972 book *Attitudes and Motivation in Second Language Learning,* Gardner and Lambert further define the attitudinal variables related to second language achievement. They were influenced by the work of Mowrer (1950) in child language development. Mowrer argued that language acquisition is motivated by children's desires to be like important members of their families and, as they grow older, of their linguistic community. Mowrer labeled this desire to imitate the parents as "identification." Drawing on the notion of "identification" in first language acquisition, Gardner and Lambert suggested parallels with second language learning. Second language learners should have the desire to identify with the target group whose language they are learning. Furthermore, this desire needs to be reinforced by a curiosity and interest in the group in order to produce the motivation needed to acquire competence over a period of time.

INTEGRATIVE MOTIVATION

Gardner and Lambert introduced the term "integrative motive" to describe the second language acquisition process similar to Mowrer's identification process in first language acquisition. They defined the term as "a willingness to become a member of another ethnolinguistic group." In the learning context integrative motivation will be manifested by a wish on the part of the learner "to learn more about the other cultural community, because he is interested in it in an open-minded way to the point of eventually being accepted as a member of that group" (Gardner and Lambert, 1972, p. 3).

For a student to have integrative motivation, he has to have specific characteristics such as inquisitiveness, openness to new ideas, and certain behavioral patterns. These qualities make him vulnerable with regard to changing his feelings toward his native community. An integratively oriented student might develop a degree of dissatisfaction with his native culture. Simultaneously, he might find out that "his new skills permitted him to leave his own cultural group and become a member of the new group whose language he had nearly mastered" (Gardner and Lambert, 1972, p. 16). This can be very damaging, since he might find himself lost between two cultures, having found fault with his own and not quite making it with the new, in other words, having feelings of anomie.[1]

INSTRUMENTAL MOTIVATION

Gardner and Lambert introduced the term "instrumental motivation" as a form of orientation that contrasts with integrative motivation. Instrumental motivation is defined as a desire to gain social recognition or economic advantages through knowledge of a second or foreign language. Learners who are instrumentally motivated have self-oriented reasons for learning the language; they hope to derive benefits from knowing the other language, such as getting a better job or meeting the "right" friends. Learners who have instrumental motivation are mainly interested in the target group for the purposes of personal satisfaction; they have little genuine interest in the language and culture of the people. Consequently, instrumentally motivated students will identify with their own native language and culture. There will be no foreign cultural interference with their sense of group belonging. In extreme cases, instrumentally motivated students may develop ethnocentric or authoritarian attitudes which can lead to strong feelings of prejudice against members of the target group.

MOTIVATIONAL INTENSITY

Another important variable in the attitudinal/ motivational dimension is the effort students are willing to invest in their studies and their persistence in studying the second language. Motivational intensity can be measured by asking students about their interest in the work required in the foreign language course, their efforts to improve their language skills outside of class, and personal desire to continue study of the language.

Gardner and Lambert stated that there should be no differences in the degree of motivational intensity that is associated with either integrative or instrumental motivation. In other words, an instrumentally oriented student can be just as intense or more so in his studies as an integratively oriented one. They hypothesized, however, that the integrative motive might be the "better" type of motivation for second language study. They reasoned that the acquisition of a new language involves much more than the acquisition of words, grammar, and sounds of the new language. Instead, they represent distinctive aspects of the behavior of the target cultural group. Since the integratively oriented learner has a greater desire to associate with and be like the new linguistic community, this orientation may be more likely to sustain a long-term effort and therefore be more effective in promoting mastery of the second language.

EARLY STUDIES
OF SOCIAL-PSYCHOLOGICAL VARIABLES

The Canadian setting

When the first French immersion program for English-speaking children was established in 1965 in the Montreal suburb of St. Lambert, there began an unprecedented opportunity to investigate more thoroughly the relationship between social-psychological variables and second language acquisition. To understand the context of this research, it is necessary to describe in detail the background of this original experiment in immersion education.

Genesee (1983) has described the first immersion program as a "community-based experiment in social change through educational innovation." Realizing that linguistic barriers divided the English-speaking and French-speaking communities in Montreal, a group of parents called for an improvement in French as a second language (FSL) instruction in the elementary schools. Their effort reflected a growing realization that young people needed bilingual skills in order to participate more fully in the social, economic, and political life of the community.

With the consultation of Wallace Lambert and Wilder Penfield of McGill University, an innovative new model of second language instruction began to take shape. In the resulting St. Lambert immersion program, the second language, French, was used as the exclusive language of instruction for the first three years of elementary school, with the addition of English language arts in third grade. The underlying assumption of the immersion model is that all normal children are innately capable of simultaneously learning a second language, without retardation of native language skills.

Lambert and Tucker (1972) provide a comprehensive evaluation of the St. Lambert experiment. Their purpose was "to assess and evaluate the impact of elementary schooling conducted in a second language on the linguistic, intellectual, and attitudinal development of the children" (p. 8). Four classes took part in their evaluation: the experimental class, a follow-up class, an English control class, and a French control class, all having been matched on intelligence and socio-economic background.

After seven years of longitudinal study, the findings of the St. Lambert program indicated:

1.   The students had suffered no deficit in cognitive development.

2.   The student's English language proficiency was comparable to that of their monolingual peers who had received all instruction in English.

3.   The student's French language proficiency approached that of native French-

speaking peers. It was significantly better than that of English-speaking peers receiving 20 to 25 minutes of daily instruction in French as a second language.

4. The students' scholastic achievement (e.g., mathematics and science) was comparable to that of their monolingual English-speaking peers.

5. The children seemed satisfied with the program and expressed no desire to transfer to a conventional program.

6. The children had developed a sensitivity toward French and English Canadians and toward the notion of cultural diversity.

In addition to providing students with the opportunity to acquire linguistic skills in French, the immersion experience also had an effect on attitudinal development, as their parents had hoped. Specifically, at the end of sixth grade the experimental students were found to identify strongly with their own ethnic group (English Canadians) as well as with French Canadians and French-speaking Europeans. Since the English control groups (who were enrolled in the FSL program) showed a similar tendency, the development of positive attitudes toward the target group was considered a result of their respective bilingual experiences. In contrast, the French Canadian control students showed sharp attitude differences which favored their own ethnic group and disfavored other groups.

Gardner and Lambert (1972) extended their attitudinal research beyond the Canadian setting in order to test the generalizability of their earlier findings. Three American settings, Louisiana, Maine, and Connecticut, were studied and an international perspective was added by their work in the Philippines. Each setting was selected on the basis of a particular constellation of sociocultural factors. In Louisiana and Maine, the participants were English-speaking American high school students studying French in bicultural communities where French language and traditions were still strong. These two groups of students were similar to those investigated in the Montreal studies. In addition to the English-speaking high school students in these two locations, French-speaking American high school students were included in the study because they represented members of a cultural minority group. These students spoke French at home but attended English language schools where they were also studying French. The Connecticut setting provided a more typical example of American high school students studying French. In this foreign language setting the reference group was European French speakers, a people very far removed from the American context. Lastly, in the Philippine setting English is the predominant language of instruction but rarely the language of the home. In each site, a comprehensive battery of standardized tests and attitudinal and motivation measures were administered.

In the American settings, there was strong evidence for the importance of language learning aptitude and intelligence in the French language proficiency of the English-speaking high school students. In all three settings, aptitude played an important role in the students' acquisition of academic French skills in grammar, vocabulary, and reading, more so in Louisiana and Connecticut than in Maine. In addition to predicting success in these more passive aspects of French, the aptitude and intelligence measures were also powerful indicators of grades received in French.

Similarly, in the three settings Gardner and Lambert found that English-speaking students who were highly motivated to learn French received good grades in French. For each context, however, there was a distinctive attitudinal basis for their high motivation. In Louisiana, parental support was found to underlie motivation. In Maine, it was the students' identification with their French teacher and sensitivity to other people's feelings which provided the basis for motivation, and in Connecticut motivation seemed to stem from an integrative motivation toward the language learning process and a realization of the usefulness of knowing French. Ethnocentric attitudes also negatively influenced student achievement in all three settings.

As mentioned, Gardner and Lambert were also interested in how members of a linguistic minority group approach the school learning of their own language. They found that the attitudes of the French-speaking American students toward their own ethnolinguistic group and the American way of life influenced their linguistic development in both French and English. Three linguistic outcomes were found—dominance of French over English, dominance of English over French, and bilingual competence. The particular outcome, they discovered, was determined in part at least by the way the students deal with their bicultural heritage. Those students who were content and comfortable with their dual linguistic and cultural background were "... psychologically free to become bilinguals" (p. 136).

The investigation of the relationship between attitudes and motivation shifted to a foreign setting in the Philippine study. Not only was there a change in setting but also a change in the target language. In the Philippines, English has become the second national language and the medium of instruction in the early grades. It is also the essential language for economic advancement. The results of the Philippine study confirmed the cross-cultural validity of many of Gardner and Lambert's basic notions, but also demonstrated that certain attitudinal dimensions are tied to the particular cultural context. For example, they found that Filipino students who were instrumentally motivated and received strong parental support were successful in developing a high proficiency in English.

Based on their studies in the Canadian, American, and Filipino settings, Gardner and Lambert conclude that where there is an urgency to learn the second language, for instance, in the Philippines, or with linguistic minority groups, instrumental motivation is more effective. On the other hand, where the language learning process is a form of enrichment as in the case of most foreign language programs, integrative motivation produces better results.

Following the Gardner and Lambert research, others have attempted to replicate their findings. Lukmani (1972) tested the English proficiency of Marathi-speaking high school students in India. In her study, English language proficiency correlated significantly with instrumental motivation, while integratively motivated students scored lower on the test of language proficiency. Lukmani concluded that "English proficiency arises from the desire to use English not as a means of entry into a reference group, but as a tool with which to understand and cope with the demands of modern life" (p. 271).

The work of Lambert and Tucker in Montreal led to the establishment of the first immersion program in the United States in the fall of 1971. Modeled after the St. Lambert experiment, the Culver City program offers the immersion experience in Spanish. Results from the Culver City Spanish Immersion Program (SIP) have been remarkably similar to the Canadian findings. Students are making steady progress in acquiring Spanish as a second language while making normal development in their first language, English. Standardized test scores indicate that at each grade they are at or above grade level in academic subjects such as reading and mathematics (Campbell, 1983).

The attitudinal development of Spanish immersion students has also been of great interest. Just as the social and political situation in Canada created compelling reasons for bilingual/bicultural education, the southern California setting reflects a similar need. Using the Cross Cultural Attitude Inventory and the Matched Guise procedure, Waldman (1975) assessed the attitudinal development of the pilot class after four years of immersion education. Her findings indicated that while both the immersion students and monolingual English controls preferred the Anglo culture over the Mexican-American, the immersion students gave the Mexican-American culture higher ratings than the other groups. The results from the Matched Guise procedure were consistent with this finding. All groups preferred the English Guise, but the immersion students rated the Spanish guise higher than the controls. Waldman concluded that the immersion students had developed less ethnocentric notions than had students in traditional English-only programs. In addition, they demonstrated more positive (or less negative) feelings toward the Mexican-American culture and Spanish speakers. Finally, the immersion students had retained the same positive attitudes toward Anglo culture and English speakers as students schooled in traditional elementary programs.

In sum, these early studies provide evidence for the separate roles played by intelligence and aptitude, and attitudes and motivation in second language development. The diversity shown from setting to setting suggests that the type of motivation most effective for second language achievement depends on the particular situation in which the language is learned. For certain communities integrative motivation serves the students best, in other communities it is instrumental motivation that is most productive, and still in other settings both integrative and instrumental motivation team to yield the best results.

RECENT DEVELOPMENTS
IN SOCIAL-PSYCHOLOGICAL RESEARCH

The pioneering work of Gardner and Lambert and others during the sixties and seventies established the importance of social-psychological factors in second language acquisition and laid the groundwork for further investigation of the effect of these factors. While respecting the contributions of previous research, many researchers today have called for the broadening of social-psychological research to encompass a wider scope. It is the purpose of this section to present recent developments in the study of the role of attitudes and motivation in second language learning.

Ethnic identity
Cziko, Lambert, and Gutter (1979) sought to investigate stable features of attitudes through the technique of multidimensional scaling.

This strategy, they felt, was a better alternative to evaluative attitude research which yielded a great deal of variation when using young children as subjects. In their study, respondents are asked to indicate how similar/dissimilar (as compared to how good/ bad) they think each of a pair of concepts is, e.g., myself/English Canadians. A comparison of French immersion and nonimmersion students revealed similar responses. Both groups perceived themselves to be more like English Canadians, thereby identifying primarily with their own ethnolinguistic group. Their reactions, however, were different toward French Canadians. The immersion students tended to perceive the English and French clusters as more similar, and likewise, tended to view themselves as more similar to French Canadians. Thus, Cziko et al. conclude that the early bilingual experience has reduced the social distance between the immersion students and the target language group. The bilingual experience "narrows the gulf," reducing the dividing influences of ethnicity.

An important finding on the development of ethnolinguistic attitudes is reported by Genesee (1983). Findings comparing the attitudes of immersion and nonimmersion students have been quite consistent, with immersion students being more positive toward members of the target language group. There is strong evidence, however, for a developmental shift in these positive attitudes. Thus, immersion students' attitudes are initially positive in the early grades, but eventually come to resemble those of the English controls by the later grades. Genesee attributes this attitudinal shift to the lack of real social contact with French Canadians, a necessary basis for sustaining positive attitudes over an extended period of time.

Day (1980) also reports evidence for a developmental shift in attitudes and linguistic preferences, though with much younger children. He looked at the attitudes and preferences of kindergarten and first grade children toward Hawaii Creole English and Standard English. Both groups of subjects came from urban elementary schools in Honolulu; one was located in one of the least desirable, industrial areas of the city, the other in a more residential neighborhood where many children of professional parents lived. Both kindergarten and first grade children in the higher socioeconomic neighborhood preferred English, as did the first graders in the lower socioeconomic school. In contrast, the kindergartners at the lower socioeconomic school expressed a preference for and had positive attitudes toward Hawaii Creole English. Thus, the attitudinal shift occurred in the first two grades of elementary school.

Motivational support

Genesee, Rogers, and Holobow (1983) have proposed to expand the parameters of the social context and its role in second language learning. They believe that the social context should not be defined solely in terms of the second language group but rather should be examined from an intergroup perspective. Specifically, it is their contention that positive attitudes and motivation toward second language learning may be necessary for learning to occur, but they may not be adequate for sustaining the entire learning process. Since it is the social context, they claim, in which learning occurs, it might be instructive to consider the extent to which learners believe or expect that their motives for learning the second language are supported by the target language group. For instance, learners who perceive the target group as supportive of their language learning effort would be encouraged and, as a result, would proceed with the steps necessary to learn the language. Consequently, these learners would demonstrate higher levels of proficiency.

The motivational support hypothesis was tested by asking adolescent English-speaking Canadian students why they were learning French as a second language and why French Canadians wanted them to learn French. Their findings indicated that second language learners' perceptions of the target language group's support were positively correlated with the learners' self-rated proficiency in French and with their willingness to

belong to social groups which include French Canadians. Based on these findings, Genesee et al. recommend that social-psychological models of second language learning need to take into account the role of intergroup factors.

Language use

The principal hypothesis in research on the role of social-psychological variables in second language learning has been the following: learners whose attitudes are highly positive will have increased motivation. This motivation is the precursor for making contacts with speakers of the second language. These language use opportunities provide the basis for the attainment of advanced proficiency in the second language. To test this hypothesis, researchers have begun to look at the relationship between social-psychological variables and language use.

In a study of the relationship between motivation and language use behavior in the French classroom, Gliksman (1976) hypothesized that the integrative motive influenced individual differences in the amount of active participation in class. Prior to the term, measures of attitudes and motivation were obtained for each subject in the study. During the term, observers rated the subjects on several specified dimensions. Gliksman's findings indicated that integratively motivated students volunteered more frequently and made more correct responses than their non-integrative counterparts.

In a study of language use outside the classroom, Genesee (1978) found that the immersion students he sampled felt more comfortable and confident when speaking French with Francophones than did non-immersion students; however, there was no evidence of greater language use outside of school. Moreover, their second language use was primarily "reactive"; the immersion students were not willing to initiate conversations, but they would respond in French when required to in interpersonal situations. Genesee attributes their reluctance to speak French to students' beliefs that their speaking skills are weak (perceptions borne out by test scores).

Snow (1979) reports on the attitudes of students in the Culver City Spanish Immersion Program (SIP). As in the Genesee study, the SIP students had very positive attitudes toward learning the second language, but in judging their own Spanish-speaking abilities, they gave less positive ratings. A majority of the students reported speaking Spanish very frequently outside of school; however, on closer inspection it was learned that their conversational partners were rarely native speakers of Spanish. Although they had contact with native Spanish speakers, most spoke English with them. Hence, positive attitudes may not be a sufficient precursor to the use of the second language in many settings, either because students lack confidence in speaking the second language or because powerful sociolinguistic factors mitigate against use of the less dominant language.

Assimilative motivation

Graham (1984) has introduced the term "assimilative motivation" to refer to the drive, particularly in younger learners, to become indistinguishable members of a particular dialect or speech community. He claims that this type of motivation is: (1) essential to normal first language acquisition; (2) the primary impetus for developing nativelike speech in a second language; (3) mainly a peer-group phenomenon; (4) strongest during infancy and childhood and gradually becomes weaker through adolescence and into adulthood; (5) capable of being disrupted even during childhood by certain external social factors.

Graham makes a clear distinction between integrative and assimilative motivation. Integrative motivation refers to the desire on the part of the language learner to acquire the target language in order to talk with or find out about members of the target language group. It does not imply or require direct contact with a target language peer group. The majority of research has identified integrative motivation by having the learners make "conscious reasoned" choices among alternatives on a questionnaire. Assimilative motivation, on the other hand, may require prolonged contact with the target language peer group. It is intuitive and often not identified by conscious processes. It can be identified only through observation.

Graham's evidence for the role of assimilative motivation comes from studies of child language acquisition, dialect studies, and bilingual immersion programs. He is not claiming that learners must be assimilatively motivated in order to develop a high level of proficiency in a second language. But, he argues, such learners will not likely acquire *all* the characteristics of native-like speech without assimilative motivation. Graham has proposed a new construct which must now be followed up by actual observational studies to confirm its validity as a social-psychological process in second language learning.

Learners' attitudes toward the learning situation

Brown (1983) suggests that a more global view of motivation is needed in social-psychological research. Her study looks at the learners' views toward the language learning situation and how these views relate to success in language learning. She is also interested in determining whether or not there is a relationship between the age of the learners and their views of the language learning situation. Her subjects were 33 students learning Spanish as part of their voluntary missionary service. Approximately half of the subjects were "young" (under 25 years of age) and half "older" (over 55 years of age).

Brown found that for the senior learners, perception of the teachers' skills and attitudes was predictive of success while overconcentration on feelings about methods and materials, and on repetition and review predicted lack of success. In contrast, for the younger learners, perceptual focus on grammar, vocabulary, and repetition and review were predictive of success; focus on time or on attitudes and emotions predicted lack of success. Thus, there is a relationship between what a learner focuses on in the language learning situation and how well the learner does. In addition, the relationship between the learner's perception of factors and success does not appear to be the same for younger and older learners.

THE ROLE OF SOCIAL-PSYCHOLOGICAL FACTORS IN THEORIES OF SECOND LANGUAGE ACQUISITION

Much of the early research on attitudes and motivation was aimed at providing empirical evidence for the vital role played by social-psychological variables in second language acquisition. The research has been convincing enough that many proposed theories of second language acquisition have incorporated these notions, some to a greater extent than others. It is the purpose of this section to provide brief descriptions of three current theories which have social-psychological components.

Schumann's pidginization hypothesis (1978) predicts that social and psychological distance will impede the language development of second language learners. He lists a series of social factors such as dominance, assimilation, and attitudes which either promote or inhibit social solidarity between two groups and thus influence the way a second language group acquires the language of the target group. Psychological distance is an individual phenomenon which can also account for successful or unsuccessful second language acquisition. The factors which create psychological distance between the learners and speakers of the target language are affective in nature and include culture shock and motivation.

A second model of second language acquisition is provided by Krashen (1981). An integral component of his theory is the Affective-Filter Hypothesis. Dulay and Burt (1978) first introduced the term "socio-affective filter" to describe the relationship between affective variables and second language acquisition. The Affective Filter Hypothesis deals with the role of personality, motivation, and other affective variables related to success in second language acquisition. It takes into account student anxiety level, motivation, and self-confidence. Krashen hypothesized that these affective factors relate more directly to subconscious language acquisition than to conscious learning. According to the Affective Filter Hypothesis, learners in a less than optimal affective state will have a filter, or mental block, preventing them from further acquiring the second language. For instance, if students are anxious or unmotivated, the input they receive will not be processed by the language acquisition device and acquisition will terminate. Thus, an optimal condition for effective language acquisition is a low affective filter.

The final model to be described is Gardner's social-psychological model of second language acquisition. Gardner, Gliksman, and Smythe (1978) propose three basic components to the model—attitudes, motivation, and second language achievement or behavior related to second language learning. The model rests on the assumption that since language is an integral part of culture, the acquisition of a second language is dependent on the learner's willingness to make aspects of another culture become part of his own personality. Consequently, learners' attitudes toward the target group influence the extent to which they acquire the second language. Variations in motivation are associated directly with variations in second language learning. Gardner contends that second language competence is an important goal of second language learning, but it is not the ultimate goal. The most important goal is "psychological integration" with the target group.

THE ROLE OF SOCIAL-PSYCHOLOGICAL FACTORS IN THEORIES OF SECOND LANGUAGE RETENTION

Recently, language educators and researchers have become interested in the factors affecting *maintenance* of the second language after formal exposure to the learning environment has terminated. Lambert and Freed (1982) provide an interesting format for a discussion of both the theoretical and practical implications of foreign or second language loss.

One of the volume's contributors, Robert Gardner, draws from the plethora of research studies on social-psychological variables to suggest parallels between the causal variables in second language acquisition and second language retention. He posits two hypotheses related to second language retention:

1. Since attitudinal/motivational characteristics are related to the level of second language proficiency, they will relate to second language retention.

2. Since attitudinal/motivational characteristics are related to indices of participation in language-related situations, they will relate to attempts to maintain second language skills once training has terminated.

Gardner and Smythe (1975) compared language "drop-outs" with "stay-ins" on aptitude, attitude and motivation, and indices of intelligence and French achievement. They found that the drop-outs had significantly less favorable attitudes toward learning French and toward French Canadians, were less interested in learning foreign languages, expressed less of an integrative and instrumental orientation, expressed less motivation and desire to learn French, experienced higher levels of anxiety in the French class, and demonstrated less favorable attitudes toward the French class. The evidence, they conclude, supports the hypothesis that attitudes and motivation are related to the decision to drop out and eventually to the loss of language skills.

Snow, Padilla, and Campbell (1984) administered a standardized language test and attitudinal questionnaire to graduates of the Culver City Spanish Immersion Program. Factor analysis yielded four attitudinal factors: interest in foreign language, integrative orientation, parental/integrative orientation, and an encouragement and pride in work factor. Three of the four factors were significantly associated with retention of the productive skills of Spanish writing and speaking, and language use (use of Spanish at home, travel to Spanish-speaking countries, use of Spanish media, use of Spanish outside of home). Their findings suggest that the attitudinal predisposition shown by the factors influences the degree to which students retain their Spanish skills in writing and speaking. In other words, students who rated high in the four factors also scored high on the writing and speaking subtests. Thus, retention of the productive skills was associated with positive attitudes and continued effort to use the second language. The four factors, however, were not related to retention of listening and reading skills. Retention of receptive skills may be a more passive process independent of attitudinal factors.

FUTURE DIRECTIONS
FOR SOCIAL-PSYCHOLOGICAL RESEARCH

The wealth of research evidence accumulated during the last four decades confirms the significant role of social-psychological factors in second language acquisition. With this confirmation comes a change in research focus. Rather than debating the importance of affective variables as in the past, researchers are now looking for new and improved ways to measure these variables. Oller (1982) notes that "extraneous variables ... may influence the validity of affective measures (and their tendency to correlate with measures of first or second language proficiency). [They] are the tendency to flatter oneself, to seek social approval ..., and the aim to merely be consistent in responding to affective questionnaires" (p. 185). Oller suggests that our confidence in attitudinal research and the ensuing interpretations of research studies would be strengthened by improving the validity of affective measures. Acton (1984) proposes a different view of the traditional attitudinal constructs. Because of the overlap among these factors, he recommends a multivariate approach to attitudinal research. In the same vein, Newcomb (1984) suggests that constructs such as integrative and instrumental motivation might better be viewed as being on a continuum, rather than as the typical dichotomy suggested in most studies. We can look to the future to see how these and other suggestions will be incorporated into research studies. These efforts will undoubtedly expand the empirical base on which social-psychological research rests and illuminate many other interesting findings.

In sum, research on social-psychological variables in second language acquisition has taken two main directions. Researchers have been interested in the role of attitudes as the foundation for motivation, that is, how attitudes serve as the basis for motivation. They have looked at the relationship between motivational levels and success in learning the second language. The second area of interest has been in determining how the bilingual experience has shaped or changed attitudes. Learning a second language goes far beyond the acquisition of linguistic forms; it raises questions of ethnic and cultural identity. Language learning viewed from this perspective is a powerful social-psychological force. As research progresses, we will learn more about how attitudes and motivation so profoundly influence the learning of a second language and conversely, how the learning of a second language significantly affects learner attitudes. From both directions should come a greater understanding of the processes underlying second language acquisition.

NOTE

1. Anomie (literally, meaning having no norms, social ties, or identity), is a concept taken from research in the sociology of industrialization (Durkheim, 1897) and describes the symptoms of adjustment difficulties faced by most people in urban, industrialized communities. This concept has been borrowed into the field of language learning in order to describe the feelings immigrants as well as bilinguals often experience in their struggle to maintain comfortable contacts with their two cultural traditions.

DISCUSSION QUESTIONS

1. To what extent can success in second language learning be accounted for by attitudes and motivation? In other words, how important are social-psychological factors compared with other learner variables such as general intelligence, learning style, language aptitude, personality, or instructional factors like method or teacher?

2. What are the implications of social-psychological research for changing learners' attitudes? Should such change be a by-product of language learning or should overt curriculum planning be carried out to instill certain attitudes? What criteria should be used for deciding "good" attitudes?

3. Rubin (1975) was interested in determining the characteristics of the "good language learner." Describe what you think such a learner's attitudinal profile might include.

4. Consider the following item from an attitude questionnaire: "The study of Spanish will allow me to gain good friends among Spanish-speaking people." How would you classify this item—integrative or instrumental? Might it be interpreted either way? What are the implications for the validity of attitude research? Do you think integrative and instrumental motivation should be considered mutually exclusive? Discuss how these constructs might have a complementary function in language learning.

SUGGESTED ACTIVITIES

1. Select a particular language learning setting with which you are familiar. On the basis of previous research and your knowledge of the setting, formulate hypotheses about the types of motivation you predict to be most important in that setting. Develop a questionnaire to test your hypotheses. Discuss your results and relate them to previous research findings.

2. One criticism of questionnaire research is that subjects will answer in a particular "response set"; that is, in their desire to please the researcher, subjects will select all positive items and in doing so will not give accurate descriptions of their true feelings. How can this problem be avoided (e.g., through instructions prior to administration of the questionnaire, questionnaire design, etc.)?

Construct a questionnaire format which avoids this research problem.

3. Recent work in Canada has evaluated the effect on attitudes of "excursions" and short-term exchanges between second language learners and target language speakers. Arrange for such a field trip. Develop and administer a pre- and posttest attitude questionnaire. Discuss your results.

4. Construct an attitude and motivation measure and administer a language proficiency test to a given population. Correlate the results of the two measures. Discuss your results.

5. You are assigned to teach English to a class of underachieving but capable Chicano students. They have a negative attitude toward American culture and little interest in learning English. How could you help them to improve their English?

SUGGESTIONS FOR FURTHER READING

*Attitudes and Motivation in Second Language Learning.
1972. R. C. Gardner and W. E. Lambert, Rowley, Mass.: Newbury House.

A report of the relationship between attitudes and motivation and second language achievement in different cultural settings. The book provides an excellent background on the development of social-psychological constructs and of measurement instruments.

*Bilingual Education of Children:
The St. Lambert Experiment.
1972. W. E. Lambert and G. R. Tucker, Rowley, Mass.: Newbury House.

A detailed description of the pilot class and follow-up groups of the first French immersion program in Montreal. A major component of the evaluation is on attitudinal development.

Studies on Immersion Education: A Collection for United States Educators.
1983. California State Department of Education.

This book provides the most up-to-date collection of readings on immersion education, both in Canada and in the United States. Each article touches on social-psychological issues, but the Swain, Campbell, and Hernandez-Chavez (particularly from the language minority perspectives) articles are most relevant.

The Loss of Language Skills.
1982. R. D. Lambert and B. F. Freed, Rowley, Mass.: Newbury House.

This book provides an interesting collection of readings on issues in language loss. The article by Gardner presents a social-psychological perspective on the parallels between second language acquisition and second language loss.

Language Learning.
30, 255–270. R. C. Gardner. On the validity of affective variables in second language acquisition: Conceptual, contextual, and statistical considerations.

Language Learning.
32, 183–189. J. W. Oller. Gardner on affect: A reply to Gardner.

Language Learning.
32, 191–200. R. C. Gardner and L. Gliksman. On "Gardner on Affect": A discussion of validity as it relates to the attitude/ motivation test battery: A response from Gardner.

These three articles provide an in-depth discussion and rather heated debate on issues in the measurement of social-psychological variables.

REFERENCES

Acton, W. 1984. Applications of attitudinal research to the classroom. Paper presented at TESOL, Houston, Texas.

Brown, C. 1983. The view of the learner: Does perception of language learning factors relate to success? Paper presented at Rocky Mountain TESOL.

Campbell, R. N. 1983. The immersion education approach to foreign language teaching. In California State Department of Education, *Studies on Immersion Education: A Collection for United States Educators*. Office of Bilingual Bicultural Education.

Carroll, J. B., and S. M. Sapon. 1959. *Modern Language Aptitude Test*. New York: The Psychological Corporation.

Cziko, G. A., W. E. Lambert, and R. Gutter. 1979. French immersion programs and students' social attitudes: a multidimensional investigation. *Working Papers on Bilingualism, 19*, 13–28.

Day, R. R. 1980. The development of linguistic attitudes and preferences. *TESOL Quarterly, 14*, 27–40.

Dulay, H., and M. Burt. 1978. Some remarks on creativity in language acquisition. In W. Ritchie (ed.), *Second Language Acquisition Research: Issues and implications*. New York: Academic Press.

Durkheim, E. 1897. *Le Suicide*. Paris: F. Alcan.

Gardner, R. C. 1980. On the validity of affective variables in second language acquisition: conceptual, contextual, and statistical considerations. *Language Learning, 30*, 255–270.

Gardner, R. C., and L. Gliksman. 1982. On "Gardner on affect": a discussion of validity as it relates to the attitude/motivation test battery: a response from Gardner. *Language Learning, 32*, 191–200.

Gardner, R. C., L. Gliksman, and P. C. Smythe. 1978. Attitudes and behavior in second language acquisition:

*Presently out of print.

A social psychological interpretation. *Canadian Psychological Review, 19,* 173–186.

Gardner, R. C., and W. E. Lambert. 1959. Motivational variables in second language acquisition. *Canadian Journal of Psychology, 13,* 226–272.

*Gardner, R. C., and W. E. Lambert. 1972. *Attitudes and Motivation in Second Language Learning.* Rowley, Mass.: Newbury House.

Gardner, R. C., and P. C. Smythe. 1975. Second language acquisition: A social psychological approach. Research Bulletin No. 332, Department of Psychology, University of Western Ontario.

Genesee, F. 1978. Second language learning and language attitudes. *Working Papers on Bilingualism, 16,* 19–42.

Genesee, F. 1983. Bilingual education of majority-language children: The immersion experiments in review. *Applied Psycholinguistics, 4,* 1–46.

Genesee, F., P. Rogers, and N. Holobow. 1983. The social psychology of second language learning: Another point of view. *Language Learning, 33,* 209–224.

Gliksman, L. 1976. Second language acquisition: The effects of student attitudes on classroom behavior. Unpublished M.A. Thesis, University of Western Ontario.

Graham, C. R. 1984. Beyond integrative motivation: The development and influence of assimilative motivation. Paper presented at TESOL, Houston, Texas.

Krashen, S. 1981. Bilingual education and second language acquisition theory. In California State Department of Education, *Schooling and language minority students: A theoretical framework.* Office of Bilingual Bicultural Education.

Lambert, R. D., and B. F. Freed. 1982. *The Loss of Language Skills.* Rowley, Mass.: Newbury House.

*Lambert, W. E. and G. R. Tucker. 1972. *Bilingual Education of Children: The St. Lambert Experiment.* Rowley, Mass.: Newbury House.

Lukmani, Y. 1972. Motivation to learn and language proficiency. *Language Learning, 22,* 261–273.

Mowrer, D. H. 1950. *Learning Theory and Personality Dynamics.* New York: Ronald Press.

Newcomb, M. 1984. Motivation as a consequence of social, economic and political variables. Paper presented at TESOL, Houston, Texas.

Oller, J. W. 1981. Research on the measurement of affective variables: Some remaining questions. In R. Andersen (ed.), *New Dimensions in Second Language Acquisition Research.* Rowley, Mass.: Newbury House.

Oller, J. W. 1982. Gardner on affect: A reply to Gardner. *Language Learning, 32,* 183–189.

*Oller, J. W., and K. Perkins. 1978. Language proficiency as a source of variance in self-reported affective variables. In J. W. Oller and K. Perkins (eds.), *Language in Education: Testing the Tests.* Rowley, Mass.: Newbury House, 103–125.

Rubin, J. 1975. What the "good language learner" can teach us. *TESOL Quarterly, 9,* 41–51.

Schumann, J. H. 1978. Second language acquisition: The pidginization hypothesis. In E. Hatch (ed.), *Second Language Acquisition.* Rowley, Mass.: Newbury House.

Snow, M. A. 1979. Self report of attitudes and language use by students in a Spanish immersion program. Unpublished M.A. Thesis, University of California at Los Angeles.

Snow, M. A., A. M. Padilla, and R. N. Campbell. 1984. Factors influencing language retention of graduates of a Spanish immersion program. Professional report, National Center for Bilingual Research.

Waldman, E. 1975. Cross-ethnic attitudes of Anglo students in the Culver City Spanish Immersion Program. Unpublished M.A. Thesis, University of California at Los Angeles.

*Presently out of print.

COGNITIVE STYLE AND SECOND LANGUAGE LEARNING

Dayle Davidson Hartnett

PROLOGUE

Before reading this chapter, please respond by selecting either choice A or choice B as answers to the following questions:

1. What is the ideal way for you to learn a second language?

   Choice A: Take a class in the second language to learn the basic rules and then live in the country where the language is spoken.

   Choice B: Live in a foreign country to soak up the language and then take a second language class to learn the rules not yet mastered by immersion.

2. What teaching method do you prefer?

   Choice A: An analytical, sequential presentation of rules followed by examples and exercises.

   Choice B: A holistic, synthetic presentation of the second language providing well-contextualized examples and exercises with few or no rules.

Now that you have made your personal decisions, consider what learning strategies and teaching strategies would complement your choices. These questions will be discussed again in the introduction to the chapter.

INTRODUCTION

In second language instruction a subject of much inconclusive research has been which method of teaching facilitates learning most effectively. No real superiority of any deductive method over any inductive method, or vice versa, has been clearly established. The successive trends in language instruction have been enthusiastically embraced at their inception, only to lose favor when teachers realize that no one method seems to succeed for all their students. It is clear that different methods require different cognitive processes. For example, the grammar-translation and cognitive-code methods seem to require an analytical cognitive style, while the direct and audio-lingual methods seem to tap holistic thought-processing modes. It is also clear that individual students tend to prefer certain methods over other methods. It seems reasonable then to assume that individual students will be most successful in a class where the method is suited to their unique cognitive style of encoding, storing, and retrieving information.

Certain evidence from cognitive style research (Witkin et al., 1977) adds credence to this approach. Such research provides evidence that two very distinct modes of thought may exist in every individual. As an individual matures, he or she tends to depend more on one mode of thought rather than the other for problem solving, and it seems that this preference may also be shaped and reinforced by the culture or society the individual lives in (Maehr, 1974). A student who prefers choice A as the response to the above questions may therefore learn best in a class where the rule is presented and followed by examples, while another student who prefers choice B may wish to synthesize the rules from the examples provided, in a manner similar to first language acquisition.

In learning and instruction (Cronbach and Snow, 1977) an important line of educational research is aptitude treatment interaction (henceforth ATI). ATI is the matching of specific learner characteristics to specific treatments to facilitate learning. The basic assumption is that any treatment or method interacts differently with different individuals. Therefore, there is no *one* best method for *all* learners, but a best method for an individual learner based on the learner's unique aptitude. Examples of possible aptitudes are: cognitive style, degree of anxiety, motivation, biographical information, prior achievement, and mental ability. According to the ATI paradigm, successful second language learning may depend on the harmonious association of the student's cognitive style with either the deductive or inductive methodology used in a particular language class.

CEREBRAL HEMISPHERIC FUNCTIONS

Evidence supporting the hypothesis that each cerebral hemisphere is responsible for a distinct mode of thought has been obtained from the following sources: (1) left-hemisphere brain-damaged patients are compared with right-hemisphere brain-damaged patients to see what tasks each can perform; (2) individual split-brain patients who have had their corpus callosum (the bridge between the two hemispheres of the brain) severed to prevent seizures are studied to see how the left and right hemispheres perform on the same task; (3) normal subjects are given extremely difficult tasks calling for what is hypothesized to be either a left-hemisphere or right-hemisphere function or ability (Nebes, 1975).[1]

In all right-handed and approximately two-thirds of all left-handed individuals, the *left hemisphere* is associated with what Bogen (1969a, b) calls "propositional" thought (choice A in the prequestions), which has been characterized as "logical, analytical, computerlike thought" (Levy-Agresti and Sperry, 1968). Since the left hemisphere of the brain (allied with the right side of the body) is associated with linguistic and mathematical functions, our western society has deemed it to be the "major" side of the brain. It is a linear processor of information and is responsible for time-related judgments, such as reporting which of two stimuli comes first in a sequence (Carmon and Nachson, 1971; Efron, 1963a; Papcun et al., 1974; Krashen, 1973). The left hemisphere focuses on features and abstract essentials from a field (Bogen, 1975).

The "other" side of the brain for right-handed and some left-handed individuals, the *right hemisphere* (allied with the left side of the body) seems involved with "appositional" thought (choice B on the prequestions). "Appositional" thought process information diffusely, simultaneously, or "gestalt-synthetically" (Levy-Agresti and Sperry, 1968; Bogen, 1969a; Kimura, 1966). The disgraphia-discopia syndrome (inability to write and copy) seen in split-brain patients suggests a right-hemisphere specialization for spatial-relations. In a number of experiments (Nebes, 1971a, 1972, 1973), it was found that the right hemisphere was superior to the left in part-to-whole matching tasks. The right hemisphere perceives and remembers visual, tactile, and auditory images that are complex, fragmented, and hard to describe or name (Nebes, 1975).

In solving a problem, it seems that the type of *response* (naming or pointing) or the type of *stimulus* (verbal or visuospatial) may influence which hemisphere is dominant in the solution; however, the salient distinction seems to be whether *serial or parallel processing* will more efficiently solve the problem. If a task can be performed equally well by either the left or the right hemisphere, the two hemispheres seem capable of accomplishing the same task by characteristically different strategies (Bogen, 1975). The two nearly symmetrical sides coexist, their individual functions complementing and sometimes standing in for one another.

Hemisphericity

There are two main types of evidence that argue for the existence of hemisphericity. First, Bogen, Dezure, TenHouten, and Marsh (1972) provide evidence that certain groups of people tend to prefer one cognitive or learning style associated with either the left or right side of the brain. They report that certain groups perform relatively better on tests favoring one cognitive style or the other, such as the Wechsler Similarities test (Wechsler, 1955) or the Street test (Street, 1931). (The Wechsler Similarities test is highly verbal, requiring logical abstraction. The Street figure-completion test is as nonverbal as possible. A one-word spoken or written answer is required to describe an outlined image.) Performance by different groups on these two tests have been compared.[2] Urban whites performed best on the Wechsler Similarities test (a test tapping primarily left hemisphere functions) followed by urban blacks, rural whites, and Hopi Indians. Hopi Indians, on the other hand, performed relatively better on the Street test, a test tapping right-hemisphere functions requiring part-to-whole judgments.

Second, the empirical data that relate the Wechsler Similarities test to the left hemisphere are based on psychological testing of adult patients with right-brain hemispherectomies or right-brain lesions whose performance on the test was not impaired (Bogen, 1969a). For example, DeRenzi and Spinnler (1966) found that when there was right-hemisphere damage, performance on the Street test was impaired.

LATERAL EYE MOVEMENT[3]

Day (1964) noted that individuals move their eyes in a characteristic direction when thinking. Bakan (1969, 1971) has claimed that this direction of initial eye movement in response to a thought-provoking question is an indicator of which hemisphere of the brain a person usually employs. It was hypothesized that subjects whose eyes move to the *right* when thinking used the cognitive style associated with the *left* hemisphere, while subjects whose eyes move the *left* used the cognitive style associated with the *right* hemisphere. Characteristics of right and left eye movers seem to correspond to left- and right-hemisphere functions.

This phenomenon of lateral eye movement (henceforth LEM) is observable even in blind subjects but is not observable in subjects without language. LEM seems related to an "internal-external or passive-active" dimension of attending (Day, 1964, 1967). Failure to produce LEM occurs when the subject is anxious or embarrassed. The movement does not seem to occur when very simple questions of fact are asked, e.g., What's your middle name? Individuals are consistent over time in direction of right and left eye movements (Bakan and Strayer, 1973). Kinsbourne (1972) and Kocel, Galin, Ornstein, and Merrin (1972) independently discovered that analytic thought produced right-eye movement and spatial thought produced left-eye movement if the examiner asked the questions from behind the subjects and recorded the eye movement by camera. Gur, Gur, and Harris (1975) replicated these findings, but they also found that subjects would maintain their preferred eye movement pattern when the examiner was seated in front asking the questions.

COGNITIVE STYLE

Individual differences have been noted in cognitive style, as well as in the related areas of hemisphericity and eye movement. Cognitive style is the "relatively stable way individuals perceive, conceptualize and organize information" (Wittrock, 1978, p. 90). In other words, an individual examines components of a stimulus, to access information-processing strategies previously acquired and stored to reorganize or reassemble these experiences in order to discover a solution. As in an individual's use of a preferred brain hemisphere and eye-movement direction, an individual's use of a specific cognitive style for problem solving seems to be stable over time, but the individual's dependence on one cognitive style can be shifted (Witkin et al., 1977). Dual-cognitive-style models seem to relate to the information-processing functions of the hemispheres of the brain. The following are models of dual cognitive styles that have been proposed by researchers.

Field-independence (FI)/field-dependence (FD)

FI (also called an articulated cognitive style) is the ability to identify a visual unit in a confusing background; FD (also called a global cognitive style) is the difficulty or inability to identify a visual unit in a confusing background. According to Witkin et al. (1977), FI individuals are more able to analyze a field and organize and impose structure on an unorganized field, whereas FD individuals have a functional fixedness in problem-solving, displaying less ability to organize or impose structure on verbal and other material. Focusing on how students learn, Witkin et al. (1977) found individual differences in students' reactions to modeling, reinforcement, mediators, class structure, feedback, elaboration, and cue salience, as well as individual differences focusing on how teachers teach. Also, when the FI and FD cognitive styles of students and teachers are matched, learning is facilitated. FI and FD are determined by use of techniques such as the Embedded Figures test or the Rod and Frame test (see Witkin et al., 1977, for a discussion of both tests).[4] Cohen, Berent, and Silverman (1973) provide evidence that electroconvulsive shock to the right hemisphere seems to reduce FD while electroconvulsive shock to the left hemisphere seems to reduce FI, suggesting an association between hemisphericity and FI/FD cognitive styles.[5] Oltman (1976) also reports correlations between degree of lateralization and FI.

Verbal/imaginal

Paivio (1971) distinguishes between verbal and imaginal coding approaches based on the assumption that "verbal and nonverbal information are represented and processed in distinct but interconnected symbolic systems" (p. 8). The *verbal* system involves the sequential rearrangement of words and other linguistic units, while the *imaginal* system encodes visual and spatial attributes. Paivio provides support for his dual coding theory from: (1) research showing individual differences in creativity measures: (2) research

showing individual differences in memory tasks; and (3) brain research citing hemisphere specialization for verbal and nonverbal information processing.

Analytic/relational

Kagan, Moss, and Sigel (1963) identified *analytical* learners as those who group objects in terms of the function or abstract qualities that the objects share, such as grouping a chair and table together because they both have legs. *Relational* learners depend on the global characteristics of a stimulus, such as grouping a chair with a table because both are used for eating. Kagan et al. (1963) found that an analytic cognitive style was related to a reflective tempo of response, while a relational cognitive style tended to be related to an impulsive tempo of response. Zelniker and Jeffrey (1976) found that reflective children use a left-hemisphere, analytic cognitive style, and impulsive children use a right-hemisphere, global cognitive style when matching figures according to their salient details. In a series of studies on the educationally disadvantaged, Cohen (1969) further clarifies the analytic vs. relational rule-sets for selection and organization of sense data in the following way: an *analytic* mode abstracts information from a stimulus or situation in a stimulus-centered orientation to reality, while the *relational* mode sees meaning only in the global characteristics of a stimulus in reference to some total context and is self-centered in its orientation to reality. Clear-cut social, psychological, and learning differences, such as differences in attention, dependence on primary groups, and language styles are extensively summarized by Cohen (1969). These individual differences in analytic abstraction and field articulation relate to the information-processing modes attributed to the hemispheres of the brain, as well as to other cognitive-style research.

Serialist/holist

Pask and Scott (1972) describe a *serialist* cognitive competency as one in which the individual consistently assimulates long se-

LEFT-HEMISPHERE FUNCTIONS	RIGHT-HEMISPHERE FUNCTIONS
1. Propositional thought (Bogen, 1969a, b)	1. Appositional thought (Bogen, 1969a, b)
2. Time-related judgments (Carmon and Nachson, 1971)	2. Spatial relations (Levy-Agresti and Sperry, 1968)
3. Linear processing (Efron, 1963a)	3. Gestalt-synthetic processing (Kimura, 1966)
4. Abstracts essentials (Bogen, 1975)	4. Part-to-whole judgments (Nebes, 1973)

RIGHT-EYE-MOVER CHARACTERISTICS	LEFT-EYE-MOVER CHARACTERISTICS
1. Higher scores on the math subtests of the SAT (Bakan, 1969)	1. Self-report clearer imagery (Bakan, 1969)
2. Higher scores on concept identification tests (Weitan and Etaugh, 1973)	2. Classical/humanistic majors (Bakan, 1969)
3. Majors in science/quantitative areas (Bakan, 1969)	3. Easier to hypnotize (Bakan, 1969)
	4. Creative, artistic, aesthetic, social (Bakan, 1969; Weitan and Etaugh, 1973)

ANALYTICAL COGNITIVE STYLES	HOLISTIC COGNITIVE STYLES
1. Field-independent (Witkin, 1973)	1. Field-dependent
2. Verbal (Paivio, 1971)	2. Imaginal
3. Analytic (Cohen, 1969)	3. Relational
4. Serialist (Pask and Scott, 1972)	4. Holist
5. Sequential-successive (Das, 1973)	5. Parallel/simultaneous

FIGURE 1 Hypothesized Relationships among Brain-Hemisphere Functions, Eye-Movement Characteristics, and Cognitive Styles.

quences of information being intolerant of irrelevant material, while a *holist* cognitive competency is one in which the individual learns and recalls information as a whole, imaging entire principles and being able to deal with extraneous information. Pask and Scott (1972) also indicate the need for appropriate instructional strategies for these distinctive and different styles. Pask (1976) fails to find a correlation between field dependence and holism as measured by the Embedded Figures test. Although the descriptions of these two styles do seem to relate to other previously mentioned cognitive styles and the propositional and appositional processes attributed to the hemispheres of the brain, one difference is that FD learners are considered intolerant of irrelevant material while holists are described as tolerant of extraneous material.

Sequential-successive/simultaneous synthesis

Luria (1966) posits that memory and reasoning are approached in either a linear or simultaneous fashion, and that these two thought-processing modes have their bases in different areas of the brain. Das (1973) found

that children from different cultures use these differing modes of problem solving possibly because of either successive or simultaneous problem-solving emphasis in the classroom environment. Das (1973) and Zelniker and Jeffrey (1976) *find neither cognitive style superior*, i.e., marked by intelligence.

To summarize, characteristics of right and left eye movers seem to correspond to analytical and holistic cognitive styles. It is thus hypothesized that there are similarities in the various definitions of cognitive styles suggesting overlapping descriptions. See Figure 1.

INFLUENCES ON COGNITIVE STYLE

It seems clear that at least two cognitive styles exist. These styles represent qualitatively different thought processes (Bogen, 1975). It is unclear how or under what circumstances these cognitive styles develop. TenHouten (1976) hypothesizes that the wealthier, more technologically advanced the group, the more analytical its members. Cohen (1969) posits either predetermination of the nature of the organism or idiosyncratic early experience as possible explanations. Following the early experience hypothesis, both Cohen (1969) and Witkin et al. (1977) claim that cultural socialization practices affect the development of cognitive style. Cohen (1969) reported that relational students had shared functions in their primary groups, while analytical students had more formal styles of group organization. Also, possibly because of cultural socialization practices, certain other groups (specifically black, Mexican-American, and low socioeconomic status students) are reported to rely more on holistic, relational cognitive styles than white middle-class groups (Ramirez and Price-Williams, 1974; Cohen, 1969). Das (1973) theorized that cognitive style may be a subcultural characteristic and found that middle-class Canadian students were reported to use simultaneous processing, while high-caste Indian students were reported to rely on successive processing. The organization of school curriculum and environment was hypothesized by Das to be the influential variable. Certainly, the type and complexity of the learning task, the student's developmental level, the student's previous experience, and the use and style of the initial and continuing processing are also factors that may influence the development of cognitive style.

Equality between cognitive styles

Holistic students starting school with the same native ability as analytical students feel disorganized and confused when faced with IQ tests which call consistently for analogy formation, logical sequencing, formal analysis and field articulation skills, and learning environments which call for knowledge of social and psychological correlates of the analytical style. This disorganization and confusion has been claimed to compound itself as the holistic student moves up through the grades (Cohen, 1969). In addition, a holistic approach to learning seems to hinder the development of an analytical approach and vice versa. Even though Witkin et al. (1977) and Zelniker and Jeffrey (1976), among others, strongly stress the importance of considering the two types of cognitive styles as equally useful (i.e., each style indicates a form of

cognitive activity, not *how much* or *what* one thinks), classroom reality tends to positively reinforce analytical thinking while discriminating against holistic thinking. *To combat this existing imbalance, a multiple-method approach is needed to complement the cognitive style of the individual learner.* Witkin and his associates (1973, 1977) report that when students and teachers having the same cognitive style are matched, more satisfaction, better student grades, and better classroom atmosphere for learning occur. Witkin et al. (1977) also cite evidence to support the ability of an individual to shift styles, suggesting the use of compensatory treatments, as well as complementary treatments, which may enable students to diversify gradually and thus broaden their ability to encode and store information presented in either mode.

Cognitive style and second language learning (L2)

L2 research has examined reflective/impulsive and FI/FD cognitive styles. Brown (1977) suggests that reflective language learners are slower and more accurate, while impulsive language learners are more fluent. Both these styles would seem to have advantages and disadvantages when learners are speaking and writing. The reflective learner would be more precise and less complicated and would provide less information, while the impulsive learner would provide more information and more varied types of structures and vocabulary, but with the greater possibility of making errors and being misunderstood. FI (the ability to abstract elements from context, reorganize a strictly organized field, impose structure on a field with little inherent structure, and focus on relevant stimuli)[4] was found to correlate significantly with language success at all proficiency levels in the Toronto Good Language Learner study (Naiman, Fröhlich, Stern, and Todesco, 1978). As mentioned previously, FI is associated with the logical-analytical thought-processing mode attributed to the left hemisphere of the brain. Brown (1977) also suggests that FI and FD may be related to Krashen's (1976) distinction between learning and acquisition. FD may be more important in acquiring natural unconscious language, while FI may be central to success in formal classroom settings. If this distinction is the case, the Toronto Good Language Learner study points to FI learners as only *successful classroom learners,* not necessarily *successful L2 acquirers.*

Krashen (1976, 1977, 1978) attempts to explain how adults understand, speak, read, and write a second language. First, many "learn" in formal environments characterized by feedback, error correction, and rule isolation; while others may "acquire" language, inducing rules as children learning their L1 do. L2 data that are "learned" are consciously applied or "monitored" when time is unlimited. When processing time is limited, only L2 data that have been "acquired" can be used. Language "learning" is conscious, ordered, step-by-step knowledge about L2, while language "acquisition" is subconscious, internalized L2 knowledge. When an individual speaks correctly and fluently, the speech is based on "acquired" competence with "learning" acting only as an "editor" or "monitor" (Krashen and Galloway, 1978).

Individual differences exist among learners and acquirers. Extreme learners seem to constantly and consistently monitor their output in a way which seriously hampers the amount of information that they communicate. Acquirers may make many mistakes but are quite fluent. General characteristics of monitor users seem to relate to an analytical cognitive style. This type of individual would prefer logical, ordered, formalized L2 instruction, where it may be the case that an acquirer would prefer any type of learning environment that stresses intake, be it formal or informal, where L2 rules could be acquired and stored in a holistic fashion. The monitor capability can correct incorrectly "acquired" forms and functions of grammar structures, or not yet "acquired," easy to remember "learned" items. "Acquisition" need not be preceded by "learning," and "learning" and "acquisition" can occur together.

Basic support for this theory comes from a number of case studies (Krashen and Pon, 1975; Cohen and Robbins, 1976). These case studies show that acquirers tend to have taken language in holistically by immersion or submersion, and they correct "by feel," whereas the monitor overuser tends to have experienced and also desires formal grammar training to aid in L2 learning. Further support comes from research on an adult "accuracy order" for grammatical morphemes. Adults acquiring English as a second language have been found to show more or less the same accuracy order as do children (Dulay and Burt, 1975; Bailey, Madden, and Krashen, 1974; Larsen-Freeman, 1975). However, when adult subjects are given more processing time this "accuracy order" is not consistent, and the number of errors decreases (Larsen-Freeman, 1975). The assumption is that exercises which give individuals time to think about or "monitor" their responses involve "learned" as well as "acquired" information.

Research comparing second language teaching methods

Another focus in second-language research has been to compare methods or treatments in order to discover which method of teaching a second language is best. The results have been unclear. Variables such as age and proficiency level of students enter in, as do certain stable elements that make a lesson successful, such as elaboration or contextualization. One possible explanation for the lack of definite superiority of one method over another is that these studies did not use the ATI paradigm of matching learner aptitudes (such as cognitive style) to methods of instruction.

Cognitive style research

Carroll (1965), in summarizing research in L2 methods, says that it makes little difference whether one uses the audio-lingual or the grammar-translation method. Valette (1969) sees no difference among strategies, except that traditional-method students are better at reading. Chastain and Woerdhoff (1968) and Chastain (1970) give the edge to cognitive-code over audio-lingual method in reading, writing, and listening. Levin (1971) suggests more learning and better student attitudes in the explicit cognitive-code method. Much research seems inconclusive, while other studies seem to favor the cognitive-code method. Prator (1979) makes the point that many of the experiments comparing language methods suffer from a "lack of clarity in the definition of methods, inability to control variables, and insufficient rigor of design."

Besides methodology, other factors are important. In an effective language classroom, Chastain (1970) concludes that students learn what they are taught. If reading is emphasized, the students will be good in reading. Meaningful contextualized drills, conversations, and discussions are superior to mechanical pattern practice. Stimulation of all the senses is important to help the student process information, e.g., multimedia presentations (music, tapes, realia, games, slide shows, video tapes, films). Maximum language practice over a short period of time leads to fluency and quality of expression (Briere, 1967). Interest of the teacher, high student motivation, prior language learning experience, high verbal ability, and prior academic success all support successful language learning.

Some research emphasizes the importance of individual student differences. Carroll (1965) feels that it is impossible to control the techniques that a student will adopt to acquire a given skill. A student who has developed a fondness for a particular method of problem solving will apply this method no matter how the information is presented. Wardhaugh (1969) feels that teachers should not rely on any one method. "We must respond to the different needs of the students, the different learning patterns they exhibit, and the different inclinations and motives that they have in learning" (p. 111).

Although cognitive and behaviorist theories have spawned the following prevalent methods, their basic orientation tends to be either deductive or inductive. The *grammar-translation method* stresses learning grammar deductively by means of memorizing rules and exceptions to rules. Students memorize long vocabulary lists and use their knowledge of rules and vocabulary to tran-

slate literature from their second language to their first. The *audio-lingual method* was developed as a reaction to the grammar-translation method, and it is based on the behaviorist theory that all learning is habit formation, a mechanical, not a mental skill. Students make conditioned responses by means of dialogue memorization and pattern practices in the target language and are reinforced by hearing the correct response. All drills are presented inductively. The *direct method* tries to mirror first language acquisition by total immersion. The *cognitive-code method* draws from the previously mentioned methods. It is based on cognitive theory, which stresses man's innate ability to learn language using his mental powers to deduce rules and create novel utterances. Rules are presented deductively to facilitate meaningful, contextualized learning, thereby moving the student from competence to performance, practicing all four skills (listening, speaking, reading, writing) from the beginning of instruction.

To summarize: (1) Language instruction methods tend to fall into two basic categories of presentation—a rule followed by examples, and examples followed by a rule; (2) there seem to be two distinct cognitive styles: analytic and holistic; (3) individuals and groups tend to prefer one mode of thinking over the other for problem solving; and (4) specific learner aptitudes have been found to interact with specific treatments to facilitate learning.

With this in mind, it seems probable that an individual who learns analytically will be most successful at learning in a deductive method class, and that a holistic learner will be most successful in an inductive class. It also seems reasonable to assume that those successful at analytic thought will differ in eye movement from those successful at part-to-whole judgments and holistic thought. The following two experiments tested these hypotheses.

Experiment 1

A study by Krashen, Seliger, and Hartnett (1974) tested the hypothesis that successful

TABLE 1 Eye Movement in the Bull and Barcia Methods

Method	Right-Eye Movement	Left-Eye Movement
Bull	104	22
Barcia	70	67

TABLE 2 Right-Eye Movers and Left-Eye Movers

Method	Right Movers	Left Movers	No Preference
Bull	9	0	4
Barcia	4	3	9

students of the Bull method of learning Spanish, a system emphasizing deduction and analysis, would show more right-eye movement than successful students of the Barcia method, a system requiring more inductive skills of the students.

The Department of Spanish and Portuguese at UCLA outlined the two-track system in the following way. The *Bull method* used the text *Spanish for Communication* by Bull, Briscoe, La Madrid, and Dellacio (1972).[6] Students intellectually understand what they are learning. Rules are presented in written and self-correcting programs, not by the instructors. Use of students' knowledge of English is transferred to facilitate learning Spanish. The instructor helps in practicing the spoken language in the classroom, not in explaining the structure of the language. The Barcia method used the text *Lengua y Cultura* by Barcia, Pucciani, and Hamel (1973).[6] The students simultaneously learn to listen, speak, read, and write Spanish. Spanish is the only means of communication in the classroom. The instructor conducts controlled conversation using a limited vocabulary, thereby permitting the students to inductively learn the grammar rules. Two hours of language laboratory per week are strongly recommended. Spanish culture is presented in humanistic terms and constitutes a single entity with the language.

Method/Subjects The subjects were 30 right-handed, native, English-speaking students from the Spanish 3 classes at UCLA. All students had received A grades in Spanish 1 and Spanish 2, and felt they would receive an A grade in Spanish 3.

Procedure The students were asked 10 questions to elicit eye movement: (1) How do you spell "journey"? (2) What is six times 12? (3) How many letters are there in the word *Washington*? (4) What is similar about salt and water? (5) What is similar about first and last? (6) Which way does Lincoln face on the penny? (7) How many sides are there on a five-pointed star? (8) Is the top stripe of the American flag red or white? (9) Is the moon now waxing or waning? (10) What is your favorite color?

The examiner sat facing the subject and noted the direction of the initial eye movement. The chairs were placed so that there would be equal space on either side of the student, and there was nothing distracting on either side of the room. One student was eliminated from the analysis because she was aware that eye movement was being investigated.

Results The findings were that students in the Bull classes made more right movements as a group than those in the Barcia class. See Table 1. Students who made 8 out of 10 movement in one direction were classified as "movers" in that direction. Over half had a preferred direction, which is consistent with other studies of this kind in the literature. Table 2 shows again that the Bull group contained more right movers. To allow for statistical analysis, the left mover and nonmover categories were combined and Fisher's exact test was applied—the Bull group was found to contain significantly more right movers than the Barcia group ($p < .02$), supporting the hypothesis.

Discussion It is possible that the differences observed between the two groups may have been due to some other difference in the teaching method; nevertheless, the results supported the hypothesis that students successful at a logical-analytic deductive system of learning Spanish will show more right-eye movement (reflecting greater left-hemisphere dependence) than students successful at a more inductive synthetic system. The finding that the Barcia group contained both right and left eye movers as well as those who showed no preference could mean that the kind of guided induction called for can be achieved through either analysis or synthesis or a combination of both.

Experiment 2

To further substantiate the finding that congruence of method and cognitive style is an important factor in second language learning, a second experiment was conducted (Hartnett, 1975) which tested the following hypotheses: (1) students in the deductive Bull method of learning Spanish show more right-eye movement, i.e., analytic learning style associated with left-hemisphere preference than students in the inductive Barcia method; students in the inductive Barcia method show more left-eye movement, i.e., holistic learning style associated with right-hemisphere preference than students in the deductive Bull method; (2) students know whether they learn best deductively or inductively and choose the method that complements their particular cognitive style; (3) students with the highest gains on the language proficiency tests in the deductive Bull method show more right-eye movements; students with the highest gains on the language proficiency tests in the inductive Barcia method show more left-eye movement; (4) there is a significant interaction between learning style preference and method when the covariates of sex,

pretest, major, and years of previous Spanish instruction are controlled.

Method/Subjects The subjects were 34 right-handed, native English-speaking students from the Spanish 3 classes at UCLA who had been in either the Bull or the Barcia track for Spanish 1, 2, and 3. There were 26 females and 8 males. Students were aware of the differences between the two methods when they enrolled in Spanish 1, and these differences were re-emphasized by the teaching assistants the first few days of class. A few students, however, chose the deductive Bull method or the inductive Barcia method on the basis of teacher reputation, scheduling problems, or relief at being assigned to any section as there were long waiting lists.

Procedure Students were given pre- and posttests both having cloze (a paragraph with every fifth or sixth word deleted) and dictation portions. The cloze and the dictation have been shown by Oller (1971), Oller and Conrad (1971) and others to be excellent measures of overall language proficiency. The two forms of the test, which were written and recorded by native Spanish speakers, were highly correlated. They were the same length and included the same major grammar points which the teaching assistants hoped the students would have mastered by the conclusion of Spanish 3, e.g., subjunctive vs. indicative, preterit vs. imperfect. The dictation was read once at normal speed, then with pauses between thought groups, and again at normal speed. The score was computed by the number of correct words on the dictation plus the number of correct entries in the cloze portion. The tests given at the beginning and the end of the quarter yielded a gain score which was used to assess the students' improvement during the quarter. The pretest was used as a covariate of the posttest (along with sex, major, and years of previous Spanish instruction) in testing for an interaction between learning-style preference and method.

Students were asked relevant demographic information, e.g., their deductive or inductive teaching method preference, major,

TABLE 3 Eye Movements in the Bull and Barcia Methods

Method	Right-Eye Movement	Left-Eye Movement
Bull (N = 16)	89	59
Barcia (N = 18)	68	91

TABLE 4 Students' Deductive and Inductive Learning Preferences

Method	Deductive	Inductive	No Preference
Bull (N = 16)	11	4	1
Barcia (N = 18)	4	13	1

and number of years of previous Spanish instruction.

Hemisphere preference was determined using the method previously mentioned. Students exhibiting greater than 50 percent consistent eye movement in one direction were classified as either left-eye movers or right-eye movers.

Results Hypothesis 1 stated that students in the deductive Bull method would show more right-eye movement, i.e., presumably a left-hemisphere preference, than students in the inductive Barcia method, and that students in the inductive Barcia method would show more left-eye movement, i.e., presumably right-hemisphere preference, than students in the deductive Bull method. Results are shown in Table 3. The data seem to indicate more right-eye movements for the Bull group, and more left-eye movements for the Barcia group.

Hypothesis 2 stated that students know whether they learn best deductively or inductively and choose the method that comple ments their particular cognitive style. Results are shown in Table 4.

Hypothesis 3 stated that students with the highest gains on the language proficiency tests in the deductive Bull method would show more right-eye movements, i.e., presumably a left-hemisphere preference, while students with the highest gains in the inductive Barcia method would show more left-eye movements, i.e., presumably a right-hemisphere preference. In the Bull method 10 students were identified as right-eye movers, and 6 were identified as left-eye movers. In the Barcia method 10 students were identified as left-eye movers, and 8 were identified as right-eye movers. Results of the t tests (Table 5) show that so-called left-hemisphere students did significantly better (p < .05) on gain scores than right-hemisphere students in the deductive Bull method. There is a strong though not statistically significant trend (p < .06) for so-called right-hemisphere students to make the greatest gains in the inductive Barcia method.

A planned comparisons test (Lindquist, 1953, p. 15) was computed on the hypothesized interaction, which is that in the Bull method presumably left-hemisphere-dominant learners (right-eye movers) would *gain more* than presumably right-hemisphere-dominant learners (left-eye movers), and that in the Barcia method presumably right-hemisphere-dominant learners (left-eye movers) would gain more than presumably left-hemisphere-dominant learners (right-eye movers). The planned comparisons test was statistically significant at the .05 level.

Hypothesis 4 stated that there is a significant interaction between presumed hemisphere preference and method when the covariates of sex, pretest, major, and years of previous Spanish are controlled. As an alternative to the above analysis of gain score, an analysis of covariance was computed, using the posttest achievement scores as the dependent variable and pretest, sex, major, and years of previous Spanish instruction as the covariables. The interaction between hemisphere dominance and method of instruction approaches statistical significance (.055) when the four covariates are controlled.

TABLE 5 Mean Gain Scores for Right- and Left-Hemisphere Students for the Bull and Barcia Methods

Method	Left Hemisphere	Right Hemisphere	t ratio
Bull	5.7 points	1.7 points	1.56*
Barcia	.25 points	2.7 points	1.72†
Combined groups	3.3 points	2.3 points	.124‡

*p < .05   †p < .06   ‡n.s.

A planned comparisons test (Edwards, 1960, p. 140–144) was computed on the hypothesized interaction, which is that Bull left-hemisphere-dominant learners (right-eye movers) would *outperform* Bull right-hemisphere-dominant learners (left-eye movers) and Barcia right-hemisphere-dominant learners (left-eye movers) would outperform Barcia left-hemisphere-dominant learners (right-eye movers). The result was statistically significant at the .01 level.

Discussion   The results of this second language learning experiment tend to confirm the hypothesis that students learn in distinctly different ways, as suggested by the research of Paivio ("verbal processes" vs. "imagery"), Bogen ("propositional" vs. "appositional"), Cohen ("analytic" vs. "relational"), and Witkin ("field independent" vs. "field dependent"). The students from the Bull method class moved their eyes to the right a majority of times, suggesting possible left-hemisphere thought processing, and students from the Barcia method class moved their eyes a majority of times, suggesting possible right-hemisphere thought processing. Almost all students were very definite in stating their preference for a deductive method over an inductive method or vice versa. If students felt the best way to learn a language was to logically and sequentially learn the rules of Spanish, they enrolled in the Bull method; but if their preference was to learn by "discovery" or induction, they enrolled in the Barcia method. The finding that students learn more if they are in a class whose methodology matches their cognitive style is consistent with logic and with research on cognitive styles (Witkin, 1973). This is also consistent with the finding that there is an interaction between method and assumed hemisphere dominance when pretest, sex, major, and years of previous Spanish instruction are controlled. A teaching presentation that is comfortable and compatible with the individual's usual thought-processing mode may ensure that his or her quality of attention and comprehension is better. If a student is in a class where the method is in opposition to the student's learning style, he or she may not learn as much. Other factors may be interacting, such as motivation or attitude, which bear on successful learning of a second language. A replication of these results is needed. Nevertheless, these findings support the notion that teaching should be individualized to the needs of each students to maximize second langauge learning.

Educational implications

Knowledge of the thought-processing modes associated with the hemispheres of the brain bears directly on what is taught, how it is taught, and how students learn. "What is taught" mirrors what is felt to be important by the teacher and school, and what is regarded as meaningful by the society. Curriculum in U.S. schools tends to emphasize left-hemisphere abilities over right-hemisphere abilities. Even IQ tests tend to measure left-hemisphere abilities over right-hemisphere abilities. Counterculture inroads have explored "alternative" schools where in many cases "how a subject is taught" is paramount to a prescribed set of subjects. "Verbal" vs. "discovery" learning has become an important methodological issue. However, the most essential element in successful teaching seems to be "how the individual student thinks." Each student is unique, with the diversity of cognitive styles ranging on a continuum from left-hemisphere thought processing to right-hemisphere thought processing.

The individual's thinking style has been shown to be consistent over time (Witkin, 1973). This consistency may be perpetuated by a student's subject-matter preference, e.g., math over English. Here a vicious circle begins where the teacher's cognitive style relates to his or her subject-matter preference, which relates to his or her deductive or inductive method of teaching that subject.

Three suggestions may help achieve more balance along with optimum facilitation of learning: (1) matching method to the learner's cognitive style, (2) classroom problem-solving training, (3) use of interacting methods in one class. Students learn more and positively evaluate their teachers when the teaching method is matched to the learner's cognitive style (Witkin, 1973). There is better teacher-student communication and vice versa. Teachers tend to value students whose cognitive style is like theirs, reinforcing a positive self-image in their students. When mismatching occurs, the student is likely to feel frustrated and hostile to the teacher, subject matter, and learning in general (Gazzaniga, 1975). Since little factual information learned in school is retained for very long, an important aspect in any school program should be to teach students how to *think* both analytically and synthetically. Research in problem solving and creativity (Davis, 1973; Davis and Scott, 1971) indicates that thought-processing strategies can be taught. Perhaps ideas unique to the individual come from using the least characteristic thought-processing mode, or a novel blending of the characteristic in conjunction with the least characteristic thought-processing mode. Wittrock's generative learning model (1974, 1975) seems an ideal marriage of both thought-processing modes. "Learning is the construction of concrete, specific, verbal and imaginal associations, using one's prior experience as part of the context for the construction" (Wittrock, 1975, p. 40). An example of the potency of this approach is the Bower and Clark study (1969) where subjects had 93 percent retention of a list of words, using the words to create a story, as opposed to 14 percent retention in the control group. Thus an ideal teaching method stimulates an interaction between both learning styles in order to facilitate optimum retention.

Implications for English as a second language
Students learning English as second language seem to be more successful and to feel more comfortable in a class which complements their cognitive style. If a school offers both deductive and inductive ESL classes, it is important that the students are aware of the differences in methodology and that they can make a free selection in line with the way they like to learn. An interest inventory, featuring simplified questions similar to those at the beginning of this chapter, can serve as an indicator of cognitive style preference. Since most schools do not offer a choice of methods, it is important for the ESL teacher to use both deductive and inductive methods in each lesson in order to stimulate both analytic learners and holistic learners, and to encourage both learning styles in each individual.

Any aspect of the language can be taught either deductively or inductively. For example, here is a conversation where a nurse talks to a patient on the phone.

Nurse: "How long have you had the sore throat?"
Patient: "I have been sick for two days."

This can be as effective an introduction to the present perfect as either the statement of rules of usage on a study sheet or a comparison of the present perfect and the simple past tense. This emphasis on variety livens the pace of the lessons, encouraging the teacher to develop creative lessons and to minimize dependence on a textbook-enforced methodology.

Imagery should be used in the ESL classroom. Audio-visual aids enhance listening and reading skills, and can create intense interest in speaking and writing. These tools can help relate the new unfamiliar language experiences to experiences in the past. Relevant pictures from magazines, drawings on the blackboard, photographs, slide shows, movies, records, tapes, and realia (e.g., menus, bus schedules, clothing, food cans) all help relate what the student is learning verbally to an image. The image improves the student's ability to retain and to retrieve the correct word and structure when needed. In children's literature the visual images are deemed as important as the words in furthering first language reading skills. However, the emphasis in most ESL texts seems to be lopsided in favor of words, with few graphics used. Learning vocabulary becomes easier if the student creates an image for each word or creates a story using a list of words. These techniques work because there is an interaction between the two learning styles to process the verbal information. ESL teachers can learn communication skills from successful educational TV shows and TV commercials which utilize the interaction of words and images.

NOTES

1. For a review of other ways to measure lateralized cerebral hemispheric functions, such as dichotic listening, see McNeil and Hamre (1974).

2. It should be noted that the interpretation of these results is controversial and that the findings should therefore be viewed as suggestive or speculative.

3. The link between eye movement and hemisphere activity is considered by some researchers to be somewhat weak and indirect. The results reported here should thus be interpreted with some caution.

4. It is not at all certain that we can generalize from visual FI/FD measures (i.e., the Embedded Figures test or the Rod and Frame test) to the auditory modality, which is also critical in second language performance. Also, note that some confusion exists in the FI/FD literature: there is a lack of comparable test measures, resulting in some conflicting results.

5. The effects of electroconvulsive shock, however, may extend over to the right hemisphere and vice versa. We do not know how "localized" a jolt of electricity remains.

6. These were the texts and methods used to teach Spanish at UCLA in the early and mid seventies. Since then, the textbooks have changed, with presumably some changes occurring in the methods as well.

DISCUSSION QUESTIONS

1. Name some factors which might influence which cognitive style an individual tends to rely on. How can an individual change from one cognitive style to another?

2. What is imagery? Can imagery include use of all the senses? How might a language teacher use imagery to facilitate memory and learning in language instruction?

3. A common complaint of second language learners is "I didn't like Ms. Smith, so I got a bad grade in French." How much do you feel this reaction might relate to an unconscious frustration at dealing with the teacher's cognitive style and method of instruction rather than other factors such as personality?

4. Give arguments for and against purely deductive and purely inductive ESL classes at the elementary, secondary, adult and university levels.

5. What aspects of the language are being tested in dictation and cloze tests? Might a person who uses the cognitive style of the left hemisphere perform better on a cloze and dictation than a person who uses the cognitive style of the right hemisphere or vice versa?

6. Of what value in a language class might it be to ask students what method of instruction they prefer?

SUGGESTED ACTIVITIES

1. Using the procedure explained in the aforementioned experiments, give the eye-movement test or the Wechsler and Street tests to right-handed bilingual students (of the same language group) in both languages to see if the so-called hemisphere preference remains the same in both languages.

2. There seem to be different styles of speakers and writers in second language learning. One individual speaks or writes quite fluently, had a wide vocabulary, and tries many different structural combinations (many

of these are ungrammatical). Another individual is not as fluent but makes sure that every proposition is syntactically correct and articulated in proper word order. Give the eye-movement test or the Wechsler and Street tests to a number of students who have been identified as using the above strategies to see if a fluent strategy of speaking and writing correlates with left-hemisphere preference and a nonfluent strategy of speaking and writing correlates with right-hemisphere preference or vice versa.

3.   Ask students in an ESL class whether they prefer a deductive or an inductive approach. Construct two grammar lessons where the same concept is taught deductively and inductively. Pretest the concept to make sure it is unfamiliar to the students. Divide the class into four groups—two groups of deductive learners and two groups of inductive learners. Teach the concept deductively to one group of deductive learners and one group of inductive learners, and vice versa. Give the students two tests to evaluate their understanding of the grammatical concept— one test directly after the lesson, and the other two weeks after the lesson. The students whose learning preference matched the presentation should score higher on both evaluations. (See Hartnett, 1980, for an example of such a study.)

4.   Using a chapter from a required ESL textbook for an adult class, creatively develop a lesson plan which will stimulate learners of both cognitive styles: analytic and holistic.

5.   Construct a discrete-point test, a dictation test, and a cloze test to evaluate students' comprehension of some grammatical structures. See Cohen (1980) and Madsen (1983) for guidance. Would students in a deductive method class perform better on a discrete-point test and students in an inductive method class perform better on integrative tests like the cloze and dictation? Explain why or why not.

6.   Discuss the methodology used in two different language departments that you are familiar with and state what you feel is the rationale behind these differing methodologies.

SUGGESTIONS FOR FURTHER READING

The Human Brain.
M. C. Wittrock (ed.) 1977. Englewood Cliffs, N.J.: Prentice-Hall.
Devoted to education and the hemispheric processes of the brain. Jerison describes recent research on the evolution of the brain. Hemispherical processes of the brain are discussed by Gazzaniga, Nebes, and Krashen. Educational implications are presented by Bogen and Wittrock.

Review of Educational Research.
H. A. Witkin, C. A. Moore, D. R. Goodenough, and P. W. Cox. 1977. 47, 1–65.
Field-dependent and field-independent cognitive styles and their educational implications. A thorough discussion of the cognitive characteristics involved in field-independent and field-dependent cognitive styles.

Left Brain, Right Brain.
S. Springer, and G. Deutsch. 1981. San Francisco: W. H. Freeman Co.
A very readable paperback that provides the interested lay reader with review and discussion of current issues and findings in brain research.

Neuropsychological Perspectives in Education.
L. Galloway. 1982. Bilingualism: Neuro-psychological Considerations.
G. Hynd (ed.) Special issue of the Journal of Research and Development in Education, 15 (3), 12–28.
This is the most extensive critical review of this literature available in English. It is written in a style accessible to non-specialists. There are implications for bilingual education and ESL.

REFERENCES

Allen, H. B., and R. N. Campbell. 1972. Teaching English as a Second Language. New York: McGraw-Hill.

Bailey, N., C. Madden, and S. Krashen. 1974. Is there a "natural sequence in adult second language learning"? Language Learning, 24, 235–243.

Bakan, P. 1969. Hypnotizability, laterality of eye movements, and functional brain asymmetry. Perceptual and Motor Skills, 28, 927–932.

Bakan, P. 1971. The eyes have it. Psychology Today, 4, 64–69.

Bakan, P., and F. F. Strayer. 1973. On reliability of conjugate lateral eye movements. Perceptual and Motor Skills, 36, 429–430.

Barcia, J., O. Pucciani, and J. Hamel. 1973. Lengua y Cultura. New York: Holt, Rinehart, and Winston.

Bogen, J. E. 1969a. The other side of the brain I: Dysgraphia and dyscopia following cerebral commissurotomy. Bulletin of the Los Angeles Neurological Society, 34, 73–105.

Bogen, J. E. 1969b. The other side of the brain II: An appositional mind. *Bulletin of the Los Angeles Neurological Society, 34,* 135–162.

Bogen, J. E. 1975. Some educational aspects of hemispheric specialization, *UCLA Educator, 17,* 24–32.

Bogen, J. E., R. Dezure, W. D. TenHouten, and J. F. Marsh. 1972. The other side of the brain IV: The a/p ratio. *Bulletin of the Los Angeles Neurological Society, 37,* 49–61.

Bower, G. H., and M. C. Clark. 1969. Narrative stories as mediators for serial learning. *Psychonomic Science, 14,* 181–182.

Briere, E. J. 1967. Quantity before quality in second language composition. *Language Learning, 16,* 141–150.

Brown, H. D. 1977. Cognitive and affective characteristics of good language learners. *Proceedings of the Los Angeles Second Language Research Forum,* UCLA, 349–354.

Bull, W., L. Briscoe, E. La Madrid, and C. Dellacio. 1972. *Spanish for Communication.* Boston: Houghton Mifflin Co.

Carmon, A., and I. Nachson. 1971. Effect of unilateral brain damage on perception of temporal order. *Cortex, 7,* 410–418.

Carroll, J. B. 1965. Contributions of research to foreign language teaching. *Modern Language Journal, 49.*

Carroll, J. B. 1972. Fundamental considerations in testing for English language proficiency of foreign students. In H. B. Allen and R. N. Campbell (eds.), *Teaching English as a Second Language.* New York: McGraw-Hill, 313–321.

Chastain, K. A. 1970. A methodological study comparing the audio-lingual habit theory and the cognitive-code learning theory: A continuation. *The Modern Language Journal, 54,* 257–266.

Chastain, K. A. 1971. *The Development of Modern Skills: Theory to Practice.* Philadelphia: The Center for Curriculum Development, Inc.

Chastain, K. A., and F. J. Woerdhoff. 1968. A methodological study comparing the audio-lingual habit theory and the cognitive-code learning theory. *The Modern Language Journal, 52,* 268–279.

Cohen, A. 1980. *Testing Language Ability in the Classroom.* Rowley, Mass.: Newbury House.

Cohen, A., and M. Robbins. 1976. Toward assessing interlanguage performance: The relationship between selected errors, learner's characteristics, and learner's explanations. *Language Learning, 26,* 45–66.

Cohen, B. D., S. Berent, and A. J. Silverman. 1973. Field-dependence and lateralization of function in the human brain. *Archives of General Psychiatry, 28,* 165–167.

Cohen, R. A. 1969. Conceptual styles, culture conflict, and non-verbal tests of intelligence. *American Anthropologist,* 828–855.

Cronbach, L. J., and R. E. Snow. 1977. *Aptitudes and Instructional Method: A Handbook for Research in Interactions.* New York: Irvington (Halsted Press).

Das, J. P. 1973. Structure of cognitive abilities: Evidence for simultaneous and successive processing. *Journal of Educational Psychology, 65,* (1), 103–108.

Davis, G. A. 1973. *Psychology of Problem Solving.* New York: Basic Books.

Davis, G. A., and J. A. Scott. 1971. *Training Creative Thinking.* New York: Holt.

Day, M. E. 1964. An eye-movement phenomenon relating to attention, thought, and anxiety. *Perceptual and Motor Skills, 19,* 443–446.

Day, M. E. 1967. An eye-movement indicator of type and level of anxiety: some clinical observations. *Journal of Clinical Psychology, 66,* 51–62.

Day, M. E. 1969. Don't teach till you see the direction of their eye movement. *The Journal of Special Education, 4,* 233–237.

DeRenzi, E., G. Scotti, and H. Spinnler. 1969. Perceptual and associative disorders of visual recognition. *Neurology, 19,* 634–642.

DeRenzi, E., and H. Spinnler. 1966. Visual recognition in patients with unilateral cerebral disease. *Journal of Nervous and Mental Disorders, 142,* 515–525.

Dulay, H., and M. Burt. 1975. A new approach to discovering universal strategies of child second language acquisition. In D. Dato (ed.), *Development Psycholinguistics: Theory and Applications.* Georgetown University Round Table on Languages and Linguistics, Washington, D.C.: Georgetown University Press, 209–233.

Edwards, A. L. 1960. *Experimental Design in Psychological Research.* New York: Rinehart and Co. Inc., 140–144.

Efron, R. 1963a. The effect of handedness on the perception of simultaneity and temporal order. *Brain, 86,* 261–284.

Efron, R. 1963b. Temporal perception, aphasia, and deja vu. *Brain, 86,* 403–424.

Gazzaniga, M. S. 1975. Review of the split brain. *UCLA Educator, 17,* 9–12.

Greene, D., and R. Lepper. 1974. Effects of extrinsic rewards on children's subsequent intrinsic interest. Unpublished paper, Stanford University, Department of Psychology.

Gur, R. E., R. C. Gur, and L. J. Harris. 1975. Cerebral activation, as measured by subjects' lateral eye movements, is influenced by experimenter location. *Neuropsychologia, 13,* 35–45.

Hartnett, D. D. 1975. The relation of cognitive style and hemispheric preference to deductive and inductive second language learning. Unpublished master's thesis in TESL, UCLA.

Hartnett, D. D. 1980. The relationship of analytical and holistic cognitive styles to second language instructional methods. Unpublished Ph.D. dissertation in education, UCLA.

Kagan, J., H. A. Moss, and I. E. Sigel. 1963. Psychological significance of styles of conceptualization. In J. C. Wright and J. Kagan (eds.), Basic cognitive processes in children. *Monographs of the Society for Research in Child Development, 28* (2), 73–112.

Kimura, D. 1966. Dual functional asymmetry of the brain in visual perception. *Neuropsychologia, 4,* 275–285.

Kinsbourne, M. 1972. Eye and head turning indicate cerebral lateralization. *Science, 176,* 539–541.

Kocel, K., D. Galin, R. Ornstein, and E. Merrin. 1972. Lateral eye movements and cognitive mode. *Psychonomic Science.*

Krashen, S. 1972. Language and the left hemisphere. Unpublished Ph.D. dissertation, UCLA, Department of Linguistics.

Krashen, S. 1973. Lateralization, language learning, and the critical period: Some new evidence. *Language Learning, 23,* 63–74.

Krashen, S. 1974. Cerebral asymmetry. *Current Trends in the Language Sciences.*

Krashen, S. 1976. Formal and informal linguistic environments in language acquisition and language learning. *TESOL Quarterly, 10,* (2), 157–168.

Krashen, S. 1977. Some issues relating to the monitor model. Paper presented at the TESOL Conference, Miami.

Krashen, S. 1978. Individual variation in the use of the monitor. *Second Language Acquisition Research.* New York: Academic Press, Inc., 175–183.

Krashen, S., and L. Galloway. 1978. The neurological correlates of language acquisition: Current research. Paper presented at the Sixth Annual Convention of SPEAQ, Quebec City.

Krashen, S., and P. Pon. 1975. An error analysis of an advanced ESL learner: The importance of the monitor. *Working papers on Bilingualism, 7,* 125–129.

Krashen, S., H. Seliger, and D. Hartnett. 1974. Two studies in adult second language learning. *Kritikon Litterarum, 3,* 220–228.

Larsen-Freeman, D. 1975. The acquisition of grammatical morphemes by adult ESL students. *TESOL Quarterly, 9,* 409–420.

Levin, L. 1972. *Comparative Studies in Foreign Language Teaching.* Stockholm: Almqvist and Wiksell.

Levy-Agresti, J., and R. Sperry. 1968. Differential perceptual capacities in major and minor hemispheres. *Proceedings of the National Academy of Science, 61,* 1151.

Lindquist, E. F. 1953. *Design and Analysis of Experiments in Psychology and Education.* Boston: Houghton Mifflin Co., 15.

Luria, A. R. 1966. *Human Brain and Psychological Processes.* English translation by B. Haigh, New York: Harper & Row.

Madsen, H. 1983. *Techniques in Testing.* New York: Oxford University Press.

Maehr, M. L. 1974. *Sociocultural Origins of Achievement.* Monterey, Calif.: Brooks/Cole Publishing Co.

McNeil, M. R., and C. E. Hamre. 1974. A review of measures of lateralized cerebral hemisphere functions. *Journal of Learning Disabilities, 7.*

Naiman, N., M. Fröhlich, H. Stern, and A. Todesco. 1978. The good language learner. *The Ontario Institute for Studies in Education, 7,* 1–112.

Nebes, R. 1971a. Superiority of the minor hemisphere in commissurotomized man for the perception of part-whole relations. *Cortex, 7,* 350–356.

Nebes, R. 1971b. Handedness and the perception of part-whole relationships. *Cortex, 7,* 350–356.

Nebes, R. 1973. Perception of spatial relationships by the right and left hemispheres in commissurotomized man. *Neuropsychologia, 11,* 285–289.

Nebes, R. 1972. Dominance of the minor hemisphere in commissurotomized man on a test of figural unification. *Brain, 95,* 633–638.

Nebes, R. 1975. Man's so-called "minor" hemisphere. *UCLA Educator, 17,* 13–16.

Oller, J. 1971. Dictation as a test of ESL proficiency. *English Language Teaching, 25,* 254–259.

Oller, J., and C. Conrad. 1971. The cloze technique and ESL proficiency. *Language Learning, 21,* 183–196.

Oltman, P. K. 1976. Field-dependence and extent of lateralization. Paper presented at the annual meeting of the American Psychological Association, Washington, D.C.

Ornstein, R. 1972. *The Psychology of Consciousness.* San Francisco: W. H. Freeman and Co., 50–73.

Ornstein, R. 1973. Right and left thinking. *Psychology Today, 6,* 86–92.

Paivio, A. 1971. *Imagery and Verbal Processes.* New York: Rinehart and Winston.

Papcun, G., S. Krashen, D. Terbeek, R. Remington, and R. Harshman. 1974. The left hemisphere is specialized for speech, language and/or something else. *Journal of the Acoustical Society of America, 55,* 319–327.

Pask, G. 1976. Styles and strategies of learning. *British Journal of Educational Psychology, 46,* 128–148.

Pask, G., and B. C. E. Scott. 1972. Learning strategies and individual competence. *International Journal of Man-Machine Studies, 4,* 217–253.

Prator, C. H. 1979. The cornerstones of method. In M. Celce-Murcia and L. McIntosh (eds.), *Teaching English as a Second or Foreign Language,* Rowley, Mass.: Newbury House.

Ramirez, M., and D. R. Price-Williams. 1974. Cognitive styles of children of three ethnic groups in the United States. *Journal of Cross-Cultural Psychology, 5,* (2), 212–219.

Smart, J. C., C. F. Elton, and C. W. Burnett. 1971. Underachievers and overachievers in intermediate French. *Language Learning, 416.*

Street, R. F. 1931. A gestalt completion test—a study of a cross section of intellect. New York: Teachers College, Columbia University Contributions to Education, No. 481.

TenHouten, W. 1976. More on split brain research, culture, and cognition. *Current Anthropology, 17,* (3), 503–506.

Upshur, J. A. 1968. Four experiments on the relation between foreign language teaching and learning. *Language Learning, 18,* 124.

Valette, R. M. 1969. The Pennsylvania project, its conclusions and its implications. *The Modern Language Journal, 396.*

Wardhaugh, R. 1969. TESOL: Current problems and classroom practice. *TESOL Quarterly, 3,* 105–116.

Wechsler, D. 1955. *The Measurement of Adult Intelligence.* Baltimore: Williams and Wilkins.

Weitan, W., and C. Etaugh. 1973. Lateral eye movements as related to verbal and perceptual-motor skills and values. *Perceptual and Motor Skills, 36,* 423–428.

Williamsen, V. 1969. A pilot program in teaching Spanish: An intensive approach. *The Modern Language Journal, 73–78.*

Witkin, H. A. 1973. The role of cognitive style in academic performance and in teacher-student relation. Paper presented at a symposium on Cognitive Styles, Creativity and Higher Education, sponsored by the Graduate Record Examination Board, Montreal, Canada, November 8–10. 1972. Princeton: Educational Testing Service.

Witkin, H. A., C. A. Moore, D. R. Goodenough, and P. W. Cox. 1977. Field-dependent and field-independent cognitive styles and their educational implications. *Review of Educational Research, 47,* 1–65.

Wittrock, M. C. 1974. Learning as a generative process. *Educational Psychologist, 11,* 87–95.

Wittrock, M. C. 1975. The generative processes of memory. *UCLA Educator, 17,* 33–43.

Wittrock, M. C. (ed.). 1977. *The Human Brain.* Englewood Cliffs, N.J.: Prentice-Hall.

Wittrock, M. C. 1978. Education and the cognitive processes of the brain. *77th Yearbook of the N.S.S.E.,* Part II. Chicago: University of Chicago Press.

Zelniker, T., and W. E. Jeffrey. 1976. Reflective and impulsive children: Strategies of information processing underlying differences in problem-solving. *Monographs of the Society for Research in Child Development, 41,* (5), 1–52.

PART II
THE LEARNER'S LANGUAGE

INTRODUCTION

In this second part of the anthology we are concerned with the language (or output) that second language learners produce as they communicate in English, trying to approximate what they perceive to be the target language system.

Hatch, Gough, and Peck, in their chapter, provide us with an excellent overview of the case study research that has been done in second language acquisition. In the other chapter in this section Celce-Murcia and Hawkins show how both contrastive analysis and error analysis have contributed to the development of interlanguage analysis, which they then proceed to explore in some detail.

After reading both chapters, the ESL teacher will recognize that second language acquisition and interlanguage analysis are both concerned not only with describing the learner's language in linguistic terms but also with explaining what learners acquire (i.e., the forms and the sequence) and how they acquire it (i.e., the processes and strategies) in psychological terms.

WHAT CASE STUDIES REVEAL
ABOUT SYSTEM, SEQUENCE, AND VARIATION IN
SECOND LANGUAGE ACQUISITION

Evelyn Hatch, Judy Wagner Gough
and Sabrina Peck

For many years, teachers have observed the errors made by their adult students learning English as a second language and they have searched for ways to account for these errors. At the same time, they have marveled at how "easy" it is for young children living abroad to acquire a second language. One of the basic assumptions about second language acquisition is that there are vast differences in the strategies, speed, and ease of child and adult in learning a second language.

Yet, in recent years, the notion that second language learning is radically different according to the age of the learner has gradually diminished in importance. In its place, the hypothesis has been formulated that the speech of a second language learner at any point in the acquisition process is a systematic language which can be described. This systematic language is not age dependent. The system, using Weinreich's earlier theory of languages in contact (1953), has been called "interlanguage" by Selinker (1972); Nemser (1971) has called it a "learning system." Richards (1971) has stated that the set of common errors shared by all students learning ESL are proof of this learning system.

While granting that differences do exist in success and motivation, Corder (1967, 1971) has called for evidence to show that language acquisition, first and second, differs in any important way. He assumes that the same *process* takes place in language acquisition despite the age range, despite differences in the first language of various learners, and in spite of the number of languages the person knows. All these factors may make the learner more or less sophisti-

cated in learning the new language, but the process remains the same.

How does one account for the language produced by the learner as he acquires a second language? A number of important causes have been identified, three of which Selinker (1972) has listed as (1) transfer from the first language; (2) learning strategies such as overgeneralization of the target language rules and semantic features; and (3) communication strategies in using the second language. None of these explanations of the form of developmental language systems has been fully tested; each writer calls for studies of second language learners, both children and adults, to study the process of second language acquisition.

This call for studies is not new. In 1945, Professor Werner F. Leopold, the father of language acquisition research in this country, published a paper calling upon linguists to carry out serious study of child language and infant bilingualism. While he noted a number of interesting theoretical papers on language acquisition, he explained that without numerous case studies of the acquisition process they could only be speculative. Nothing useful, as Dr. Leopold said, can come from speculative thinking until second language acquisition has been studied in tangible case histories.

By the early 1970s, ESL teachers and researchers began to realize the importance of second language acquisition studies. This research is useful and valuable for the language teacher for three basic reasons. First, it can help explain the "errors" students make, not as isolated mistakes but as part of the language acquisition process. And, second, it

TABLE 1 Case Studies of Second Language Acquisition Cited Here (Arranged by Age of Subject)

Subject Name(s)	Age	Languages	Investigator(s)	Year
Hildegard	Complete record. Emphasis on 1st three years	English, German	Leopold	1939–1949
Louis	1st 3 years	German, French	Ronjat	1913
Sven	2–4	Swedish and Estonian	Oksaar	1973
Takahiro	2:6–3:1	Japanese, English	Itoh	1973
Paul	5	Taiwanese, English	Huang	1970
Rune, Reidun	6, 3:9	Norwegian, English	Ravem	1968
Homer	5:11	Assyrian, Persian, English	Gough	1974
10 unnamed Ss	Range 4:11–5:9	Spanish, English	Adams	1974
12 unnamed Ss	5–7	English, Spanish	Flores	1973
Alma, Juan, Enrique	Range 5:6–6:6	Spanish, English	Young	1974
Ken	7	Japanese and English	Milon	1974
Male child	10	French, Spanish, English	Chamot	1972
Ricardo	13	Spanish, English	Butterworth	1972
Zoila	Adult	Spanish, English	Shapira	1975

can give the teacher information on the general sequence followed in acquiring the language under natural conditions (rather than in the classroom). This is important in relation to the pedagogical sequence followed for introducing the structures of English to second language learners. Third, such studies can show us important differences among individual learners. As Selinker has noted, "a theory of second language learning which does not provide a central position of individual differences among learners *cannot* be considered acceptable" (1972, fn. 8, 213).

This paper is an attempt to summarize case studies in second language learning in relation to these three basic areas. Since the ESL curriculum includes the verb system of English, we will concentrate on the parts of the language which involve tense, modals, and progressive and perfective aspect, that is, the development of the AUX system. While examining our data we will try to answer the following questions:

1. Are there systematic language errors common to all learners?

2. Can we outline a general sequence of language learning?

3. Can we explain why this sequence occurs and why there are variations from it?

4. Is this sequence similar for both first and second language learners?

5. What individual differences exist among language learners?

To answer these questions, data from approximately 17 observational studies of 40 second-language backgrounds are drawn on. In all cases the learners acquired their second language naturally; that is, they were not taught the language in formal language classes. Subjects are referred to by name rather than by investigator; the age range is from 2 1/2 to 34 years. Most of the data cited here are from observational studies that were completed in the early 1970s, probably the richest period for case studies in second language acquisition research. The remaining data are from research published before 1940. A list of the observational case studies cited in this paper is in Table 1.

LOOKING FOR SYSTEMATICITY IN LANGUAGE LEARNER ERRORS

In trying to account for the language of the learners, we first looked at our data for evidence of first language interference. Although we found errors which could be explained as interference, we could not ignore problems with this explanation since (1) many errors could not be explained as interference; (2) where we might expect to find interference errors, there are often none; and (3) what appears to be interference can be also explained as a systematic development of the second language, or interlanguage. Two examples of errors which at first glance may seem to be interference involve WH-fronting and copula deletion.

WH-fronting

In English WH-questions, the question word (who, what, where, or when) is fronted so that "You are (AUX) going where?" becomes transformed into "Where are (AUX) you going?" Inversion involves the AUX rather than the entire verb form.

In Spanish interrogatives, the question word QUE is also fronted, but the entire verb form itself is inverted. If interference were to occur as predicted by the contrastive analysis theory, we would expect a Spanish speaker to produce WH-questions with subject-verb inversions and no do-support:

> *What like you?
> *Where watch you it?
> Who is he? (positive transfer)
> *What watch you on TV yesterday?
> *Where eat you your dinner yesterday?

If we examine the data on Ricardo, an adolescent whose native language is Spanish, we find that his speech errors in using WH-questions are not caused by interference from Spanish. Sometimes his question words occur at the end of the phrase, resembling neither Spanish nor English syntax:

> You like what?
> You watch where?
> He is who?

Even the predicted positive transfer (Who is he?) does not occur—i.e., Ricardo says (He is who?). Although Ricardo fronts the WH-question word in the majority of his questions, he still makes none of the required AUX inversions and omits do support.

Copula deletion

In the dialect of Taiwanese spoken by 5-year-old Paul, the omission of the copula "shi" in an NP + NP pattern occurs only in affirmative sentences where the first NP is a demonstrative pronoun. In such cases the copula may be omitted, but it is not a mandatory deletion. When we examine the data reflecting Paul's English language development, we notice many two-word utterances where the copula is deleted:

You+++Edmond.	Paul+++baby.
Me+++Paul.	This+++freeway.
Bozo+++clown.	This+++not freeway.

In most of these cases the first NP is either a proper noun or a pronoun. We could say that "This+++freeway" is an interference error according to the rules of Taiwanese; however, such an analysis would not account for what appears to be an identical language rule in the other utterances listed above.

The language rules in these two examples are not idiosyncratic; when we examine the data collected on other second language learners, we also find similar errors involving copula deletion and WH-fronting (see Table 2). The occurrence of such forms is independent of age and language background; they appear in observational studies where the learner has received no formal language training and in the data Richards (1971) has collected on students in ESL classes who come from all over the world.

Both WH-fronting and copula deletion provide evidence for a developmental language system. Because of widespread examples of these patterns, we have reason to believe that they are not mere slips of the tongue nor are they random mistakes. We are unable to substantiate claims of interference or idiosyncratic rule formation as the errors occur independent of the language background of the learner and seem to occur in the data of all learners. It is more reasonable to suggest that they are evidence of a system for organizing language data in communication and that this system reflects the learner's grammar at a particular moment in his language development.

SEQUENCES IN LANGUAGE LEARNING

If this is true, we should be able to outline a general sequence of language development for all second language learners. Therefore, we looked at the data next for evidence of a shared sequence in acquisition of the AUX system of English.

Most learners began with neither AUX nor main verb in their utterances:

This kite. Me Paul.	(Paul)	I my cat to Andy.	(Homer)
It hot. I okay.	(Zoila)	Me good. He champion.	(Ricardo)

A large percentage of the two-word utterances were "introducer" "That . . . *noun*" sentences. Some verbs do, of course, appear in early data, and in these the verb is in base form and is unmarked for tense:

Push in. (Hildegard)	Me watch TV. Me exercise.	(Ricardo)
Wash hand. (Paul) I fall down again. (Rune)	Mrs. L. tell me. You go in school.	(Zoila)

TABLE 2 Typical Developmental Errors

I. *Omission of Inversion*
    Where you was?
    What you was doing?   }   Hildegard (German)

    What was called the film?
    How many brothers she has?
    When she will be 15?   }   Richards (1971) data, adults
    Why this man is cold?

II. *Omission of Do*
    Why we not live in Scotland?
    What Jane give him?   }   Rune (Norwegian)

    Where put it?
    Why you speak French?   }   Chamot data (Spanish and French)

    What you said?
    What time you up now?   }   Zoila (Spanish)

    Why you went?
    How long it takes?
    Where it happened?   }   Richards (1971) data, adults

III. *Be-deletion*
    He champion.
    This Cisneros.
    Me good player.   }   Ricardo (Spanish)

    What this?
    This Misty?   }   Homer (Persian)

    It hot.
    I okay.   }   Zoila (Spanish)

    What you reading to-yesterday?
    What her going to market?   }   Rune (Norwegian)

    He born England.
    He disgusted.
    When Jane coming?
    What she doing?   }   Richards (1971) data, adult
    They running very fast.
    The industry growing fast.

Be begins to appear, first as *is*, then moving later to *'m* and *'r*. *-ing* is the first appearance of aspect, usually beginning as *-ing* alone:

I no pushing. (Paul)	She no looking. (Zoila)
Elizabeth coming. (Homer)	We climbing. All crying. (Rune)
You playing (Enrique)	You necessary working. (Ricardo)

and then, as the learner develops *be*, it too begins to appear along with the *-ing*, but there are many lapses with either the *be* or the *-ing* dropped as the form is developed:

I'm write.
I'm open the table.   (Paul)

One man is talk ... uh ... play trumpet.   (Ricardo)

Some learners acquire the "going to" future at the same time as the -ing form; others acquire it much later. For those who acquire be + ing first and then the going-to future, the addition of the going-to form usually requires them to sort out all the forms once again. There is more evidence of be deletion and some confusion as to just what gets marked with the -ing:

He no gonna do purple.
I no going to be your friend.   (Enrique)

When you're going to doing the car?   (Juan)

Later going to pickup Alisha.   (Zoila)

Modal acquisition order varies a great deal from learner to learner. Some acquire can't first, then can in questions and finally in statements; others reverse the order. We will have more to say on can later.

Tense acquisition on the main verb also varies. For Adams' subjects, three learned past tense first; four learned present first; one acquired them simultaneously; and two left the verb unmarked for tense during the two years of observation. Other learners (cf. Ravem, 1968) appeared to learn the present/past distinction simultaneously, though they seem to have had more difficulty in producing the third person singular endings for present tense than the -ed endings for past. Since the base form of the verb is used except for third person singular, it is difficult to use the 80 percent or 90 percent criterion level as evidence of present tense acquisition. As long as the person is not talking about he, she, or it, he does not have to mark the verb. This gives a high count number for present tense which may be quite misleading. The perfective verb forms were used only rarely and then only in the studies which covered two or more years of observation. The perfect forms in the data usually had either tense or participle form "errors."

Question formation also follows a sequence. First, rising intonation is used or transferred from the first language:

This tree?
We're going home?   (Paul)

This name?
This Canada?
You studying?   (Homer)
I'm going UCLA?

Is good?
Play blocks?   (Adams data)

You will finish?
Tomorrow is Saturday?   (Chamot data)

You see?
You go?   (Zoila)

This is quickly supplemented by tag questions in the data of most subjects:

George come to school, no?   (Ken)

You Joe, okay?
Sit here, okay?   (Paul)

You want tea, no?   (Zoila)

WH-questions begin with WH-fronting frequently before the copula has developed:

Where my ball?
What you doing me?   (Hildegard)
What you knitting?

What you reading to-yesterday?
                            (Rune)
What her going to making?

For most learners, tense has not yet been acquired and since there is no *do*-support, *do* does not appear in questions:

What Jane give him?
                            (Rune)
Why we not live in Scotland?

Where you put it?
                            (Chamot data)
What you said?

When you up?
                            (Zoila)
When you go your house?

Modal inversion seems to be the first inversion to take place, but it may well be "formula-learned" rather than a true inversion:

How can I finish?   (Chamot data)

Can Ken have some juice?
Can I play?   (Paul)
Jim, can you play with the ball?

Some subjects try verb inversion, but there are very few examples of this phenomenon:

Like you ice cream?
Drive you car yesterday?   (Rune)
Like you me not?

What say that?
Where goes the eraser?   (Adams data)
What draw a tree?

When verb inversion does take place, it is usually explained as first-language interference (the examples given above are from Norwegian and Spanish speakers where these forms are possible in the first language). Yet, they could also be attributed to rule testing. That is, learners realize something is to be inverted so they test out moving the whole verb as one rule possibility.
Be inversion

Is it Misty   Are you a good boy?
            (Homer)   (Paul)
Are you play,   Is this yours house?

occurs before *do*-inversion:

What you did in Rothbury?   (Rune)

Why he don't run?   (Juan)

When *do*-inversion finally does occur, there is often confusion over what should get marked for tense (e.g., did he walked? do he walking?). During the whole sequence, however, all learners use rising intonation as the preferred form for all questions, thereby avoiding inversion completely:

> You don't want to go?
> This is my name?   (Paul)
> Jim is coming too?
> You put the belt on?

Here we have briefly outlined just two examples of sequence in the acquisition of English: a general sequence for the AUX system, and a more clear-cut sequence for question formation. Although we have sketched out only two sequences, it is also possible to provide similar sequences for almost all other structures of English such as the pronoun system, noun phrase development, and negation formation. Since such sequences can be shown to exist, we can then turn to the more important questions involving universals of language acquisition. The first have to do with questioning the sequence: how universal is this sequence and how clear is it?

First, the sequence is not universal in the sense that every learner acquired each item in exactly the same order. For example, Paul never had a "Where ball is?" stage; all his WHERE-Qs included *be*-inversion right from the start. His *can* questions also appeared with *can* inverted ("Can I play?") rather than inside the sentence ("Where I can play?"). Most of the other learners, however, did go through an intermediate step before inverting *can*.

Second, the sequence is not always clear. There is a great deal of overlapping in stages, and the amount of overlapping varies from learner to learner. Paul, for example, moved from stage to stage with a minimum of overlapping of old forms. To be sure, he still avoided question inversion through all five months of his observational study, but in looking at the data, the switch from stage to stage is neat and clear. He is a real "rule-former." His data are very nice to work with for that reason. Other children, for example, Homer, are what we have called "data-gatherers." If we analyzed a typical two-week period for Homer, setting an 80 percent or 90 percent criterion for the appropriate use of a structure in obligatory cases, we would have to conclude that Homer had acquired nothing over the two weeks. Still, the tape recordings from that period would reveal that Homer's speech was becoming more and more fluent, and more and more forms would be appearing, although Homer would not seem to be sorting them out. Of course, there are also some researchers like Paul, and some like Homer: some people begin organizing or sorting their data almost before they start collecting; others gather and gather and the organization or sorting out seems to be minimal as they go along. Both types of people, learners or researchers, seem to function well. Sorting, even for data-gatherers, seems to go on but not in a way that is always obvious to us.

ACCOUNTING FOR SEQUENCES AND VARIATIONS WITHIN SEQUENCES

While accepting individual differences in organizing language data and accepting some variation in the order of acquisition from learner to learner, we do believe that the sequence of acquisition is reliable. It has been corroborated by case studies (Hakuta, 1974; Cancino, Rosansky, and Schumann, 1978) and in a large-scale experimental study of over 100 children by Dulay and Burt (1974). Rosansky and others have questioned whether individual variation may not outweigh the similarities.

However, if we do accept the similarity of sequence in acquisition, the most important question is, why *this* sequence: why are the data ordered the way they are and why are there certain variations within the order of acquisition? That is, can we find explanatory universals that might account for the sequence?

In some cases we can easily explain the occurrence of a pattern. If we look at the input data (in the few studies where they have been included), it is obvious why the data included so many "This . . . *noun*" sentences and "This

... *noun?"* questions in the beginning stages. The learners in all these "natural, non-teaching observational" studies are in fact being taught. In an attempt to get *some* data in the initial observations, the "observers" are subjecting the learners to a constant barrage of "What's this?" or "Is this a *(noun)?"* questions. It's small wonder the "This ... *(noun)"* utterances predominate and "This ... *(noun)?"* questions appear first.

In other cases the explanations are not easy to find. The confusion in the acquisition of *can* is a case in point. Some learners seem to learn *can* first in questions, others in negative statements, and others in affirmative statements. Part of the problem is lack of input data to show which form is used most frequently in language addressed to the learner. The other part of the problem is that we haven't bothered to look at the semantic content of *can*. In some of the data where questions with *can* appear first, they seem to be concerned with asking permission while the *can't* form learned later is used to express inability. To explain variations in acquisition patterns, we need to go back over the data to sort out "permission/ability/probability" meanings of *can,* and to look at the frequency of each in the input data as well.

In addition to frequency in the input data, semantic function and linguistic complexity play an important part in determining the sequence. Input alone cannot explain the sequence. Observers in the Huang study continually asked Paul "What are you doing?" and "Are you VERBing?" questions. If input were the only criterion for language acquisition, we would expect Paul to have learned the progressive by the end of the 5-month study. This was not the case, however. Paul rarely produced the coveted 'Subject + Be + V+ing' response on his own, despite the well-sequenced "teaching techniques" of his "observers."

At first, the semantic content of "What are you doing?" confused Paul, and he would not make the required analogy between "doing" and "VERBing." Paul continued to omit either the *ing* or the *be.* These additional morphemes were just too difficult for him to

handle at this stage. Here is a sample of a dialogue between Paul and his observer:

Observer	Paul
Paul, are you writing?	Yeah.
What are you doing?	I'm write.
Paul, are you writing?	Yeah.
What are you doing?	I'm writing.
What's the baby doing?	Baby cry.
Is the baby crying?	Yeah.
What's the baby doing?	Baby is crying.

This drilling resembles the exercises found in language teaching texts. As we shall see, although Paul was able to produce the progressive when guided through a dialogue, it did not mean that he had acquired the progressive form in his free speech production. Only fifteen lines later, the conversation looked like this:

Observer	Paul
What are you doing now?	I'm sleep.
Sleeping!	

Not to be discouraged, the observer persisted with his questions. Finally, perseverance paid off, and both observer and language learner came to terms; it appears to have been a peaceful surrender:

Observer	Paul
What are you doing on the chair?	I'm sit down on the chair.
I'm sit down on the chair. Okay.	

Paul, as we see, sifted through the language data, using those symbols he needed to express an idea. In context, "I'm sit down on the chair" offers as much semantic information as does "I'm sitting down on the chair." Oftentimes, the language necessary for communication is far simpler than the linguistic system of the native speaker, for all languages have a certain amount of built-in redundancy. The reduction of these redundancies, sometimes called simplification, is a very common strategy among language learners and offers an explanation for the occurrence of certain linguistic patterns.

The simplification principle can help us explain WH-fronting, for example. A sentence, such as "Where you was?" contains all the semantic elements necessary for asking a question. Although inversion of the subject and verb makes the sentence syntactically correct, it does not add new meaning. While learning about WH-questions and simultaneously sorting out other kinds of language rules, it is easier to attach a WH-question word to a sentence with declarative word order. This strategy simplifies the linguistic task while asking for the necessary information. At a later date, the learner will be ready to apply the English inversion rule as well as supply do-support in all required contexts.

Copula deletion can be explained in a similar manner. If Ricardo or another learner includes the proper form of the copula in an equational sentence (He *is* champion), he does not provide any additional semantic information to the listener. From the context in which the sentence is uttered, the listener knows that the two noun phrases are linked and he is also able to determine the time period referred to from the context. Utterances such as:

This kite. (Paul) or
I okay. (Zoila)

are clear for the same reason.

Still another explanation for the language system of second language learners is the principle of overgeneralization, that is, the learner's inappropriate extension of a linguistic rule in the target language. For example, having learned "likes to," a learner may produce "enjoys to" because of the analogy he has created between "verb + infinitive" to express desire. Learners have a strong tendency to couple a linguistic rule with a semantic notion. Richards (1971) found that when instructed students learned "make" in the same lesson as "enable it to" "allow it to" and "permit it to," 13 out of 23 students produced "The policeman made the driver *to*

get out of his car." However, in English as in other languages, it it not uncommon to find semantically analogous situations which require different patterns. This is especially true of the English prepositional system.

For the learner, overgeneralization is an efficient method of initially sorting and storing language data. In addition, learners first acquire the most general rules, which can apply to the greatest amount of language data. Rules for linguistic exceptions are not learned until later (Slobin, 1973), especially when those exceptions are not necessary for the communicative process. (There are some apparent exceptions to this principle, since irregular past tense verb forms are acquired early. This exception is more apparent than real, however, since those past tense forms appear to be memorized forms which have high frequency in the input data. When the learner acquires the past tense rule, he then applies it to irregular past tense forms as well.)

Even when a sentence is correctly produced, we must guard against assuming that the acquisition of form means acquisition of function. This is especially clear when we look at the acquisition of tense. We have said that the *ing* form is the first marker of aspect to appear, and that is true. The *ing* form appears, but its function is not yet acquired. That is, the *ing* form is used to talk about past, present, the moment of speaking, and both future probability and future time by our learners. This occurs in the data for Zoila, Ricardo, Enrique, Juan, and Homer. Homer even used it as an imperative. Why then does it appear so early? One reason may be the frequency of *ing* in the input data. We do not have enough input data to be sure about this, but Legum's (1969) study shows the *ing* form is the most frequent form in kindergarten through third grade classroom language. In Brown's count of parental speech samples (1973), the progressive ranked highest in verbal inflections for Eve's parents and second highest in samples from Adam and Sarah's parents. Since *ing* is also phonologically salient, learners' frequent use of *ing* could also be accounted for by Slobin's perceptual saliency principle. This principle holds that a phonologically salient form will be easily recognizable and will therefore be learned early. But because the progressive has a variety of temporal-time functions (I'm eating at six tonight, He's eating now, etc.), its true boundaries are difficult to learn. It covers not only the moment of speaking but also various future and extended present functions. In acquisition studies we need to go through the data to look at function along with form.

A learner may use a form before acquiring its function, and perhaps while continuing to use a non-English form. A good example of use of structures which are not really acquired is in Enrique's data. While he had a great deal of difficulty with the definite article *the*, he finally reached the 90 percent criterion level on it. One month later, he suddenly began using something new: Spanish articles and an invented article *le*. *Le* seemed to be an amalgam of a Spanish article and English *the*. Perhaps rapid development of other parts of the language system caused the regression in article production, or perhaps he still had not really sorted out the function of the article system at all.

After looking at all the data, it seems very clear that knowledge of input language is extremely important. In the few cases where we do have both production and input data, we can show fairly clearly that frequency of structures in the input data does influence the order of acquisition. Table 3 shows how the questions asked of Paul in the input data influenced his own question development. The stages referred to are months 1 and 2 for stage 1; the third month for stage 2; and the fourth month for stage 3. The questions in the input data are ranked by frequency. The table shows that questions asked frequently may be learned as formulas and then acquired as rules, dependent, of course, on their complexity. Frequency of question type in the input data does influence the kinds of questions that Paul acquires. Tracing the development of *where*- and *can*-questions explains why these were learned without the intermediate stage most learners go through. The two question types were extremely frequent in the speech of people talking to

him. More interesting, perhaps, is why he learned some but not all the questions frequently asked of him. That is, why did he not acquire questions requiring *be*-inversion and *do*-support? Both these forms appeared very late in his production data. Partly it is a matter of a required change in word order. Yet, while changes in word order increase difficulty, he was able to acquire *can*- and *where*-questions which also represent word order change. The difference must have to do with the semantic content of *can* and *where* as opposed to *be* and *do*. *Do* is a tense carrier and *be* has a number of functions as linker, classifier, and as an equivalence marker of sorts. None of these functions carry the semantic weight of *can* or *where*. Since *do* and *is* lack any clear semantic function, it is not surprising that the correct form of such questions was acquired late despite their frequency in the input language. The variety of patterns for *be* (is, am, are, was, were) and *do* (do, does, did) also adds to the difficulty of acquisition.

So far, we have presented evidence based on studies of second language learners to support the theory of a developmental sequence in language acquisition. We have found that any comprehensive interpretation of the language learning process must include an analysis of the input data as well as the learner's production data and of form as well as function. While we do not wish the reader to misinterpret this to mean that imitation can account for more than the most trivial part of the language learning process, frequency of forms occurring in the input data does seem to have an effect on the rate of acquisition. What we have learned from the data so far is that communication is the goal of all learners, and parts of the language system which are not important to communication are learned slowly. However, if a structure is extremely frequent in the input data, the learner will produce it. The effects of frequency are modified in a number of ways. If a form has low semantic power, it will be learned late. If a form requires changes in word order, it will be learned late. If there are a variety of forms for a morpheme (e.g., regular plural endings with /s/, /z/, and /əz/ forms), it will be acquired

TABLE 3 Input Frequency and Question Production

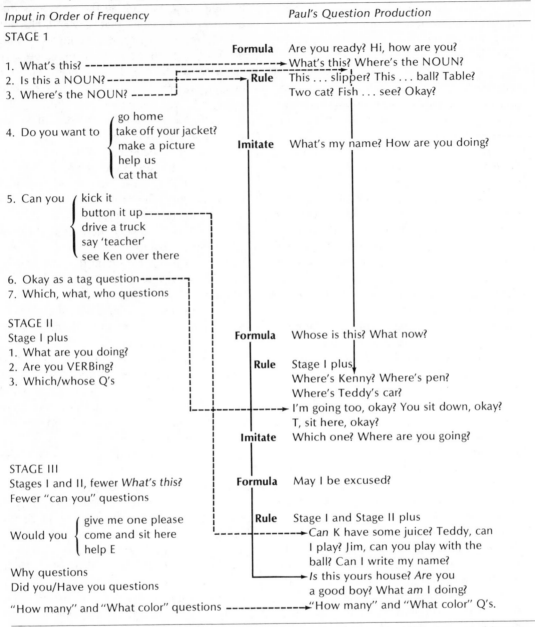

Input in Order of Frequency	Paul's Question Production

STAGE 1

Formula — Are you ready? Hi, how are you?
1. What's this? ──────────────→ What's this? Where's the NOUN?
2. Is this a NOUN? ────────→ **Rule** — This . . . slipper? This . . . ball? Table?
3. Where's the NOUN? ──────┘ Two cat? Fish . . . see? Okay?

4. Do you want to { go home / take off your jacket? / make a picture / help us / cat that } **Imitate** — What's my name? How are you doing?

5. Can you { kick it / button it up / drive a truck / say 'teacher' / see Ken over there }

6. Okay as a tag question
7. Which, what, who questions

STAGE II
Stage I plus
1. What are you doing?   **Formula** — Whose is this? What now?
2. Are you VERBing?
3. Which/whose Q's   **Rule** — Stage I plus
                          Where's Kenny? Where's pen?
                          Where's Teddy's car?
                          I'm going too, okay? You sit down, okay?
                          T, sit here, okay?
                          Imitate — Which one? Where are you going?

STAGE III
Stages I and II, fewer *What's this?*   **Formula** — May I be excused?
Fewer "can you" questions

Would you { give me one please / come and sit here / help E }   **Rule** — Stage I and Stage II plus
                          Can K have some juice? Teddy, can
                          I play? Jim, can you play with the
                          ball? Can I write my name?
Why questions   *Is* this yours house? *Are* you
Did you/Have you questions   a good boy? What *am* I doing?

"How many" and "What color" questions ──────→ "How many" and "What color" Q's.

From E. Hatch and J. Wagner Gough (1976), Explaining sequence and variation in second language acquisition, *Language Learning*, special issue No. 4, 39–57. Reprinted with permission of the editor.

late. Any combination of these variables will make the form more difficult to learn and will consequently delay its acquisition. Forms of low frequency, low semantic power, requiring rules for changing word order, having a multiplicity of form and a multiplicity of function, and receiving tertiary stress (or no stress) will take the longest to learn.

These ideas are not new. Slobin, Brown, and others have talked of them frequently in

TABLE 4 AUX and QUESTION Development in First Language Acquisition

Period 1	Period 2	Period 3
See hole?	What book name?	Does the kitty stand up?
I ride train?	What the dollie have?	Does lions walk?
No ear?	What soldier marching?	Oh, did I caught it?
Mommy eggnog?	Why you smiling?	Which way they should go?
What doing?	Why not me drink it?	What he can ride in?
Where Ann pencil?	You can't fix it?	Where my spoon goed?
Where milk go?		Is mommy talking to Robin's grandmother?

discussing first language acquisition. We find that the learning strategies of generalization and simplification apply to both first and second language acquisition. Although we are not prepared to make claims which are as strong as Corder's, we find that there are striking similarities in the sequence of question formation for both first and second language learners.

COMPARING SEQUENCES FOR SECOND AND FIRST LANGUAGE ACQUISITION

In their classic study of three small children learning English as a first language, Klima and Bellugi (1966) reported on the development of WH-questions. In Table 4, we can see that the first stage in question formation for children is very similar to that for second language learners. The utterance primarily consists of nouns and verbs that are un-inflected for tense and number; the copula is omitted, too. There is no AUX and no subject-verb inversion. WH-interrogatives are fronted, and questions are signaled with rising intonation.

As we can see, there is a lot of over-lapping between each period. In period 2, there are still no modal auxiliaries in affirmative sentences and only two negative forms (*don't* and *can't*). *Don't* and *can't* are usually the first negative markers to be acquired after *no* and *not* (this too is true of second language learners). Also in this period, the progressive is marked only by the *ing* affixed to the verb, which is also characteristic of second language acquisition.

In period 3, be-inversion is present as is do-support, although there is some confusion over which form of *do* is appropriate. Even at this stage, the child expresses preference for WH-fronting without do-support. Although this comparison does support Corder's theories, no strong claims can yet be made. Bever, Fodor, and Weksel (1965) in a theoretical paper claimed that first and second language learning are irreconcilably different. And based on real language data, Cancino, Rosansky, and Schumann (1978) have found that there are, indeed, differences between first and second language acquisition. It is clear that both first and second language learners use prior knowledge for new learning. Since second language learners' prior knowledge includes a first language and since second language learners are also older and therefore more cognitively mature, we should expect differences. However, until we have more comprehensive studies of both first and second language acquisition, we cannot make strong claims about the relationship between learning a first and second language. We need to examine input data along with the learner's speech production to thoroughly evaluate both form and function. Until such data become available for study, we cannot establish a basis for making a comparison between first and second language learning.

ACCOUNTING FOR DIFFERENCES AMONG LANGUAGE LEARNERS

While searching for evidence of language learning universals, it is important to recognize individual differences among learners. By discarding "exceptional data" we may be omitting information that could be valuable to other researchers trying to account for what appears to be an "exception to the rules" in their data.

We have shown that there are differences in the way some learners process language by identifying rule-formers and data-gatherers. The speed at which language is learned also seems to vary greatly. Five-year-old Paul, with 2-1/2 hours of exposure to English a day, learned English so rapidly that in 5 months it was difficult to find ways in which his language differed from that of his peers (Huang, 1970; Huang and Hatch, 1978). Alma, in over a year of observation, said only a few words of English given even greater exposure to English each day (Young, 1974). Takahiro was very reluctant to speak English, while Homer began to use English words 2 weeks after his arrival in the United States (Itoh, 1973). Leopold's Hildegard, learning two languages simultaneously, always showed a preference for one of her two languages (depending on which country she was in), while Ronjat's Louis used both of his languages, switching with no apparent difficulty according to the language of the person he spoke to.

The extent to which there are differences among language learners seems dependent on that vague term "personality." However, we cannot ignore evidence for other contributing factors.

Interference differences

The nature and amount of interference vary greatly among learners. With a few exceptions, some interference does occur in most of the studies we looked at. In the cases where there is no interference, the children still frequently explained new vocabulary items to themselves or to others in their first language. There is a nice example in Homer's data where he simply explains away new vocabulary he doesn't understand. Mark, his playmate, had been warning Homer to be careful of the blocks that they were using to build with. "Quit making it so tall," he commanded. When Homer questioned, "What is it /sulta/?" Mark responded by merely repeating his command: "Don't make it so tall." Again Homer asked for the meaning of "so tall" and when no response was given, he spoke in his first language, Assyrian, to verbalize a rational explanation for this "thing" /sulta/:

Mærın muile sulta. Mærın mærεle sulta khæmεndile. Mærın lıt khæmεndile. (I ask what is this /sulta/. He says /sulta/ is something. I say there's no such thing.)

The amount of language mixing varies markedly from subject to subject. Some learners never mixed. Others used their first language, substituting second language vocabulary items as they learned them (making second language learning look like a relexification of the first language). This was particularly so in the first-year Spanish immersion program for Anglo children in Culver City. As these kindergarten children began acquiring Spanish, they tried to communicate with the teacher by using as many Spanish words as they knew:

> *Si*, I think. I got a quarter for *leche*.
> I'm gonna get a drink for *agua*.
> *True* more *dias* and we're going to the zoo.
> I'm a *avion*. I have a *bicicleta roja*.

Obviously more than relexification took place because after two years in the program the children are speaking Spanish.

Some subjects used a large number of words from their first language even when speaking to monolinguals who did not understand their first language. Few of the mixed words were verbs; most were nouns and there were a large percentage of these which were cognates for the two languages:

No speak too *mucho* him.
Me no *posible* go Los Angeles   (Ricardo)
He go for *Europa.*

There were many examples of repetition of vocabulary items in both languages:

Is no *bueno,* no good.
En mi, my house.   (Adams data)

Ohisama, Okay the sun.   (Takahiro)
Zoosan, eff—(attempt at elephant)

While it is not always clear from the data, repetitions seem to be used frequently when the learner either wishes to emphasize his point or when the expected reaction is not immediately forthcoming from the listener. They were usually said with stronger stress and raised pitch, with paralinguistic support.

Some learners occasionally said sentences which appear to be direct translations from the first language to the second or vice versa. It should be emphasized that these are exceptional examples, not typical of the subjects' utterances:

Je suis fini. ("Je suis pret" from "ich bin fertig") Un bateau faire. Je veux mes pantoufles mettre. Sur ce chemin on peut facile marcher. Mama sais de tres jolies choses peindre. (French verbs placed in German word order) (Louis)

Du kannst haben das. Das ist nicht in da. Ich kann spielen mit ihr morgen. (English word order in German) (Hildegard)

The water hot is ready. Two paper white. Is very well. (Spanish word order in English) (Zoila)

The number of "direct translations" can easily be increased by giving the learner a translation task where no time delay is allowed (cf. Swain, et al., 1972; Adams, 1974).

Many children produced "blends":

sloo "beat," from Swedish *sla* and Estonian *loo*   (Oksaar data)
kats "cats," from Swedish *katt* and Estonian *kass.*

and loan translations:

Butterfliege (butterfly) and meinselbst (myself)   (Hildegard)

The problem again is that it is not always clear whether these are all cases of language interference, whether they have a social basis instead, or whether, in some cases, they are simply creative play with the two languages. Oksaar (1973) has shown in her Swedish-Estonian case study that mixing of the languages by an incipient bilingual can be attributed to the same factors that are given for mixing or switching of languages by fluent bilinguals. The person spoken to, topics of conversation, and place of conversation all cause children to switch to the language they judge appropriate for discourse. If they have not yet acquired fluency in the language they judge appropriate, they will use as much of it as they can. Children mix languages to heighten emotional effect, to wheedle what they want out of particularly affectionate adults, and to quote others. They may mix languages because a particular word in one language appeals to them more than its equivalent word in another. A case in point is one child who would never say *blomster* but always said *flower* because she felt that the word sounded better in English. Vocabulary impoverishment, and therefore interference from the dominant language, may account for some mixing. In other cases, particularly in the simultaneous acquisition of two languages, the child is quite adept at soliciting and learning vocabulary for each language. Many researchers have commented on children's interest in finding out "how X says this" and "how Y says it."

Another label for at least some of the examples given in this section could be communication strategies with social and psychological causes. On the other hand, they all may be examples of "interference" from the first language. The label really depends on what is included in this frequently vague cover term, "interference." Certainly mixing or borrowing do not occur in first language data. That much can be said. We also need to look at interference phenomena over the age range of the learners. Interference and language mixing may not be as age-graded as has been thought; mixing may be related as much to "personality" as to age. It is true that the young children showed the least phonological interference, but there is a great deal of variation in this area among both children and adults. Evidence on syntactic and semantic interference over an age range simply is too sparse to allow us to make statements.

Age differences

The relationship between age and second language learning is still not clear. Taken as a whole, the research does not strongly support any optimal age hypothesis—neither "the younger the better" nor "the older the better." In an experimental study, Snow and Hoefnagel-Höhle (1978) found that older learners surpassed younger learners in the early stages: teenagers did best, then adults, then young children. Patkowski's study (1980) strongly supported the hypothesis that native-like proficiency in the syntax of a second language is possible only if the learning occurs before the end of puberty. In a review of optimal age studies, Krashen, Long, and Scarcella (1977) suggest that adults do better in initial learning but that younger learners do better in the long run. While this position is supported by their careful review of the literature, we feel that it is still too soon to make strong claims. More research on second language learning and age is needed. Researchers need to control for the same factors, and specify subject traits, the language skills tested, the testing methods, and the types of language exposure and instruction. For theoretical discussions on the effect of age on language learning processes see Lenneberg (1967), Penfield and Roberts (1959), and Ausubel (1964).

One age-related difference we do have evidence for is that more is expected of an adolescent (and we assume of adults, too)

learning a second language than from a child. The nature of the language input we have for Ricardo, a teenager, is far more complex both linguistically and semantically than the language input we have for children who have spent the same amount of time in the United States. It is no wonder that children appear to learn a language so quickly. We simplify their task, tolerate their errors, and marvel at how quickly they are able to string an uninflected verb to a noun. These attitudes and expectations may well determine the ease with which a second language is acquired.

If we look at the input data for Paul, a 5-year-old child, there is a strong correlation between language production, perception, and motor activity. The stimuli surrounding him provide the springboard for communication. That which he can see, identify, and act upon becomes the topic for conversation. In fact, the most common sentence patterns in months 1 and 2 are questions asking for identification (What's this? Is this a NP?), questions involving location of the object (where's NP?), and imperatives, which account for over half of the input data for this period of time. Furthermore, much of what Paul is told to do needs few language cues, since gestures, tone, and context provide most of the information. An outstretched hand, for example, suffices to clarify, "Hold my hand."

Table 5 outlines a conversation between Paul and his observers after 3 months of daily

	Paul
	2. Yeah.
	4. P. (didn't understand)
	6. Yeah.
	8. Jim's doggy.
	10. Yeah.
	12. Step.
e a dog?	14. No.
;gy out.	16. Open, open.
	18. Yeah, this is orange.
	20. No more orange.
	21. Two truck.
	23. Yeah.
	25. Other one?
	27. Truck? This.
	29. (Paul showed a car.)
my car?	31. Yeah.
	33. Joe's car.
	35. What are you doing?
	37. I'm going to.
	39. Yeah.
	41. Stop that (P. stopped).
	42. Oh! Airplane.
	44. One, two, three. Ma name is Paul. How are you?
	46. Fine.

exposure to English. We can see that language patterns are constantly recycled into the dialogue with vocabulary substitutions made (1, 5, 7, 17; 11, 13; 24, 32; 26, 28). We also find formulas of polite social discourse, such as "My name is Paul. How are you?" and "Fine, thank you," which are juggled back and forth between Paul and his language partners.

It is not uncommon for Paul to offer an inappropriate response to a question. Sometimes this is an error of interpretation; sometimes it is simply a response made for the pleasure of speaking. Sometimes a series of "inappropriate answers" can inject a Mad Hatter logic into the conversation (34–36), especially when produced with confidence as is often the case with children. Yet, the rhythm of the dialogue does not seem to suffer from such happenings. The importance of learning the rules of social discourse has not been discussed in our studies on language learning. What we mean by social discourse is the learner's ability to perceive the speaker's point of view and to respond to what has been said. Besides learning about language as symbolic representation, Paul is also learning about its function in social discourse. This may explain his inappropriate answers and the willingness of his investigators to let them pass. There are times when the uninterrupted flow of the dialogue, the conversational turn-taking rhythm, appears to be more important to Paul and the investigators than the actual exchange of information (1, 2, 3; 34–46).

In summary, Paul does not appear to be totally immersed in a new language environ-

TABLE 6 Sample Dialogue (Adult/Adolescent)

Observer	Adolescent (Ricardo)
1. Do you know what a question is?	2. Question mark.
3. Yeah. What do we mean when we say question?	4. Question?
5. What do we mean by question marks? What do we mean? What does question mark mean?	6. This a (points).
7. Yeah. But why do we put that mark there?	8. This.
9. Why do we put that mark there? See, we don't have it there. We just have a period there.	
10. Do you wrestle?	11. No.
12. No?	13. I like look.
14. You like to watch.	15. No me wrestle.
16. You don't like to do it yourself. You'd rather watch. Let's say "watch."	17. Hm?
18. Say "watch." Same thing. Look-watch, look-watch.	19. Watch.
20. Watch. You like to watch.	
21. What are you gonna do tonight?	22. Tonight? I don't know.
23. You don't know yet? Do you work at home, do the dishes or sweep the floor?	24. Water (garbled).
25. You water?	26. Flowers.
27. Flowers.	28. Mud.
29. Oh, You wash the mud down and all that. What else do you do at home?	30. Home?

ment. Because he is a child, there is a very limited body of graded language data that he is expected to handle. Language patterns in the input data are simple; many are formulas. Verbalizations complement the activity Paul and the people around him are engaged in. Language, then, is a medium for describing environmental stimuli. Learning the rules of social discourse also appears to be an important function served by speech, which may explain why the dialogue is allowed to flow as it does.

Ricardo had a very different language experience. After having the same amount of exposure to English as Paul (3 months), he was expected to interpret and respond to much more difficult concepts and linguistic patterns. In Table 6 we find that the sentences addressed to him have no particular linguistic pattern; they contain embedded clauses, idioms, and a wide range of vocabulary that Ricardo has a difficult time understanding (2, 3, 6, 8, 18, 31). Moreover, he is asked to supply reasons (for quite obscure questions, 1–7) including WHY-questions which are simply not found in the data on children until the very late stages of their language development. The explanation of causality requires more complex language patterns and thought processes than do location and identification.

Most of the dialogues between Ricardo and the investigators focus on activities that are displaced in time (22–31). That is, they relate to past and future events or to those things that Ricardo usually does during the day. This type of discourse requires a higher degree of abstraction than the language of commands and NP location or identification. There are also less obvious context clues to aid Ricardo in the interpretation of the input data. Even a well-devised pantomime (Table 7) is not as helpful as stimuli that are visually present as they almost always were for the child Paul.

Adults who tried to simplify their speech when talking with Ricardo still used more complex language and included a larger lexicon than those who talked with Paul and the other observed children. This is probably because the very nature of adult-adult com-

TABLE 7 Butterworth's Attempt to Contextualize with Ricardo

Observer	Ricardo
1. In Colombia, do they (lobsters) have claws?	2. Claws?
3. Claws. Do they have . . . the lobsters, do they have claws (form my hands into claws)?	4. Octopus?
5. No. The lobsters. Do the lobsters have hands?	6. Huh?
7. I don't know how to say it. I know . . . I am a lobster. This is my, this is my . . . I am a lobster. This is my claw (hands formed like claws).	8. Hm. Hm.
9. Do lobsters in Colombia have claws? Like this, you know? They pinch people.	10. Lobster?
11. On Sunday do you catch many lobsters?	12. Eh, huh?
13. Yeah, do you get many?	14. Eh. Dictionary?
15. Oh, do you want to go get your dictionary?	16. No, no necessary.
17. How many, how many do you get? How many do you catch?	18. Catch?
19. On Sunday. Yeah. How many do you catch on Sunday?	20. Thirty or forty.
21. Thirty or forty?!	22. Depend.
23. What do you do with them?	24. Huh?
25. The lobsters. What do you do with the lobsters?	26. You do?
27. Yes, where do they go?	28. In morning.

munication is different from that of adult-child or child-child discourse.

Just what effect these more complex input data have on an adult is difficult to measure. The effect will probably depend largely on the personality of the individual. We do know that Ricardo became more and more frustrated with English and more self-conscious about his inability to express himself. Whereas he had initially been very enthusiastic about learning English, at the study's end it was difficult to prove that any progress in rule formation had been made. The extremely high linguistic demands made on him as an adult learner of English may have been the cause of his frustrations and the reason for his lack of perceptible progress.

CONCLUSION

In conclusion, we see that language learning is a process which functions in much the same way for all learners. We have found evidence for discussing sequences in language learning based on common systematic errors among learners. In explaining reasons for these sequences, we have mentioned variables such as input data, semantic function of a form, its perceptual saliency, and the linguistic complexity of a given structure and its function.

Among the strategies the learner may employ to facilitate the learning and communication task are simplification and overgeneralization. Interference errors may be a learning or communication strategy as much as being a "menacing" intrusion of a first language on a second. We do need to examine and define what we mean by interference more precisely. In addition, we need to sort through the data again to examine linguistic form and its relationship to semantic function.

It is the blend of all these variables that is responsible for the language learning process. This blend is slightly different for each person so that no two individuals acquire language in exactly the same manner (see Wong-Fillmore, 1979). Age may play a significant role in determining the form of the input data as well as the expectations placed on the learner acquiring a new language. Just as important is the personality of the learner, which may be responsible for more than we usually credit it with in our studies.

While recognizing differences, the similarities in language development across age and language background are striking, enticing us to further explore the second-language-learning system. From such studies the teacher should develop a stronger understanding as to why students make errors during the learning process. Information about a natural sequence in second language learning should also tell us much about the potential effectiveness of any pedagogical sequence we might choose for use in our ESL classes.

DISCUSSION QUESTIONS

1.   A French speaker (47 years old) who learned English first by study in France and later by immersion in the United States, after 18 years in the United States still tends to use the base form of the verb for the progressive. He has also taken two advanced courses in English at the university. In this chapter we noted that *ing* appears early because of its high frequency and its perceptual saliency. How can you reconcile these two facts? Why has this French speaker not mastered the progressive? Have any of your students shown similar tendencies?

2.   What are the functions of *be*? Which functions should appear first in natural data? Consider the forms of *be*. Why should *is* occur first? What order would you predict for the other forms? Do you teach all forms and functions simultaneously?

3.   What order of acquisition would you predict for the English pronoun systems? How can you explain confusion of you/I in second language data? Most languages do have this distinction; so why should it be confusing for the learner?

4.   What could be learned about language acquisition from "forgetting" studies? In what areas do your students seem to "forget" the most (vocabulary, pronunciation, grammar)? Forgetting rates for young children appear to be even faster than acquisition rates. Does this vary with age? How much is lost over summer vacation? How much is communication influenced by what is forgotten?

5.   *Who, what,* and *where* questions usually appear in speech before *when* and *why* questions. What reasons would you give for such sequencing?

6.   In this chapter we have discussed language acquisition in terms of natural sequencing, simplification, overgeneralization, analogy, perceptual saliency, semantic complexity, and interference. How might a language teacher use any or all of these ideas to speed up the language acquisition process for his or her students?

SUGGESTED ACTIVITIES

1.   Collect data from a second language learner. Transcribe the data. Choose one area and try to describe the data: plurals tenses, pronouns, articles. How would you account for the "errors" made by your subject?

2.   Observe a child who is learning English by immersion. What strategies does he use for communicating with other children? How much does he rely on paralinguistic (gestures, exaggerated intonation, etc.) strategies?

3.   Elicit word associations from someone who is just beginning to learn a second language. Make sure that you allow for other-language "first thoughts" as well as forms in the new language. How many translations are given? Include abstract nouns as well as concrete, prepositions, verbs, etc. Are there differences in speed of response to various word classes? Does the "interference" come from the last-learned language or the person's first language? You may want to ask for multiple responses (as many as she or he can think of during 30 seconds). Ask your subject about "borrowings" she or he makes from other languages when speaking.

4.   Examine sequencing of language forms in a beginning English text. What structures would you choose to present first? Which would you save for later in the course? Why? How would you treat "errors" made in speech? Would you treat them any differently from errors in written work?

5. Here are some examples of negatives produced by Spanish speakers:

No is pain, is nerves. I no can see.
Children no is here. The pronunciation no is good.

Can you make a strong case for Spanish interference from these data? If so, how would you account for the following?

Is no good. (Persian) No heavy (English first language)
This no is chicken (French) That no mommy. (English first language)
You no can go. (Japanese) No can go. (English first language)
I no like small (Japanese) No singing song. (English first language)

If you feel there really are no differences, please read Cancino, Rosansky, and Schumann (1978) on the differences between first and second language learner's production of negative elements.

6. If you are living with a family or a roommate who speaks a language with which you are not familiar, try not to speak in English at all but rather to interact solely within their language environment. What strategies do you use to "understand" your environment? What strategies do you use to communicate? When is it easiest to understand what is going on? When is it the most difficult? Do you ever feel comfortable speaking? Under what circumstances?

7. The word *for* has many functions in English. What are they? In what ways do the following examples from a Spanish speaker violate English rules? What are the functions of *for* in the data? Are they all examples of interference from Spanish?

In house one machine for hot (a space heater) You for me (You and me)
One man is clean for clothes Father for son (Father and son)
There is shoes for water ice (ice skates) One animal go for eye, for hair
He's for English (English teacher) ... (a bug)
For eat is good I do soap for clothes
My father me go for lobster He look the clocks for time
He clean for teeth Coffee for he
Maybe go for Los Angeles (to) People go for San Silvestre (to)
Me working for 40 hours a week Go for sands in car (dune buggy)
 May be for Mr. Nixon pow!

8. If you are (or someone you know) is a language mixer, tape record a few sessions when you're talking with other mixers. Can you explain why you mix or switch languages at the places you do? Observe when mixing occurs in the speech of your students. Are they usually single word items, filler words, or words already borrowed from their language into English? Can you account for such examples of mixing in a different way than you would for your own data?

SUGGESTIONS FOR FURTHER READING

Speech Development of a Bilingual Child: A Linguist's Record.
1939, 1947, and 1949. W. F. Leopold. 4 vols. Evanston, Ill.: Northwestern University Press.

This is the classic in the field of second language development. In diary form, it allows one to see the development not only of Hildegard's phonology, vocabulary, and syntax in English and German but also of the development of the child in all aspects. Her reactions to the bilingual situation and the anecdotes included make it a delightful reading experience. Because of the care given to accurate annotation from the linguistic standpoint, it gives any researcher comparison data not just for a few months of observation but from earliest childhood to the teenage period.

Archives de Psychologie.

1938, 26, 104, 322–266. A. Kenyeres and E. Kenyeres. Comment une petite Hongroise de sept ans apprend le Français.

While Leopold's study traces the simultaneous acquisition of two languages, the Kenyeres study looks at the addition of a second language. Again, the care with which the data are described makes it a classic in the field.

Second Language Acquisition: A Book of Readings.

1978. E. Hatch. Rowley, Mass.: Newbury House.

This book contains excerpts from the classic studies in this field, along with original studies of second language learning in nonteaching environments. The studies include: (1) simultaneous acquisition of two languages; (2) sequential acquisition of a second language (3 to 8 years); (3) sequential acquisition of a second language for older children, adolescents, and adults; (4) experimental studies; (5) theoretical papers based on comparative data from a large number of studies.

REFERENCES

Adams, M. S. 1974. The acquisition of academic skills and a second language through a program of total immersion. Unpublished M.A. TESL thesis, UCLA.

Ausubel, David P. 1964. Adults versus children in second language learning: psychological considerations. *Modern Language Journal, 48,* 420–424.

Bever, T. O., J. A. Fodor, and W. Weksel. 1965. On the acquisition of syntax. *Psychological Review, 72,* 464–482.

Brown, R. 1973. *A First Language.* Cambridge, Mass.: Harvard University Press.

Butterworth, G. 1972. A Spanish-speaking adolescent's acquisition of English syntax. Unpublished M.A. TESL thesis, UCLA.

Cancino, H., E. J. Rosansky, and J. H. Schumann. 1978. The acquisition of English negatives and interrogatives by Spanish speakers. In E. Hatch (ed.), *Second Language Acquisition.* Rowley, Mass.: Newbury House.

Chamot, A. U. 1972. Grammatical problems in learning English as a third language. Unpublished Ph.D. dissertation, University of Texas, Austin, Texas. A shortened version is available in Hatch (1978).

Corder, S. P. 1967. The significance of learners' errors. *International Review of Applied Linguistics, 5,* 161–169.

Corder, S. P. 1971. Idiosyncratic dialects and error analysis. *International Review of Applied Linguistics, 9,* 2, 147–159.

Dulay, H. A., and M. K. Burt. 1974. Natural sequences in child second language acquisition. *Language Learning, 24,* 1.

Flores, M. 1973. An early stage in the acquisition of Spanish morphology by a group of English-speaking children. Unpublished M.A. TESL thesis, UCLA.

Gough, J. W. 1975. Comparative studies in second language acquisition. Unpublished M.A. TESL thesis, UCLA.

Hakuta, K. 1976. A case study of a Japanese girl learning English as a second language. *Language Learning, 26,* 2.

Hatch, E. 1972. Studies in second language acquisition. Paper presented at the 3rd International Congress of Applied Linguistics, Copenhagen, August.

Hatch, E. 1974. Second language—universals? *Working Papers in Bilingualism,* No. 3.

Hatch, E. 1978. *Second Language Acquisition: A Book of Readings.* Rowley, Mass.: Newbury House.

Huang, J. 1970. A Chinese child's acquisition of English syntax. Unpublished M.A. TESL thesis, UCLA.

Huang, J., and E. Hatch. 1978. A Chinese child's acquisition of English. In E. Hatch (ed.), *Second Language Acquisition.* Rowley, Mass.: Newbury House.

Itoh, H. 1973. A Japanese child's acquisition of two languages. Unpublished M.A. TESL thesis, UCLA.

Klima, E. S., and U. Bellugi. 1966. Syntactic regularities in the speech of children. In J. Lyons and R. Wales (eds.), *Psycholinguistic Papers,* Edinburg: Edinburgh University Press, 183–208.

Krashen, S., M. Long, and R. Scarcella. 1977. Age, rate and eventual attainment in second language acquisition. *TESOL Quarterly, 13,* 4, 573–582.

Legum, S. 1969. On recording samples of informal speech. Unpublished working paper, Southwest Regional Laboratory, Inglewood, California.

Lenneberg, E. 1967. *The Biological Foundations of Language.* New York: Wiley.

Leopold, W. F. 1939, 1947, and 1949. *Speech Development of a Bilingual Child: A Linguist's Record.* 4 vols. Evanston, Ill.: Northwestern University Press.

Milon, J. P. 1974. The development of negation in English by a second language learner. *TESOL Quarterly, 8,* 2.

Nemser, W. 1971. Approximative systems of foreign language learners. *International Review of Applied Linguistics, 9,* 2, 115–123.

Oksaar, E. 1973. Implications of language contact for bilingual language acquisition. Paper presented at IX International Congress of Anthropological and Ethnological Sciences, Chicago, Illinois.

Patkowski, M. 1980. The sensitive period for the acquisition of syntax in a second language. Ph.D. dissertation, New York University.

Penfield, W., and L. Roberts. 1959. *Speech and Brain Mechanisms.* Princeton: Princeton University Press.

Ravem, R. 1968. Language acquisition in a second language environment. *International Review of Applied Linguistics, 6,* 175–185.

Richards, J. C. 1971. A non-contrastive approach to error analysis. *English Language Teaching, 25,* 3, 204–219.

Robinett, B. W., and J. Schachter (eds.). 1983. *Second Language Learning.* Ann Arbor: University of Michigan Press.

Ronjat, J. 1913. *Le developpement du langage observé chez un enfant bilingue.* Paris: Champion.

Selinker, L. 1972. Interlanguage. *International Review of Applied Linguistics, 10,* 209–231.

Shapira, R. 1973. Observational log on an adult Spanish speaker learning English. Paper for English 260K, Psycholinguistics and Language Teaching, UCLA.

Slobin, D. I. 1973. Cognitive prerequisites for the development of grammar. In C. Slobin and D. I. Slobin (eds.),

Studies in Child Language Development. New York: Holt, Rinehart & Winston.

Slobin, D. I. 1970. Universals of grammar development in children. In G. B. Flores d'Arcais and W. J. M. Levelt (eds.), *Advances in Psycholinguistics.* Amsterdam: North Holland, 174–186.

Snow, C., and M. Hoefnagel-Höhle. 1978. The critical period for language acquisition. *Child Development, 49,* 1114–1128.

Swain, M., N. Naiman, and G. Dumas. 1972. Aspects of the learning of French by English-speaking five-year-olds. Paper presented at the 3rd International Congress of Applied Linguistics, Copenhagen, August.

Weinreich, U. 1953. *Languages in Contact.* New York: Linguistics Circle of New York.

Wong-Fillmore, L. 1975. The second time around: cognitive and social structures in second language acquisition. Ph.D. dissertation, Stanford University.

Wong-Fillmore, L. 1979. Individual differences in second language acquisition. In C. J. Fillmore, D. Kempler, and W. Wang (eds.) *Individual Differences in Linguistic Ability and Linguistic Behavior.* New York: Academic Press.

Young, D. I. 1974. The acquisition of English syntax by three Spanish-speaking children. Unpublished M.A. TESL thesis, UCLA.

CONTRASTIVE ANALYSIS, ERROR ANALYSIS, AND INTERLANGUAGE ANALYSIS[1]

Marianne Celce-Murcia *and*
Barbara Hawkins

In the sixties and early seventies a rather heated debate took place as to whether contrastive analysis (CA) or error analysis (EA) or perhaps some combination of both of them should provide information for constructing the materials used in language teaching. CA advocates claimed that a systematic comparison of the source language and the target language[2] at all levels of structure (i.e., phonological, syntactic, lexical) would predict areas of difficulty in the target language for speakers of the source language; furthermore, they maintained that the best teaching materials would emphasize those features of the target language that differ markedly from corresponding features of the source language.

A number of EA advocates then came forward and challenged the usefulness of the existing contrastive studies done on syntactic topics while admitting that on the phonological level such studies had been fairly successful. The counterclaim of the EA proponents was that a careful study of a large corpus of errors committed by speakers of the source language while attempting to express themselves in the target language would provide factual, empirical data—rather than theoretical speculation—on which to base teaching materials.

Since the mid-seventies, however, both CA and EA have been partly absorbed and superseded because of the development and evolution of interlanguage analysis (IA). IA is concerned with describing and understanding the total system that the second language learner uses in attempting to communicate in the target language. Sometimes IA is carried out with reference to the source language and the target language, in which case CA survives in IA as "language transfer"; i.e., the source language is one of many causes (or explanations) of the learner's "systematic deviations" from the target language system. However, a learner's interlanguage may also be studied as a system that exists independent of either the source or the target language—much as one might study the structure of a pidgin or creole language. For the latter type of IA all vestiges of CA and EA have become irrelevant.

This chapter will, first of all, examine the rationale for both CA and EA along with the claims made by their supporters and the criticisms raised by their detractors. Second, since IA is a vital and developing area of research in applied linguistics, the chapter will give the reader some notion of the various approaches to IA that different researchers have been exploring.

CONTRASTIVE ANALYSIS

CA has had a long and impressive list of proponents, beginning perhaps with Fries (1945):

The most efficient materials are those that are based upon a scientific description of the language to be learned, carefully compared with a parallel description of the native language of the learners (p. 9).

Lado (1957) provided the earliest procedural statement of this approach. The approach as a whole was developed by the structural linguists based on their behaviorist model of language acquisition. This model made the following assumptions: (1) a language is a set of habits; (2) old habits (i.e., the native language) are hard to break while new habits (i.e., the second or foreign language) are hard to acquire; (3) the native language will of necessity interfere with the learning of a second or foreign language; (4) the differences between the native language and the foreign language will be the main cause of errors; (5) a linguistic CA can make these differences explicit; (6) language teachers and textbook writers must take the linguist's CA into account when preparing teaching materials.

There followed a deluge of contrastive studies in the late fifties and early sixties, most of which are mentioned in Hammer's 1965 bibliography. Other publications of historical interest are the Contrastive Structure Series, with volumes comparing the phonological and grammatical structures of English and German, English and Spanish, and English and Italian (University of Chicago Press, C. Ferguson, general editor), and the Georgetown Round-table Papers devoted to CA, Alatis (1968). Subsequent introductions to the field of CA by di Pietro (1971) and James (1980) attest to a continued interest in CA despite the CA/EA controversy.

A number of shortcomings and limitations inherent in the CA hypothesis have long been recognized.[3] First, CA is pedagogically relevant only in those language learning situations where all or many of the students speak the same native language. Second, its results are more reliable on the phonological level than on the syntactic or lexical level. Finally, certain kinds of differences between two languages seem to cause greater difficulty than others; this in turn has prompted discussion of a "hierarchy of difficulty," discussed rather fully in theoretical form in Stockwell et al. (1965), but for which little empirical verification has been presented to date.

Wardhaugh in his 1970 evaluation of the validity of the CA hypothesis states:

It [the contrastive analysis hypothesis] exists in strong and weak versions, the strong one arising from evidence from the availability of some kind of metatheory of CA and the weak from evidence from language interference. The strong version of the hypothesis is untenable and even the weak version creates difficulties for the linguist. Recent advances in linguistic theory have led some people to claim that the hypothesis is no longer useful in either the strong or the weak version (p. 123).

Wardhaugh leaves us with an image of a theory under attack, one that had lost its prestige and popularity. Given such a situation, it is not surprising that a new and different theory was proposed and well received. In this case, the newly elaborated alternative, EA, follows closely the psycholinguistic search for an alternative to the behaviorist's habit-formation theory of language acquisition—an alternative that attempts to explain the essentially creative nature of the language acquisition process (e.g., Chomsky, 1965).

ERROR ANALYSIS

Trained and sophisticated language teachers have undoubtedly applied EA to one degree or another for decades. They have studied their students' recurring mistakes, classified them into categories, and used them as the basis for preparing lessons and materials designed to help students overcome such errors. Lee (1957) provides one of the early comprehensive statements of this practice and further develops the procedure, which is simple in concept but laborious and complex in practice. Lee proposes that for language learners with the same mother tongue errors be collected at all learning stages (i.e., beginning, intermediate, and advanced) so that persistent errors—errors still being made by advanced students—can be distinguished from the earlier self-correcting errors typical of beginners. Lee encourages the use of CA to explain errors whenever possible and cites some examples of errors which could not be interpreted without the use of CA.

Richards (1971), also a proponent of EA, suggested a three-way classification of errors: (1) interlingual errors, (2) intralingual errors, and (3) developmental errors. Richards' interlingual errors are those caused by interference of the learner's mother tongue. The intralingual errors are those originating within the structure of the target language itself. Complex rule-learning behavior is typically characterized by overgeneralization, incomplete application of rules, and failure to learn conditions for rule application. When the complexity of the target language encourages such faulty generalization, all learners, regardless of background language, tend to commit similar errors. Richards' developmental errors reflect the strategies by which the learner acquires the language. These errors show that the learner—often completely independent of his native language—is making false hypotheses about the target language based on limited exposure to it in much the same way that a child acquires the target language as a first language. Richards provides the reader with a number of charts exemplifying certain intralingual and developmental errors that could not be explained on the basis of CA.

While Richards did not totally reject CA, we see that he clearly minimized its role, when we compare his position with that of previous researchers:

Interference from the mother tongue is clearly a major source of difficulty in second language learning, and contrastive analysis has proved valuable in locating areas of interlanguage interference. Many errors, however, derive from the strategies employed by the learner in language acquisition, and the mutual interference of items within the target language. These cannot be accounted for by contrastive analysis. Teaching techniques and procedures should take account of the structural and developmental conflicts that can come about in language learning. (p. 214).

During the 1970s a great deal of research was carried out in the EA paradigm. Two useful references for anyone interested in gaining a better understanding of this work are Richards (1974) and Corder (1981).

CRITICISMS OF CONTRASTIVE ANALYSIS AND ERROR ANALYSIS

Two kinds of criticism were leveled at CA: (1) total rejection and (2) modification. Newmark (1966) argued that CA was irrelevant and unnecessary. He claimed that errors that appeared to be caused by interference from the native language merely represented a gap in the learner's knowledge of the target language. The learner made up for this deficiency by substituting something he already knew (i.e., his native language), thereby producing incorrect structures in the target language. The cure for such "interference," Newmark concluded, is merely the cure for ignorance: *learning*. Once the learner knew what he should do in the target language, such errors would disappear. In other words, for Newmark, there was no active interference of the native language, but rather "padding" on the part of the learner, whose knowledge of the target language happened to be incomplete.

The more moderate critics of CA called for two types of revision or modification. One group argued the need to complement CA with EA. The positions of Lee (1957) and Richards (1971), for example, have already been discussed. To this list we can add the voices of Banathy and Madarasz (1969), who concluded:

Contrastive linguistics—no matter how refined—can only point toward a potential learning problem or difficulty. On the other hand, error analysis can tell us the intensity of this difficulty or the size of the problem. Thus it appears that in designing a pedagogical grammar, both are needed with error analysis complementing the findings of contrastive linguistic analysis (p. 92).

A different type of criticism came from Paul Schachter (1967) and Celce-Murcia (1972), who argued for universalist perspective and a consideration of the kinds of evidence available in language typology studies. Celce-Murcia claimed that to understand how similar or how different two languages are with respect to some feature, one should know what many other languages are like with respect to that feature. Schachter commented that while previous syntactic CAs had emphasized differences, one should not overlook similarities among languages. If the native languages of ESL students were limitlessly different from English, how could one explain that students do in fact learn English after having been taught fairly little? He concluded that mastering of the structure of one's native language automatically involved mastery of a substantial part of the structure of any other language—the reasons for this being that deep or underlying structures are very similar—almost universal. The differences would be in the rules that produced surface structure: in different languages, different transformational rules produce different surface structures.

EA, likewise, did not go uncriticized. Jacquelyn Schachter (1974) demonstrated that students of English as a second or foreign language sometimes take advantage of the paraphrase potential of the syntactic component to avoid constructions they find difficult—her test case being restrictive relative clauses in English. In her study Schachter first undertook a CA of restrictive constructions in Persian, Arabic, Chinese, and Japanese—comparing each language with English. Based on various parameters, she predicted that the English construction would be easier for native speakers of Persian and Arabic than for native speakers of Chinese and Japanese. She then proceeded to examine written compositions—of equal number and length for all four language groups, with a native English control group, too, and got the following results (the number of errors made in using relative clauses is indicated before the total number of relative clauses used by speakers of each group):

Persian	43/174
Arabic	31/154
American English	0/173
Chinese	8/76
Japanese	5/63

Schachter's interpretation of the results is that the speakers of Persian and Arabic felt comfortable using the fairly similar restrictive relative clause construction in English and used it with about the same frequency as English speakers did but made numerous errors because they had not learned to observe some minor ways in which the English construction differed from their own. The Chinese and Japanese speakers, however, used the totally unfamiliar construction sparingly, avoiding it when possible, producing it only when they felt very secure about their accuracy—thus making many fewer errors. In other words, certain syntactic errors that a CA would predict may occur rarely or not at all in the language learner's speech and

writing and perhaps go completely undetected in an EA. Combined with a rigorous CA, however, EA can be used to demonstrate this avoidance phenomenon.[4] A subsequent study by Kleinmann (1977) further supported Schachter's notions on avoidance.

Another potential pitfall of the EA approach is to overgeneralize Richards' interlingual/intralingual distinction mentioned earlier (Richards, 1971). For example, several EA studies were carried out at UCLA.[5] which assumed that errors in English made by both (1) speakers of a specific background language and (2) a mixed group of non-English speakers representing various other background languages were of necessity intralingual rather than interlingual. While such assumptions could in some cases prove accurate, they might also be misleading. Consider, for example, the contrastive use of plural reflexive and reciprocal pronouns in English sentences such as "They were talking to themselves/They were talking to each other." Many languages, perhaps the majority of other languages, would use one form, i.e., their equivalent of the plural reflexive morpheme, to signal both meanings—allowing the context to disambiguate. The results of a statistical EA might tend to classify the reciprocal/reflexive distinction as an intralingual error; however, this would not explain why speakers of German do not misuse these forms while speakers of French, Spanish, West African languages, etc., do. Only a CA or a typological survey which makes explicit the fact that German like English has two contrasting plural pronominal forms (i.e., *sich* and *ein ander*) whereas many other languages have one form for both reflexive and reciprocal plural pronouns can explain this discrepancy. Thus one must be extremely cautious when claiming to have identified intralingual rather than interlingual errors. The distinction is not as transparent as one might at first think.

These and other limitations of EA are presented in Schachter and Celce-Murcia (1977), which concludes that the claims made by proponents of EA had been overinflated and that EA had not in fact totally supplanted CA—that EA (like CA) was only one of many tools for the analysis of language performance.

The criticisms leveled at both CA and EA suggested that a richer model for analyzing and explaining the second language learner's output was necessary, and they thus paved the way for the development of interlanguage analysis (IA).

THE ROOTS OF INTERLANGUAGE ANALYSIS

In three important articles Corder did a great deal to move EA toward IA (a more sophisticated view of the language learner's evolving system, which many researchers follow today). In "The significance of learner's errors" (1967) Corder argues that first and second language learning share basically the same processes and that whatever differences exist are explainable in terms of motivation. He cautions that random errors of the types that even native speakers may make (i.e., *mistakes*) must be carefully distinguished from errors which are systematic in nature and reflect a learner's transitional competence (i.e., *errors*). By paying attention to the learner's errors, Corder feels we will come to better understand his needs and stop assuming we know what he should learn and when he should learn it. He claims that errors can be significant in three ways: (1) they tell the teacher how far the learner has come and what he still must learn; (2) they give the researcher evidence of how language is learned (i.e., strategies and procedures used); (3) they are a device the learner uses to test out his hypotheses concerning the language he is learning.

In a later article, "Describing the language⋅ learner's language" (1971a), Corder explicitly distinguishes remedial EA (described above in item 1) from developmental EA (described in item 2)—the former facilitating teacher evaluation and correction, the latter being used for research to describe the successive transitional dialect of a language learner.[6] In "Idiosyncratic dialects and error analysis" (1971b), Corder further discusses transitional dialects, arguing that groups of second language learners can be said to speak a dialect in two ways. First, the second language learner's spontaneous speech is systematic and rule-based (i.e., it has a grammar). Second, since some sentences of the learner's language are the same as sentences in the language he is acquiring, his approximative system and the target language are—by linguistic definition[7]—dialects of sorts. A similar proposal suggesting the linguistic nature and independence of the learner's system was made by Nemser (1971).

The greatest single impetus, however, undoubtedly came from Selinker's influential article "Interlanguage" (1972), which provided the name[8] and theoretical underpinnings for many later IA studies. In this article Selinker stated that interlanguage is the systematic result of a second language learner's attempt to produce a target language norm and that the psychologically relevant data for analyzing second language learning are utterances of the target language (by native speakers) and of the native language and interlanguage by second language learners. Most successful second language learners, according to Selinker, can reorganize their interlanguage so that it identifies more and more with the target language. For Selinker, five processes are involved in such a reorganization: (1) language transfer, (2) transfer of training, (3) strategies of second language learning, (4) communication strategies, and (5) overgeneralization of target language data.

In this article Selinker also coined the term "fossilization," which he described as a mechanism that underlies nontargetlike forms or rules that learners keep in their interlanguage performance no matter how much exposure (or instruction) they get in the target language. In other words, when the learner (for whatever reason) stops reorganizing his interlanguage so that it more closely approximates the target language, fossilization of the interlanguage has begun. There have been a number of attempts to explain why fossilization occurs, among them Vigil and Oller (1976) and Stauble (1981).

INTERLANGUAGE ANALYSIS

Since neither CA nor EA proved to explain all the problems of learners, the emphasis in research has switched from purely contrast-based and/or error-based analyses to interlanguage analyses. Researchers (e.g., Andersen, 1984) believe that the interlanguage of learners has a greater capacity for revealing the learner's system of communication, and that it is their task to uncover this system and the processes guiding its development. Concentrating only on learner errors results in a built-in target-language bias that will not reveal the principles underlying what the learner is doing; i.e., it will tell us what he is *not* doing, but its focus will not tell us much about how his system develops.

It is thought, then, that the interlanguage of learners provides the raw data for elucidating the acquisition process, the process being more complicated than either CA or EA would have at first led us to believe.

In confronting the task of interlanguage analysis, various researchers have adopted different approaches. The approaches have been aimed at both describing the interlanguage of learners and also accounting for the appearance of interlanguage features, with the hope of enlightening us as to the second language acquisition process. In general, the approaches ask two questions: (1) What does the interlanguage of learners look like, and (2) Why does it take the form it does? Neither question is easily answered, of course, and attempts made at interlanguage analysis have revealed many different points of view, mostly with regard to interpretation of the interlanguage data. The following review will summarize some of the major approaches with respect to interlanguage analysis. While we have separated these areas for the purpose of discussion, we want to remind the reader that there is considerable overlap among the four areas.

The language universals approach

Researchers looking at interlanguage data from the perspective of language universals do so by examining linguistic elements which are believed to be common to all languages. The following quote from Gass (1984) explains the emphasis clearly:

By universals we do *not* intend universals of second language acquisition, that is, those elements/processes/ strategies which are common to all second language learners, but rather universals of language, those linguistic elements which are common to all languages (in the form of absolute or statistical universals) (p. 125; emphasis the author's).

As Gass notes, universals may be considered either absolute or statistical. Those which are absolute are considered to be true for all languages, whereas those which are statistical are considered to be true for most languages. The latter are often expressed in terms of universal tendencies (Comrie, 1981).

The connection between language universals and interlanguage (IL) is that the universals serve as "an overall guiding principle in second language acquisition, interacting with the native language and the target language systems, at times resulting in violations of a proposed universal, at times being consistent with a given universal" (Gass, 1984, p. 129). Interlanguage, then, should reflect universal constraints on languages at some level.

Let us consider an example. Kumpf (1982) presented evidence suggesting that the tense/aspect system of the learners she studied did not reflect either their native languages or the target language. She suggests that the IL system of the learners "reflects the capacity of humans to create . . . unique form to meaning to function relationships," and that the newly created forms of her subjects correspond to universal principles of natural languages. She used evidence from languages of the world and from child language acquisition to show that what she had found in her subjects' ILs corresponded to predictions that would follow from universal principles.

The picture is not always so clear, however. Returning to Gass' (1984) summary of the connection between second language acquisition and universals, there are apparently times when what is found in the IL of learners is not consistent with proposed universals. This poses two problems. The first is to account for how it is possible for violations of universals to appear in interlanguages. The second is, given that we can account for violations of universals, how can we predict when IL features will be consistent with universals and when they will violate them? In other words, let us suppose that there exists a proposed universal which guides the possible forms a grammatical relation can take. Let us further suppose that we find an impossible form, in relation to the proposed universal, in the IL of a learner. How are we to account for this violation? Second, how will we predict if and when the violation will or will not occur? Eckman (in press) suggests that the feature will be a result of influence from either the native language of the learner or from the target language, if it does violate a universal, implying that features which both violate the universal and appear in neither the source nor the target language will not appear in the IL.

Gass (1979) found that the IL of her learners, with respect to the acquisition and use of relative clause types, generally followed the universal accessibility hierarchy of relative clause types proposed by Keenan and Comrie (1977), in terms of accuracy of production, avoidance of structure, frequency of production, and judgments of grammaticality. At the same time, source and target language factors played "a counterbalancing role, resulting in nonhierarchical ordering in some instances" (Gass, 1984). It would seem, then, that universals are considered to play a major role and the influence of the source and target language a more minor role.

Even if this is true, generally speaking, it still does not solve the question as to the predictive powers of universals with respect to IL. It is not at all clear in any precise way when the influence of the universal will appear in the interlanguage of learners rather than a violation of it based on influence from either the source or the target language.

A third question arises when we consider the power of the influence of the source and the target language versus the power of universals. In the case that the influence from both the target language and the source language, as well as that from universals, all support the appearance of certain features in the IL of learners, how is the researcher to determine the contribution of each? Is the universal always the overriding influence? In this sense, the contribution of each needs to be defined more tightly by those who ap-

proach IL study from a universals point of view. Untangling the influence of each is a difficult process that demands a clear understanding of transfer (influence from the source language), input (influence from the target language), and the nature of universals.

Finally, one last controversy involved in the universals approach to IL study is that of whether universals are best predicted by natural languages or by ILs. This is to say, are we using universals arrived at on the basis of what happens always or most often in natural languages to predict what will or will not appear in ILs, or are we using ILs as the testing ground for universals? In a sense, this is asking the question of how universals are determined in the first place. For example, if violations of universals are found in the IL of learners which are not easily accounted for by L1 or target language influences, do we question the universal, or do we look for other explanations? Coupled with this question is that of whether or not what we agree upon as universals actually taps "what the learner is doing" in constructing his IL. That is, is there a set of linguistic universals that we can actually define and which we can say the learner uses as the basis for building his IL system?

All these questions are known to those looking at IL from a universals approach. Much of their research deals with, and will continue to deal with, answering them.

Markedness theory
Linguistic markedness theory—like research into language universals—derives from the work of Prague School linguists such as Trubetzkoy (1939) and Jakobson (1941). It distinguishes the members of a pair of related forms or structures by assuming that the marked member of a pair contains at least one more feature than the unmarked one. In addition, the unmarked (or neutral) member of the pair is the one with a wider range of distribution than the marked one. For example, in the case of the English indefinite articles (a and an), an is the more complex or marked form (it has an additional sound) and a is the unmarked form with the wider distribution.

Celce-Murcia (1972) for lexicon and Eckman (1977) for phonology and syntax have proposed that markedness theory is a way to refine CA in order to predict areas of difficulty more accurately when learners of a given source language are acquiring a given target language. In the domain of EA, Santos (1984) extends markedness theory to error evaluation and shows that native speakers are more likely both to notice and to be irritated by a marked form being substituted erroneously for an unmarked form than vice versa. In other words, markedness theory can explain why native speakers of English are more apt to notice and be irritated by 1 than by 2:

1. He is an European.
2. I ate a apple.

Markedness theory has been used in first and second language acquisition to explain a variety of phenomena. In first language acquisition the theory predicts that the unmarked form will be acquired first and the marked form later. The work of Donaldson and Balfour (1968), which demonstrates that children understand the unmarked form *more* before they can comprehend the marked form *less*, provides some empirical support for this prediction, for example.

From the perspective of second language acquisition (SLA), Rutherford (1982) has proposed markedness theory as an explanation for results of certain SLA studies in which researchers uncover an order for morpheme acquisition but do not provide any general principle to explain the order they find. For instance, Rutherford draws on markedness theory to show why learners of English as a second language acquire singular *he* before plural *they*, *on* before *under*, *where* before *why*, and the phonologically simple possessive forms /s, z/ before the phonologically more complex one /ǝz/.

Jordens and Kellerman (1978) use psycholinguistic notions of markedness to explain transfer tendencies and strategies in interlanguage in terms of three constraints, the second of which involves markedness: (1) if the learner's perception of typological distance between his native and the target language is small, transfer will occur more readily and transfer errors will be more numerous; (2) the more marked the learner perceives an item in his native language to be, the less likely it is that it will transfer; and (3) the learner's knowledge of the target language—real or assumed—will systematically influence language transfer.

To illustrate principle 2, Jordens and Kellerman carried out several experiments demonstrating that Dutch learners of English of various age groups all felt that the Dutch verb "breken" (to break) could be readily translated into English as "break" only when "breken" was used in a core or unmarked meaning such as "to break a stick" or in some clear extension of the unmarked meaning (e.g., to break someone's heart). The same Dutch speakers felt that noncore or marked meanings of "breken" as in Dutch equivalents of "his voice broke" or "to break an oath" would not transfer, even though transfer would have been perfectly acceptable in these cases.

Language transfer
Although transfer does not represent a specific approach to IL study, it is an area of research that has undergone quite a bit of scrutiny and development as a result of IL studies. Even though the idea of "interference" from the native language, as predicted by CA, is not longer tenable, it has proved impossible to ignore the influence of the native language (L1) in interlanguage data. Transfer is impossible to ignore mainly because it represents one of the effects of prior learning that the second language learner brings to the task of learning the new language. In other words, a second language learner has already learned his first language, and he has formed many ideas about language based on his first language experience. Of course, the problem is that we do not always know exactly what these ideas are and to what degree he uses them in learning the second language (L2). Hatch (1981) summarizes the important, yet elusive, nature of prior learning as follows:

Our problem . . . is not one of convincing each other that prior learning affects second language acquisition. Rather, it is to define as precisely as possible *what* prior knowledge the learner is most likely to use in making his hypotheses about how one does the new language. Are these predictions about the new language likely to be based on language typology information? Are they likely to be based on "universals" of processability? Are they based on how exotic the learner thinks the new language might be? In other words, we need to know *which* of all possible prior knowledges the learner will try out (p. 104, emphases the author's).

Interlanguage studies in more recent years have dealt with transfer mainly at a linguistic level with the aim of defining constraints, and thus increasing its predictive powers. One of the basic problems when dealing with the question of transfer becomes apparent when we see elements in the IL of a learner which resemble very closely elements from his L1. Is it reasonable to assume that those elements are directly transferred by the learner from his L1? On the surface of it, this may seem a logical conclusion, but the solution is not so easy when the same elements also appear in the IL of a learner whose L1 does not have these elements. Transfer cannot be the only explanation if the learner does not even have these elements in his L1 to bring to the L2 learning task. The fact that elements which resemble the L1 of the learner are found in his IL does not necessarily mean therefore that transfer, as a process, has taken place. The issue for those studying transfer is to determine exactly when and under what conditions the process of transfer does occur.

Zobl (1980a, 1980b, 1982) views transfer and developmental influences as interacting. By developmental influences are meant those developmental stages that all children pass through in acquiring their native languages. He suggests that if there is a natural developmental stage in the L2 that corresponds to a pattern in the learner's L1, then the learner will persist in using that pattern longer in his interlanguage than if the pattern did not exist in his L1, in that there are two forces—developmental and L1—which promote its usage. To illustrate, let us look at a Spanish speaker learning to negate in English. Spanish has simple, preverbal negation: "(Yo)

no voy" (I'm not going). Likewise, children acquiring English as a native language go through a simple, preverbal negation stage in their language development: "I no go." In this sense, because simple, preverbal negation represents a developmental stage in the target language, *and* because the pattern exists in the L1 of the learner, the learner would be expected to produce simple, preverbal negation in his IL for a prolonged period of time. Other learners whose L1s do not have simple, preverbal negation may also manifest this pattern of negation in their English ILs, but it will not persist as long as it does for the learner whose L1 has the pattern.

Another view of transfer is found in Andersen's (1983b) transfer to somewhere (TTS) principle. In positing his principle, Andersen tries to outline the necessary (but not always sufficient) conditions for the operation of transfer from a learner's native language to either promote or delay acquisition of a given form or construction in the target language. His principle, which draws on the work of Weinreich (1953), Slobin (1977), Zobl (1980a, 1980b, 1982), Larsen-Freeman (1978), and Naro (1978), reads as follows:

A grammatical form or structure will occur consistently and to a significant extent in the interlanguage as a result of transfer *if and only if* (1) natural acquisitional principles are consistent with the L1 structure *or* (2) there already exists within the L2 input the potential for (mis-)generalization from the input to produce the same form or structure. Furthermore, in such transfer, preference is given in the resulting interlanguage to free, invariant, functionally simple morphemes which are congruent with the L1 and L2 (or there is congruence between the L1 and natural acquisitional processes) and the morphemes occur frequently in the L1 and/or the L2 (Andersen 1983b, p. 182).

In stating the TTS principle, Andersen brings together several different contributions from other researchers, and it is necessary to review them briefly in order to understand the principle. By "natural acquisitional processes" are meant those operating principles which govern the nature of language. He relies on Slobin's (1977) "four charges to language":

1.   Be clear.
2.   Be humanly processible in ongoing time.

3. Be quick and easy.
4. Be expressive.

These four charges to language have evolved out of Slobin's (1973) operating principles that guide L1 development.

We are now ready to return to Andersen's (1983b) first point in the TTS principle, that a grammatical form or structure will occur as the result of transfer if natural acquisitional principles are consistent with the L1 structure. This is somewhat similar to Zobl's position (1980a, 1980b, 1982), which we discussed earlier.[9] Put very simply, it is saying that an L1 structure which is consistent with developmental processes (or natural acquisitional principles) is likely to be transferred and appear in the IL of the learner.

The second point of Andersen's (1983b) principle offers a second condition under which transfer can occur if it does not occur under the first. In stating this second condition, Andersen takes into account the idea of input. By input is meant the L2 that the learner is exposed to during the acquisition process. In listing this second condition under which transfer can occur, Andersen (1983b) states that the learner must find potential evidence in the input that the form he is carrying over from his L1 exists in the L2. For example, Andersen looks at the acquisition of the possessive form in English by Marta, a child who is a native Spanish speaker. Marta's English IL showed a *noun + of + noun* construction to express possession. Typical examples were *The books de Mommy* and *The mother of my mother*. Neither form is of course a standard L2 construction. Yet, the *noun + of + noun* construction does in fact exist in standard English (i.e., "the arm of the chair"). In addition *noun + de + noun* is the usual Spanish possessive construction. The fact that the form is usual in Marta's L1 *and* that it does exist in the L2 input qualifies it under the second condition of the TTS principle as an example of transfer. Under this condition, the potential for Marta to misgeneralize her own *noun + de + noun* possessive construction exists in the L2 input in the form of the *noun + of + noun* construction in English.

Finally, Andersen (1983b) further refines his TTS principle by stating preferences for certain forms over others under the second condition. He states that preference will be given to "free, invariant, functionally simple morphemes which are congruent with the L1 and L2." Morphemes which are free are not bound (example: English articles are free whereas plural markings are bound). Those which are invariant will always be the same (example: English *-ing* is invariant whereas the form of the past tense varies /ə d, d, t/). Those which are functionally simple are more explicit in the sense that they directly indicate only one grammatical function (example: possessive "of" is functionally simple whereas third person, singular present /ə z, s, z/ is functionally complex, indicating three grammatical functions: third person subject, singular subject, present tense). These forms are congruent with the L1 and L2 when there is a similarity in patterns (example: *noun + of + noun/noun + de + noun* to indicate possession). In the case of Marta given above, the *noun + of + noun* construction fits all the criteria: "of" is a free morpheme, it is invariant, functionally simple, and the pattern is congruent with the L1 and L2. Finally, preference is given to the morphemes that meet the above conditions when they are also frequent in the L1 and/or the L2. There is, of course, other work which has been done on transfer (see, for example, many of the chapters in Gass and Selinker, 1983), but the examples given serve to point out that the issue of defining constraints on transfer is by no means simple. In the case of Andersen's (1983b) TTS principle, we can see that it attempts to take into account several forces which all act as constraints on transfer which either promote or delay SLA.

Input

As has been noticed in the preceding discussion on transfer, researchers have found it necessary to look at the input the learner receives in accounting for the appearance of his IL. Input, defined in a very general way, is the target language that the learner is exposed to. In his task of acquiring the L2, the learner is constantly trying to incorporate into his IL system messages he receives in the L2, which are both around him and directed at him. If certain features of the input are more salient and/or more frequent, it is possible that such factors can help to account for the appearance of these features in the IL of learners.

Dulay and Burt (1974) conducted a cross-sectional study in which they elicited natural speech data (by means of the bilingual syntax measure[10]) from 55 Chinese-speaking and 60 Spanish-speaking children who were 6 to 8 years old. Dulay and Burt then analyzed the speech samples of the children for the production of 11 morphemes. Their basic question was whether or not the subjects, from such dissimilar source language backgrounds, would show the same sequence of acquisition for the 11 morphemes. They concluded from their results that the accuracy orders for the 11 morphemes by the two groups of children were virtually the same.

Bailey, Madden, and Krashen (1974) replicated the Dulay and Burt (1974) study, but they used adult ESL learners as subjects instead of children. The subjects were 33 native Spanish-speaking adults and 40 adults who were native speakers of other languages. Their results showed that for their adult subjects the accuracy order for the 11 morphemes was quite similar to the order that Dulay and Burt had found for their child subjects.

Larsen-Freeman (1978), in an attempt to find an explanation for the accuracy orders found by both Dulay and Burt (1974) and Bailey, Madden, and Krashen (1974), tried to measure and compare the frequency of morphemes in input and output data. In other words, she looked at the frequency of the morphemes likely to be in the input of native speakers and then compared this with the frequency of the morphemes in the output of the L2 learners from whom she had collected speech data. Her rationale in doing so was as follows:

Perhaps the frequency counts of morphemes on the speaking task reflect their actual occurrence in real com-munication. Thus, if a subject encountered certain morphemes more than others, he was likely to score higher on those morphemes, all other things being equal (Larsen-Freeman, 1978, p. 376).

As her independent measure of morpheme frequencies, Larsen-Freeman used the morpheme frequencies determined for three sets of native English-speaking parents of subjects that Brown (1973) had used in one of his studies. Brown's counts were made from the transcripts of recordings taped during periodic visits by researchers to the subjects' homes. Larsen-Freeman then ranked these morphemes in order of frequency and compared the order obtained with the accuracy orders found by Dulay and Burt (1974) and Bailey, Madden, and Krashen (1974). She found that significant correlations existed between her frequency order and Brown's frequency order and also the accuracy orders of both of the other studies. From these results, Larsen-Freeman arrives at the tentative conclusion that "morpheme frequency of occurrence in NS [native speaker] speech is the principal determinant for the oral production morpheme accuracy order of ESL learners" (p. 377). In her discussion, she notes that second language researchers should pay more attention to the input to which the learner is exposed than had been done in previous research.

Also included in input studies is the phenomenon of foreigner talk (FT). FT is the language used by native speakers (NSs) in communicating with nonnative speakers (NNSs). The reader will note that Larsen-Freeman's (1978) study relied on NS speech addressed to other NSs, under different conditions, for her independent measure of frequencies of morphemes. FT studies, on the other hand, examine the speech of NSs as it is addressed to NNSs.[11] It has become apparent that the language NSs use in FT is modified in specific ways. Among other things, FT is characterized by a slow rate of speech, high-frequency vocabulary, simple propositional syntax, and WH-questions restated as yes/no or alternative questions. (For a summary of FT features and their possible benefits to the learner, see Hatch, 1983).

Our question is, of course, how FT, as input, influences the appearance of the IL of learners. In order to answer this question, researchers need to know the effects of FT on the learner. Hatch (1983) suggests three functions of FT: "it promotes communication, establishes an affective bond, and serves as an implicit teaching mode" (p. 64). The exact connection between these functions of FT and the output of learners is not, however, always so easy to pinpoint, since the interest is not solely on the acquisition of L2 forms but rather on how conversational interaction determines frequency of forms and how it shows language functions evolving. Depending on the nature of the interaction, then, the learner is exposed to a variety of forms and functions, some of which he might acquire. Some of these incoming forms may be syntactic forms which subsequently appear in the learner's IL. Some of the forms, however, may have nothing to do with syntax. That is, the learner may be learning many things including vocabulary, chunk utterances, and discourse routines. (Again, see Hatch, 1983, for a summary of the possible benefits of FT to the learner.) In analyzing the IL of learners, then, the researcher must look beyond syntax to discover how FT influences the appearance of forms and functions in the IL sample.

Let us see how this might work. Peck (1978) describes conversation in NNS-child–NS-child discourse and in NNS-child–NS-adult discourse. In her study, she asks what the child L2 acquirer might be learning about English syntax, phonology, and semantics in his conversations with another child and an adult, both of whom are NSs. In general, she found that the child-child situation gave Angel, the learner, many chances to practice syntax and phonology, and the child-adult situation offered him many chances to practice syntax and semantics (Peck, 1978, p. 394). As an example, notice how Angel's syntax evolves in this bit of conversation with Joe (the child NS):

J: That's like on—Ernie and Bert—(roar)
A: No, like a crazy boy! (laugh)

J: (laugh) That's more like it. (high pitch:) What?
A: (chuckling) Like a crazy boy!
J: (even higher) What?
A: (softer) Like a crazy boy.
J: Like a mazy – like a – a –
A: Crazy!
J: I – I mean – li' li (pretending to stutter) I mean – I – I – I mean – I mean – I mean – I mean – I mean –(normal voice:) I mean a crazy?
A: A crazy.
J: A crazy what, a crazy daisy?
A: No, a crazy you.
J: Oh! Oh! Oh!
A: //You are//
J: //Oh!//
A: Crazy.
J: Oh! (10X).

(Peck, 1978, pp. 394–95)

Angel's original utterance, "No, like a crazy boy!" becomes "You are / crazy" during the interaction. Peck provides several other examples of language play between the two boys which gave Angel the chance to practice English sounds.

Hatch (1978) provides excerpts of a conversation between two adults, one a NNS and the other a NS, that shows the learner soliciting vocabulary from the NS, and then driving the NS to restate his comments in summary fashion:

Rafaela: I like men American but I no no . . . I no . . . have nothing . . .
NS: Oh, I see. You don't have a boyfriend here.
R: No boyfriend American.
Rafaela: Before here three, two months I live my mother.
NS: For two months you lived with your mother.

The interaction in these excerpts shows the NS producing, through the interaction, both lexical and syntactic reformulations for the NNS. As this happens, there is the possibility for the NNS to learn.

In a final example from Hawkins (1982) an adult ESL learner, Jaime, is trying to indicate to his NS interlocutor, Stephen, that he has a picture of an airplane (in the first picture he is supposed to describe to Stephen):

J: Number one is, uhm, ... you know, the ..."Trrrr" (laughing and trying to imitate Stephen's noise for the plane)
S: ... The what?
J: The ... flu— ... flap?

(p. 250)

Later on, in retrospective comments on his conversation with Stephen, Jaime made the following remark in Spanish about his use of the word "flap" (translation by Hawkins):

In the restaurant (where J works), a bug came in once and Lisa (a co-worker) said it was "flapping" around. She taught me the word "flap" and moved her arms to show me. I didn't know how to say "plane" or "fly," so I said "flap." (p. 250)

This excerpt, together with the retrospective comment, shows us that input during interaction can be a source of learning which manifests itself in the IL of the learner. The interaction in the restaurant with Lisa provided Jaime with a new lexical item that later appeared in his interlanguage in the interaction with Stephen.

How do these kinds of analyses help us predict what the IL of learners will look like? In fact, they don't make strong predictions about what will be found in the IL of learners in the same way that the morpheme studies do. Rather, these analyses are looking for the processes that will explain why the features that appear in the IL of learners are there. They underscore the importance of interactional input in the acquisition process, emphasizing that the input received by the learner in interaction with speakers of the target language is no small influence on the IL of the learner. An implication of this is that researchers must take into account the input that a learner receives if they wish to understand his IL.

CONCLUSION

In this chapter we have endeavored to show how CA, EA, and the various approaches to IA

have evolved and how they have all contributed to descriptions of the forms that ILs take and possible explanations for these forms. Within the broader framework of IL, we observe that an earlier pedagogical focus on "interference" within the CA tradition has shifted toward a more neutral view of "transfer"[12] as one of several influences on second language development. At the same time, EA has developed into a study of what the L2 learner does with input in his attempt to approximate the target language. The search for language universals and markedness in IL overlaps with both transfer and input.

There are some other aspects of IA that we have not explored in this chapter. We have not, for example, discussed how ILs at the lowest level resemble pidgins. This area of IL has been discussed at some length by Schumann (1978a, 1978b, 1982), Stauble (1978), Stauble and Schumann (1983), and Andersen in his introduction to Andersen (1983a). We have mentioned only in passing those types of studies which deal with interlanguage without any reference to the target and source languages because the perspective emphasized here of expected development toward a native norm is the one we feel offers greater immediate relevance to classroom language teachers. In addition, we have focused on syntax and morphology in IL to the detriment of phonology and lexicon;[13] however, this merely reflects the heavy bias toward syntax and morphology in the existing literature.

We would like to close this discussion by pointing out that both CA and EA are still developing in areas that are of interest to language teachers. For example, Hartmann (1980) has proposed a new area, contrastive textology (a combination of CA and discourse analysis) as a way of discovering systematic differences between two languages at the discourse level. Moreover, the level of discourse function has been shown by Schachter and Rutherford (1979) to be a promising means of extending EA and CA so that certain types of language transfer at the discourse level can be explained in terms of major organizational differences in language typology between the learner's source language and the target language (e.g., whether a language exhibits topic prominence, subject prominence, etc.). A relatively new area within EA is error evaluation (Santos, forthcoming), which analyzes the reactions of native speakers to a variety of IL errors to determine which of the errors made by L2 learners are most noticeable and/or most irritating to native speakers of the target language.[14] The expectation is that findings in this area will help establish priorities for language teachers and learners.

We are confident that other developments will occur in the future to add new dimensions and insights to the growing body of research that we have described here as contrastive analysis, error analysis, and interlanguage analysis.

NOTES

1. The authors wish to thank Roger Andersen for his thorough reading of and insightful comments on an earlier version of this paper. We are fully responsible, however, for any inaccuracies and infelicities that remain.

2. The term *source language* represents the native language of the learner, while the term *target language* refers to the second or foreign language the learner is trying to acquire.

3. Despite this, many of our M.A. TESL students at UCLA—especially the nonnative speakers of English—have been intrigued by the CA hypothesis and have felt it to be worthwhile, with the result that phonological (e.g., Bejarano, 1977), syntactic (e.g., Shintani, 1974), discourse (e.g., Wu, 1982), lexical (e.g., Vander Werf, 1969), and cultural (e.g., Bernaldo, 1970) CA studies have been carried out as M.A. theses. By far the largest number of such theses have been done in the area of syntax.

4. Schachter's paraphrase and avoidance theory also explains the greater success of phonological CA: there is no such thing as a phonological paraphrase, and therefore the avoidance phenomenon is difficult, if not impossible, to identify at the phonological level (Schachter, 1974).

5. See, for example, Kleinmann (1973), Suwatthigul (1973), and Khampang (1974).

6. Such descriptive studies can, of course, be carried out with children learning a first or second language or adolescents or adults learning a second, third, etc., language.

7. Linguistically, two languages sharing a significant number of grammatical rules are dialects.

8. The term "interlingual" was first used by Weinreich (1953), whose work on languages in contact was an acknowledged inspiration to Selinker.

9. The difference between Zobl's and Andersen's positions is that Zobl maintains that for transfer to occur, the developmental stage must exist in the L2 and that this must correspond to a pattern in the learner's L1, while Andersen proposes that transfer may occur if a feature in the L1 structure is consistent with developmental processes.

10. For more information on the bilingual syntax measure, see Burt, Dulay, and Hernandez (1973).

11. Some researchers (notably Long, 1980) have looked at NS-NS data and NS-NNS data produced under the same conditions in order to ensure a more accurate description of the differences in NS speech to NNSs as opposed to other NSs. Long (1980, 1981) found that interaction modifications appear with greater significance in FT discourse than do linguistic input modifications.

12. Transfer is a cover term for both negative transfer, which produces erroneous forms, and positive transfer, which produces acceptable forms. In this context "positive" should not be equated with "good" or "negative" with "bad."

13. Readers interested in IL phonology should see Tarone (1976) and Kumpf (1984), while those interested in lexicon should see Yoshida (1977) and Meara (1982).

14. The study of error evaluation—as we refer to it here—is distinct from the study of error correction or corrective feedback. See Chaudron (1977), Salica (1981), and Day et al. (1984) for examples of this other type of research.

DISCUSSION QUESTIONS

1. What are the major differences between the data used in doing CA, EA, and IA? How do the goals of CA, EA, and IA differ?

2. Corder has said that the three main phases of EA are identification, description, and explanation. What specific activities would be carried out in each of these phases?

3. Can you suggest some reasons why CA has been more successful (i.e., a better predictor of errors) on the phonological level than on the syntactic or semantic level?

4. Why might the methods and results of language typology studies be of interest to those engaged in CA, EA, or IA?

5. There has been much anecdotal evidence and some experimental evidence (see

Lazghab, 1973) indicating that a well-established second language can cause as much or more interference or transfer than the native language if the learner is acquiring a third language. Why do you suppose this is possible?

6. Two native Spanish speakers of the same age and sex and equivalent education have studied English the same number of years, and both have lived in the United States for 4 years. However, their interlanguages are very different, with that of one of the speakers being much closer to English than that of the other. What factors might account for such noticeable individual differences in interlanguage?

SUGGESTED ACTIVITIES

1. Read the chapter on "The Hierarchy of Difficulty" in Stockwell et al. (1965) or the Stockwell and Bowen article on the same topic in Robinett and Schachter (1983). Can this hierarchy—or any aspect of it—be tested empirically? If so, suggest a number of ways that such testing might be carried out.

2. Collect 10 compositions written by speakers of a language/dialect—other than standard English—that you are familiar with. Identify and categorize the errors made. Describe the errors that were clearly due to "interference" or "transfer." What percentage of the errors have you accounted for? What other types of errors do the remaining data suggest?

3. Using your knowledge of English and some other language or dialect, do a CA of a narrow syntactic or lexical topic for which you know there will be major differences. State the differences clearly. Then construct a pilot test to determine whether these differences cause transfer errors on the part of speakers of the foreign language or dialect in their use of English. Administer your test to at least two or three subjects. Describe the results in terms of the CA you did and your own expectations.

4. Ask a nonnative speaker of standard English if you could record him or her telling a story relating some past experience. After you have made the recording, transcribe it carefully. Write down exactly what the speaker said. What can you say about the speaker's interlanguage (IL)? Can you find systematic rules in the IL that differ from rules in both the source language and the target language? If so, what might be the explanation for such rules?

5. With permission of the speakers, record a 10-minute conversation between a native and nonnative speaker of English. After you have made the recording, transcribe it carefully. Write down exactly what the two speakers said. Is there any evidence of "foreigner talk" on the part of the native speaker? Is there any evidence that the nonnative speaker is using the native speaker's input to achieve certain segments of his communication with the native speaker?

6. Read the papers on avoidance by Schachter (1974) and Kleinmann (1977) (reprinted in Robinett and Schachter, 1983). Think of other English structures that nonnative speakers might consciously or unconsciously avoid. Design an experiment that would detect avoidance of one of the structures you have identified.

SUGGESTIONS FOR FURTHER READING

Languages in Contact: Findings and Problems.
1953. U. Weinreich. New York: The Linguistic Circle of New York. Reprinted in 1963 by Mouton & Co. in The Hague.

If you can find a copy of this seminal classic, by all means read it. It has influenced Selinker, Andersen, and a host of other researchers working in interlanguage; it is as valid today as it was when it first appeared.

Second Language Learning: Contrastive Analysis, Error Analysis, and Related Aspects.
1983. B. W. Robinett, and J. Schachter. Ann Arbor: University of Michigan Press.

This anthology contains a comprehensive collection of articles that have defined research in CA, EA, IA, and related areas of second language acquisition from the late fifties to the eighties.

New Dimensions in Second Language Acquisition.
1981. R. W. Andersen. Rowley, Mass.: Newbury House.

A collection of articles that considers many factors in second language acquisition relevant to interlanguage including age, personality, pidginization, input, etc.

Discourse analysis and second language acquisition.
1978. E. Hatch (ed.). *Second Language Acquisition: A Book of Readings.* Rowley, Mass.: Newbury House, 401–435.

Psycholinguistics: A Second Language Perspective.
1983. E. Hatch. Rowley, Mass.: Newbury House, 152–187.

These two references are some of the best expositions on how input and communicative interaction play a major role in second language acquisition. The second reference synthesizes most of the available research up to 1983.

Interlanguage as chameleon.
1979. E. Tarone. *Language Learning* 29, 1, 181–191.

A good overview of the variables that affect the form of interlanguage and the causes of variation within interlanguage.

The Interlanguage Studies Bulletin
Published by the University of Utrecht in the Netherlands, this is a journal devoted exclusively to interlanguage research and should be consulted by anyone interested in this area.

REFERENCES

Alatis, J. 1968. *Contrastive Linguistics and Its Pedagogical Applications*, 19th Annual Round Table. Washington, D.C.: Georgetown University Press.

Allen, H. B., and R. N. Campbell. 1972. *Teaching English as a Second Language: A Book of Readings*, Second Edition. New York: McGraw-Hill.

Andersen, R. 1983a. *Pidginization and Creolization as Language Acquisition.* Rowley, Mass.: Newbury House.

Andersen, R. 1983b. Transfer to somewhere. In S. Gass and L. Selinker (eds.), *Language Transfer in Language Learning.* Rowley, Mass.: Newbury House.

Andersen, R. 1984. Autonomous analysis of interlanguage systems: a methodological inquiry. Paper presented at the Edinburgh Seminar on Interlanguage. April 1984.

Bailey, N., C. Madden, and S. Krashen. 1974. Is there a "natural sequence" in adult second language learning? *Language Learning*, 24, 235–244. Reprinted in Robinett and Schachter (1983).

Banathy, B. H., and P. H. Madarasz. 1969. Contrastive analysis and error analysis. *Journal of English as a Second Language*, 4, 3, 77–92.

Bejarano, Y. 1977. A practical American English pronunciation course for native speakers of Hebrew. Unpublished M.A. thesis in TESL, UCLA.

Bernaldo, A. 1970. A contrastive analysis of some American and Filipino attitudes. Unpublished M.A. thesis in TESL, UCLA.

Brown, R. 1973. *A First Language.* Cambridge, Mass.: Harvard University Press.

Burt, M., H. Dulay, and E. Hernandez. 1973. *Bilingual Syntax Measure* (Restricted Edition). New York: Harcourt Brace Jovanovich.

Celce-Murcia, M. 1972. The universalist hypothesis: some implications for contrastive syntax and language teaching. In UCLA *Workpapers in TESL*, vol. 6, 11–16. Reprinted in Robinett and Schachter (1983).

Chaudron, C. 1977. A descriptive model of discourse in the corrective treatment of learners' errors. *Language Learning*, 27, 1, 29–46.

Chomsky, N. 1965. *Aspects of the Theory of Syntax.* Cambridge, Mass.: MIT Press.

Comrie, B. 1981. *Language Universals and Linguistic Typology.* Chicago: University of Chicago Press.

Corder, S. P. 1967. The significance of learner's errors. *IRAL*, 5, 4, November, 161–170. Reprinted in Robinett and Schachter (1983).

Corder, S. P. 1971a. Describing the language learner's language. CILT Reports and Papers, No. 6.

Corder, S. P. 1971b. Idiosyncratic dialects and error analysis. *IRAL*, 9, 2, May, 147–160.

Corder, S. P. 1981. *Error Analysis and Interlanguage.* Oxford University Press.

Day, R., N. A. Chenoweth, A. E. Chun, and S. Luppescu. 1984. Corrective feedback in native—non-native discourse. *Language Learning*, 34, 2, 19–45.

*di Pietro, R. J. 1971. *Language Structures in Contrast.* Rowley, Mass.: Newbury House.

Donaldson, M., and G. Balfour. 1968. Less is more: a study of language comprehension in children. *British Journal of Psychology*, 59, 461–472.

Dulay, H., and M. Burt. 1974. Natural sequences in child second language acquisition. *Language Learning*, 24, 37–53.

Eckman, F. 1977. Markedness and the contrastive analysis hypothesis. *Language Learning*, 27, 2.

Eckman, F. In press. Universals, typologies and interlanguage. In W. Rutherford, and R. Scarcella (eds.) *Second Language Acquisition and Language Universals.* Amsterdam: John Benjamins Press.

Fries, C. C. 1945. *Teaching and Learning English as a Foreign Language.* Ann Arbor: University of Michigan Press.

Gass, S. 1979. Language transfer and universal grammatical relations. *Language Learning*, 29 (2), 327–344.

Gass, S. 1984. A review of interlanguage syntax: language transfer and language universals. *Language Learning*, 34, 2, 115–132.

Gass, S., and L. Selinker. 1983. *Language Transfer in Language Learning.* Rowley, Mass.: Newbury House.

Hammer, J. 1965. *A Bibliography of Contrastive Linguistics.* Washington, D.C.: Center for Applied Linguistics.

Hartman, R. R. K. 1980. *Contrastive Textology: Comparative Discourse Analysis in Applied Linguistics.* Heidelberg: Julius Groos Verlag.

Hatch, E. 1978. Discourse analysis and second languge acquisition. In E. Hatch (ed.), *Second Language Acquisition: A Book of Readings.* Rowley, Mass.: Newbury House, 401–435.

Hatch, E. 1981. Discussion of "Input from the inside: the role of a child's prior linguistic experience in second language learning." In R. Andersen (ed.), *New Dimensions in Second Language Acquisition Research.* Rowley, Mass.: Newbury House, 104–108.

*Presently out of print.

Hatch, E. 1983. Simplified input and second language acquisition. In R. Andersen (ed.), *Pidginization and Creolization as Language Acquisition*. Rowley, Mass.: Newbury House, 64–86.

Hawkins, B. 1982. Comprehension in foreigner-talk disicourse: an observational study. Unpublished MA thesis in TESL, UCLA.

Jakobson, R. 1941. *Kindersprache, Aphasie, und allgemeine Lautgesetze*. Uppsala: Almqvist and Wiksell.

James, C. 1980. *Contrastive Analysis*. London: Longman.

Jordens, P., and E. Kellerman. 1978. Investigations into the "transfer strategy" in second language learning. Paper presented at the fifth AILA Congress in Montreal. Published in the Proceedings of the Congress (1981) 195–215.

Keenan, E., and B. Comrie. 1977. Noun phrase accessibility and universal grammar. *Linguistic Inquiry, 8* (1), 63–99.

Khampang, P. 1974. Thai difficulties in using some selected English prepositions. Unpublished M.A. thesis in TESL, UCLA.

Kleinmann, H. 1973. Transformational grammar and the processing of certain English sentence types. Unpublished M.A. thesis in TESL, UCLA.

Kleinmann, H. 1977. Avoidance behavior in adult second language acquisition. *Language Learning, 27,* 1, 93–107. Reprinted in Robinett and Schachter (1983).

Kumpf, L. 1982. An analysis of tense, aspect, and modality in interlanguage. Paper presented at the 16th Annual TESOL Convention, Honolulu.

Kumpf, L. 1984. Prosody in interlanguage. Paper presented at a Colloquium on Interlanguage and Interlanguage Development, May 26, 1984, UCLA. Forthcoming as Ph.D. dissertation in applied linguistics.

Lado, R. 1957. *Linguistics across Cultures*. Ann Arbor: University of Michigan Press.

Larsen-Freeman, D. 1978. An explanation for the "morpheme accuracy order" in learners of English as a second language. In E. Hatch (ed.), *Second Language Acquisition: A Book of Readings*. Rowley, Mass.: Newbury House, 371–379.

Lazghab, S. 1973. Tunisian Arabic and French Phonological Interference with English as a Second Foreign Language: Stress and the Phoneme /h/. Unpublished M.A. thesis in TESL, UCLA.

Lee, W. R. 1957. The linguistic context of language teaching, *English Language Teaching*, vol. 11, April-June, 77–85. Reprinted in Allen and Campbell (1972) and Robinett and Schachter (1983).

Long, M. 1980. Input, interaction and second language acquisition. Unpublished Ph.D. dissertation in Applied Linguistics, UCLA.

Long, M. 1981. Input, interaction and second language acquisition. Paper presented at the New York Academy of Sciences Conference on Native Language and Foreign Language Acquisition. New York, January 15–16, 1981. To appear in the *Annals of the New York Academy of Sciences*.

*Presently out of print.

Meara, P. 1982. Vocabulary acquisition: a neglected aspect of language learning. In V. Kinsella (ed.) *Surveys 1: Eight State-of-the-art Articles on Key Areas in Language Teaching*. London: Cambridge University Press.

Naro, A. 1978. A study on the origins of pidginization. *Language, 54,* 314–347.

Nemser, W. 1971. Approximative systems of foreign language learners. *IRAL, 9,* 2, 115–123.

Newmark, L. 1966. How not to interfere with language learning, *IJAL, 32,* January, 77–83. Reprinted in Allen and Campbell (1972).

Peck, S. 1978. Child-child discourse in second language acquisition. In E. Hatch (ed.), *Second Language Acquisition: A Book of Readings*. Rowley, Mass.: Newbury House, 383–400.

Richards, J. C. 1971. A non-contrastive approach to error analysis. *English Language Teaching, 25,* 3, 204–219. Reprinted in Robinett and Schachter (1983).

Richards, J. C. 1974. *Error Analysis: Perspectives on Second Language Acquisition*. London: Longman.

Robinett, B. W., and J. Schachter. 1983. *Second Language Learning: Contrastive Analysis, Error Analysis, and Related Aspects*. Ann Arbor: University of Michigan Press.

Rutherford, W. E. 1982. Markedness in second language acquisition. *Language Learning, 32,* 1, 85–108.

Salica, C. 1981. Testing a model of corrective discourse. Unpublished M.A. thesis in TESL, UCLA.

Santos, T. 1984. Markedness theory and error evaluation: an experimental study. Unpublished Ph.D. qualifying paper in applied linguistics, UCLA.

Santos, T. Forthcoming. Professors' reactions to the academic writing of non-native speakers of English. Ph.D. dissertation in Applied Linguistics, UCLA.

Schachter, J. 1974. An error in error analysis. *Language Learning, 24,* 2, 205–214. Reprinted in Robinett and Schachter (1983).

Schachter, J., and M. Celce-Murcia. 1977. Some reservations concerning error analysis. *TESOL Quarterly, 11,* 4, 441–451. Reprinted in Robinett and Schachter (1983).

Schachter, J., and W. E. Rutherford. 1979. Discourse function and language transfer. *Working Papers on Bilingualism, 19,* 3–12. Reprinted in Robinett and Schachter (1983).

Schachter, P. 1967. Transformational grammar and contrastive analysis. *UCLA Workpapers in TESL*, vol. 1, 1–7. Reprinted in Allen and Campbell (1972).

*Schumann, J. H. 1978a. *The Pidginization Process: A Model for Second Language Acquisition*. Rowley, Mass.: Newbury House.

Schumann, J. H. 1978b. The relationship of pidginization, creolization, and decreolization to second language acquisition. *Language Learning, 28,* 367–379.

Schumann, J. H. 1982. Simplification, transfer, and relexification as aspects of pidginization in early second language acquisition. *Language Learning, 32,* 2, 337–366.

Selinker, L. 1972. Interlanguage. *IRAL, 10,* 3, 209–231. Reprinted in Robinett and Schachter (1983).

Shintani, M. 1974. A contrastive analysis of relativization in English and Japanese. Unpublished M.A. thesis in TESL, UCLA.

Slobin, D. 1973. Cognitive prerequisites for the development of grammar. In C. Ferguson and D. Slobin (eds.), *Studies of Child Language Development.* New York: Holt, Rinehart & Winston.

Slobin, D. 1977. Language change in childhood and history. In J. Macnamara (ed.), *Language Learning and Thought.* New York: Academic Press, 185–214.

Stauble, A. 1978. Decreolization: a model for second language development. *Language Learning, 28,* 29–54.

Stauble, A. 1981. A comparative study of a Spanish-English and Japanese-English second language continuum: verb phrase morphology. Unpublished Ph.D. dissertation in Applied Linguistics, UCLA.

Stauble, A., and J. Schumann. 1983. Toward a description of the Spanish-English basilang. In K. Bailey, M. Long, and S. Peck (eds.). *Second Language Acquisition Studies.* Rowley, Mass.: Newbury House.

Stockwell, R. P., J. D. Bowen, and J. W. Martin. 1965. Hierarchy of difficulty. Chapter 11 in *The Grammatical Structures of English and Spanish,* Contrastive Structures Series, Chicago: University of Chicago Press.

Suwatthigul, P. 1973. Thai students' performance in the usage of modal auxiliaires in English. Unpublished MA thesis in TESL, UCLA.

Tarone, E. 1976. Some influences on interlanguage phonology. *Working Papers in Bilingualism, 8,* 87–111.

Tarone, E. 1979. Interlanguage as chameleon. *Language Learning, 29,* 1, 181–191.

Trubetzkoy, N. S. 1939. *Grundzüge der Phonologie.* Prague: Cercle Linguistique de Prague.

Vander Werf, W. 1969. Lexical analysis and comparison: English and Persian. Unpublished MA thesis in TESL, UCLA.

Vigil, N., and J. Oller. 1976. Rule fossilization: a tentative model. *Language Learning, 26,* 2, 281–295.

Wardhaugh, R. 1970. The contrastive analysis hypothesis. *TESOL, 4,* 2, 123–130. Reprinted in Robinett and Schachter (1983).

Weinreich, U. 1953. *Languages in Contact: Findings and Problems.* New York: Publication No. 1 of the Linguistic Circle of New York.

Wu, Z. 1982. Logical connectors in Chinese and English written discourse. Unpublished M.A. thesis in TESL, UCLA.

Yoshida, M. 1977. A Japanese child's acquisition of English vocabulary. Unpublished M.A. thesis in TESL, UCLA.

Zobl, H. 1980a. The formal and developmental selectivity of L1 influence on L2 acquisition. *Language Learning, 30,* 2, 43–58.

Zobl, H. 1980b. Developmental and transfer errors: their common bases and (possibly) differential effects on subsequent learning. *TESOL Quarterly, 14,* 4, 469–482.

Zobl, H. 1982. A direction for contrastive analysis: the comparative study of developmental sequences. *TESOL Quarterly, 16,* 2, 169–184.

PART III
THE LEARNING ENVIRONMENT

INTRODUCTION

In this third section of the anthology we look at the learning context and address the following question: under what conditions does classroom instruction tend to be productive or unproductive?

In their chapter, McGroarty and Galvan examine the role of culture in the language classroom and show us how the source and/or target culture can influence both student and teacher behavior; furthermore, these authors emphasize how important it is for teachers and students alike to develop cultural sensitivity and awareness in order for the learning environment to be optimal. Since relatively little empirical research has been carried out in this area, the authors write primarily based on their experiences in teaching seminars on intercultural communication to ESL teachers.

Bailey's chapter, an excellent overview of classroom-centered research, discusses effective classroom behaviors from the point of view of both the ESL student and the teacher; it also exposes us to the diverse research methods available to us should we wish to carry out classroom research. In this respect Bailey's contribution is a fine transition to the next part of this anthology, where we consider the research process in greater detail.

CULTURE AS AN ISSUE IN SECOND LANGUAGE TEACHING

Mary McGroarty *and*
José L. Galvan

One of the most significant developments for the field of language instruction has been the recognition of the close relationship that exists between language and culture. Yet in spite of that recognition, the role of culture in second language learning/teaching by and large continues to be ignored by language researchers and curriculum planners alike. Courses dealing with the role of culture in language learning are not commonly included as part of the core curricula of TESL programs in the United States. In fact, most American TESL programs do not even offer such courses as electives (Black, 1978).

Perhaps the main reason that culture is not dealt with adequately is that it is difficult to describe. Even though culture is reflected in all forms of human behavior, most of us are largely unaware of its effects on our communications with others. Furthermore, there is no obvious or uniform linguistic system to describe the culturally determined patterns of language use that affect the grammar of a language. Arvizu and colleagues (1980) provide many useful guidelines for helping teachers describe culture in pedagogically useful ways. They note that culture may be defined as a set of ways of behaving; possession of a high level of education; or a particular style of artistic expression in areas like art and music. As they note, teachers need to understand all these aspects of culture, and the first is particularly important and elusive.

CULTURE FOR WHOM AND FOR WHAT?

When teacher trainers decide to include a course in culture as part of a TESL program's curriculum, they must consider carefully what the course content should be, based on a number of possible desired objectives. For instance, should the course concentrate on one specific culture or should its focus be more general? Some TESL programs are designed to train teachers for very specific assignments (e.g., Spanish-English bilingual education classrooms, university EFL assignments in Asia, etc.); thus it may be desirable for the course to limit its focus to one or two cultures. However, because most TESL programs train teachers for a range of assignments, either in the United States or abroad, it is more common for such a course to deal with culture as a general field of inquiry. Specific cultural details are then used merely as examples of general trends or patterns.

Similarly, it will be necessary to determine what the course goals should be—e.g., whether the course should be about culture as a field of study or about cultural awareness as part of the student teacher's personal growth and experience. Both are important objectives, but each TESL program must decide on its own priorities for its own students.

Effective ESL teachers should be aware of specific aspects of their own and other cultures and as a consequence should understand how the cultures of the world relate to one another. In addition, prospective teachers should understand and accept the notion of cultural relativity, i.e., that cultural "norms" are societal conventions, that these conventions develop arbitrarily over time, and that they are subject to the same evolutionary influences as language. Thus, cultural awareness is an important training objective for a TESL program to encourage.

It would be possible to make a case for *general* awareness of culture as a useful tool for ESL teachers. However, general sensitivity to the varieties of cultural experience is not enough; such sensitivity would not provide ESL teachers with the specialized understanding of themselves and the role that their work demands. Instead, ESL teacher training programs should offer a course tailored specifically to the needs of second language teachers.

There are three main reasons why ESL teacher trainees would benefit from such a course. First, ESL teachers as well as their students are culture bearers. Second, culture shapes one's views of language and education in profound ways, and these views affect expectations regarding the nature of language teaching and learning in the classroom and in other situations. Third, many culturally derived expectations regarding language and education are unconscious; thus they are not available for analysis and reflection unless made explicit.

Teachers and students as culture bearers

The statement that ESL teachers and their students are culture bearers seems obvious. Observers are often struck by the cultural as well as the linguistic diversity within most ESL programs and by the differences between ESL students and their host country peers. In ESL classes, students often ask numerous questions related not just to points of grammar and pronunciation but also to cultural matters such as customs and practices. Even in well-defined contexts like university ESL classrooms, many areas of potential cross-cultural misunderstanding may arise (Althen 1981; Dunnett et al., 1981, pp. 53–57).

The need for second-language teachers to respond to the cultural diversity of the learners they serve has long been axiomatic in the field. The early days of ESL in the United States saw heavy emphasis on Americanization as the goal of English language study (Los Angeles City Schools, 1975). This emphasis shifted to a more balanced view that treated the students' culture as a useful source of knowledge. Some years ago, Finocchiaro (1958, 1969) listed "gaining insight into the linguistic and cultural background of their pupils" and "studying the educational and cultural backgrounds of their students" as the two most important skills that new ESL teachers should have (1969, p. 24). Morain (1977) has also offered several good practical

strategies for incorporating cultural awareness into the methodological training of language teachers (pp. 84–85, 100–101). Brown (1980) has noted the centrality of culture to the language learning enterprise in general, observing that "culture, as an ingrained set of behaviors and modes of perception, becomes highly important in the learning of a second language" (1980, p. 124).

More recent commentators have echoed these prescriptions. Additional examples of cultural topics related specifically to teachers are given by Altman (1981). Selecting the potential descriptors of skills needed by ESL teachers from a recent TESOL conference program, he found that 20 of the 85 descriptors dealt with cultural topics: among other things, an ESL teacher was to be "expert in dealing with the problems of refugees," "trained in sociolinguistics," "a skillful developer of communicative competence in the classroom," "a dialectologist," "a specialist in teaching culture," "a values clarifier," "an expert on tone and register in language," and "a communications analyst" (1981, pp. 11–13). All these titles attest to the teacher's role as cultural expert and mediator. Entry into the world of ESL teaching may well bring cultural questions into sharp focus for the new teacher. (See Gavin, 1981, and Wei, 1982, for additional examples of the ESL teacher's responsibility for teaching culture.) Indeed, Morain (1983) calls for all language teachers to increase their attention to cultural topics.

Yet the cultural diversity of ESL students is only part of the reason that teachers need a course in cross-cultural communication as part of their professional training. More important by far is the concept of teacher as culture bearer. It is not only second language students who bring a culture to the classroom; second language teachers do as well. Because education is a process continuously negotiated between teachers and students (Wilkinson, 1982; Cook-Gumperz and Gumperz, 1982; Mehan, 1979), we need to know what the teacher brings to the negotiation as well as what the students provide. In ESL teaching, the teacher obviously brings

English language skill to bear. Less obvious but vital are the teacher's culturally determined assumptions regarding the roles of teachers and students and the types of techniques and activities suitable for language teaching.

There are two sources for a teacher's attitudes and performance in the ESL classroom setting: the teacher's individual cultural history and the teacher's professional cultural morés. As individuals and members of families with specific cultural patterns, teachers have undergone different kinds of experiences which shaped their beliefs about the way the world works. Landes (1976, pp. 401ff.) has described the background of a group of educators who investigated their own family patterns; most of these family histories were characterized by, among other common attitudes, belief in achievement as a means to upward mobility in the United States. That teachers share this almost universal American belief is not surprising; what is surprising is that they themselves did not realize how common this was. As Spindler has stated so eloquently, "Most teachers are idealistic, many are quite liberal in their political and social beliefs, but they *are products of their culture* and live within the framework of values and symbols that are part of that culture" (1974, p. 153). Individual cultural background plays a major role in determining the attributions of meaning to one's own behavior and that of others (Jaspars and Hewstone, 1982, pp. 132–143); so it is important to become aware of one's individual cultural predispositions in order to understand why certain judgments are made.

However, individual cultural history is not the only source of a language teacher's cultural framework. A teacher's professional socialization is also culture-specific. In a wide-ranging study of American teachers, Lortie (1975) found that teacher training embodied "grand ideals and scant strategy" (p. 69); this training did not provide many specific guidelines for the "endemic uncertainties" (pp. 134–161) teachers faced in their work. Teachers were, he concluded, left on their own to evolve most of the pedagogical techniques they used.

A major source of their pedagogical techniques was their own informal "apprenticeship-of-observation" (p. 67) during which they developed their own techniques based on what they saw in classrooms coupled with their "prior conceptions of good teaching" (p. 66). This pattern of professional socialization means that beginning teachers typically have few models from which to draw, for their training has not included systematic exposure to a broad range of recurrent classroom problems. They are thus left to devise their own approaches to teaching; many of these approaches, resting as they do on personal background and experience, reflect "a strongly biographical orientation to pedagogical decision-making" (Lortie, 1975, p. 81). Hence, because of the absence of comprehensive training in a range of alternative approaches to instruction, the professional preparation of teachers magnifies the influence of individual background with all the cultural predilections which that implies.

Some of these cultural predilections are especially relevant to the teaching of language. In an attempt to explain certain tendencies of second language teachers, Walmsley (1982, pp. 79ff.) has proposed the concept of "teacher value system" to describe some apparently contradictory behaviors. He argues that the way teachers treat language learners in the classroom often provides evidence of a "teacher" value orientation which promotes quiet, order, and structural accuracy over speech, creativity, and communicative use of the second language. Such an orientation reduces the opportunities for learners to develop mastery of the second language (pp. 86–87). It is thus important for ESL teachers to come to terms with their cultural predilections in the area of teaching in general and language teaching in particular in order to understand why they act and react in certain ways in their roles as teachers.

The concept of teacher may also vary cross-culturally. Radford (1980) found that Arab students' perceptions of a "good teacher" are quite different from those of American students. Chen's (1984) study of

Chinese scholars doing graduate work in the United States makes a similar point.

Culture affects expectations

Both education and language use are marked by many cultural norms which are often unstated. Culture-specific expectations regarding the role and training of teachers were discussed in the previous section. There are some additional cultural considerations that affect language learning, teaching, and use. These include the value a culture places on formal education; the expected outcomes of such education; and the role of education in individual and societal development.

Recently sociolinguistic researchers have articulated the critical relationship between language use and these broad social concerns. Cook-Gumperz and Gumperz relate these concerns specifically to mastery of communication through language: "Critical for any consideration of communicative competence is the need to see the sociolinguistic practices of speaking and interacting within the wider context of the educational assumptions and ideologies held by members of the society" (Cook-Gumperz and Gumperz, 1982, p. 17). Many recent ethnographic studies offer impressive anthropological evidence for differing views of language learning and use within and across widely varying societies. The research described in the works of Heath (1983), Cazden, John, and Hymes (1972), Gumperz and Hymes (1972), Bauman and Sherzer (1974), and Blount and Sanches (1977) demonstrate how profoundly language use is molded by cultural influence.

In the area of cultural norms related to language use, unstated differences in expectations can also lead to difficulty in communication. In discussing the television series "Crosstalk," which depicts the problems that sometimes arise between speakers of British and Indian English, Baxter and Levine (1982) point out that awareness of culturally derived differences is vital for ESL teachers who must teach learners to interact with speakers of many different first and second language varieties of English. In doing so, cultural con-siderations such as conceptions of the proper way to express polite deference or provide personal information may be as important as reasonably accurate grammar and pronunciation. Fillmore (1981) enumerates several possibly "unexpected ways" (p. 30) that culture might influence children's second language learning; among these are the influences of the discourse patterns, cognitive approaches, and social orientations of the native culture, all of which may shape children's learning strategies in a second language.

Awareness as an element of change

Awareness of the cultural differences that affect communication and language use is not always easily achieved. Cultural assumptions are largely unconscious and thus not available for reflection unless made explicit. Two areas strongly shaped by cultural influences yet not always obvious areas of inquiry for language teachers are those of nonverbal communication and the conventions of argumentation.

Emphasis on teaching students to attain communicative competence, interpreted to mean all the forms of communication used in any speech community, has led to renewed interest in the study of nonverbal communication. In a fine discussion of the communication system related to the Palestinian Arabic school in which he taught, Klassen (1981, pp. 30–35) demonstrates how understanding the local system of nonverbal signals made him a more effective ESL teacher. He notes that awareness of nonverbal communication systems is critical for second language teachers, although such awareness is "submerged and inadvertently hidden to them" (p. 27) unless they make special efforts to analyze it. A course devoted to intercultural communication can provide methods for becoming aware of nonverbal aspects of communication and thus assist second language teachers in broadening their understanding of communicative skills that complement verbal language (Nine-Curt, 1975, p. 1976).

The second culturally influenced area that affects the work of second language teachers and yet is not always obvious to them is that of cultural conventions shaping argu-mentation, definitions of fact, and uses of evidence to support a point. These conven-tions affect written communication dramati-cally, but they also mold other aspects of language use as well. Condon and Yousef, whose text has been a basic tool in the study of intercultural communication for several years, remark that "what is 'reasonable' is not fully separable from cultural assumptions" (1975, p. 213). They point out that the processes of rendering social value judgments and con-structing arguments both reflect cultural influences; and, furthermore, they emphasize that we are probably unaware of these influ-ences unless they are challenged (pp. 47–90; 209–249). A course in culture offers a forum for challenging culturally derived expecta-tions in these areas and thus making language teachers aware of them.

Furthermore, experimental psycholo-gists have demonstrated that, at least in a few cases, even basic perceptual processes may sometimes be influenced by cultural back-ground (see Pick and Pick, 1978, for a thor-ough review of related issues). The differences noted by those psychologists who studied widely varying groups resulted principally from exposure to literacy and modern educa-tion; often persons with little or no literacy training were more accurate in perceiving differences in optical illusions than the better-educated group, which suggests that educa-tion may change one's view of the world both figuratively and literally. Thus, in education as in other areas of behavior permeated by cul-ture, we remain unaware of many influences until they are tested or otherwise raised to consciousness; such information can help second language teachers understand them-selves and their students more completely.

Many ESL teachers are already per-suaded of the need for improved training in intercultural communication. Indeed, through contact with foreign students or students from subcultures other than their own, or as a result of previous training, many ESL teachers have become aware of their own cultural predilec-tions. They realize that their role as language teachers carries with it a responsibility to serve

as a cultural as well as a linguistic resource. Contact with persons from another culture can make teachers curious about their own cultural background and ready to reinterpret it from a fresh perspective. This kind of experi-ence may thus prepare teachers to become cross-cultural mediators in the language class-room. A scholar engaged in the study of cultural mediation has noted, "a person does not usually become aware of the gaps in his knowledge of his own society until he comes into contact with members of other cultures who, through their curiosity about his origins, push him into the role of cultural ambassador and explicator" (Bochner, 1981, p. 13). The actual teaching of ESL may thus be a catalyst for growth in the teacher's own cultural understanding, with pedagogically useful results.

CULTURE AS CONTENT

ESL teachers may need guidance about ways to present cultural information along with the language. Thus, a course in culture designed for ESL teachers must also deal with culture as content. The two major questions a second language teacher faces are what to teach and how to teach it. How does an ESL teacher know that a particular cultural detail is impor-tant or relevant? Once a given cultural area has been identified, what are some appropriate ways to present the cultural information in the second language classroom?

Determining what to teach

Even though it may seem obvious that certain cultural elements need to be covered, it is important that the language teacher take care-ful stock of her or his particular classroom en-vironment at the beginning of the term. The crucial variables are (1) the setting, (2) the learner characteristics, and (3) the extent of the language teacher's familiarity with the learner's background and/or the availability of appropriate resources.

Where is the class being taught and under what conditions? A university-level class in a large metropolitan area of the United States may require lessons on such specialized topics as everyday etiquette and the use of mass transportation in addition to such generalized topics as American dating rituals and classroom comportment. In contrast, a large elementary school EFL class in central Mexico would more appropriately deal with American national holidays and geography.

Who are the students and what are their expectations? Student characteristics can affect the content of a culture lesson in a number of ways. For instance, a homogeneous class might lend itself to a more specialized kind of lesson planning than a heterogeneous class. Similarly, students who are temporary sojourners in the host country have different needs and expectations than immigrants (Dunnett et al., 1981, p. 56). The ESL teacher can address these different needs by varying the content of the culture component.

How well does the teacher know the students' culture? A teacher who has firsthand knowledge of a particular culture may find it easier to identify appropriate cultural topics than one who knows little or nothing about that culture. If the teacher is not familiar with the students' cultural background, many libraries hold extensive collections of cultural descriptions that would be appropriate background reading for the teacher or might even be appropriate as assigned reading for the more advanced students. (A selection of these descriptions is given in Appendix B, which follows this article.)

A word of caution is in order when discussing descriptions of specific cultures, however. Any description of a culture is, of course, limited by the nature of the author's experiences with that culture; i.e., whether that person is a native of that culture or not. Thus, we should remember that generalizations about any given culture oftentimes are limited and therefore can be dangerous. It is important to understand that there is a difference between making a simple observation about another person or culture and making a judgment about it. Extended observations can sometimes lead to valid generalizations, but because they are often colored by the observer's preconceptions, they can limit the

range of interpretations for a specific behavior or culture. It is therefore preferable to assume that observations about any culture will constantly be subject to reinterpretation as new information becomes available to the observer.

Approaches to the teaching of culture
There are several possible approaches to the teaching of culture. As we have noted with regard to course objectives, the approaches used in any culture course should specifically reflect the goals of the overall ESL/EFL training program; depending on the trainees served, the type of institution involved, and the language background and location of the students whom the trainees will eventually teach, certain approaches will be more appropriate or feasible than others. Here we list a wide variety of approaches that culture course designers may wish to consider.

1. Conventional Academic Approaches. a. *Lectures* can be an efficient means of conveying new information or offering new perspectives on what students already know. They can be easily combined with other techniques. In addition, if experts in a particular field are available in addition to the course instructor, they can be invited to give guest lectures in order to give the class the benefit of their special expertise.

b. *Readings* from textbooks on intercultural communication, other scholarly sources, related disciplines, and additional useful sources such as feature articles in good magazines and newspapers are essential to a comprehensive culture course at any college or university. By reading these materials, students have access to detailed treatments of issues related to culture and to information about specific cultures that they can analyze individually and with other members of the class. The bibliography and Appendix C included in this chapter offer a point of departure for selection of relevant readings; again, the amount and type of reading to be done depend on the nature of the course, the training program, and the students.

2. Observational Approaches.   a. *Native informants or long-time sojourners* from a country of interest can be invited to come to the class and answer questions. This is particularly appropriate if students in the class are being trained for a specific area and have a specific role: if they will serve as ESL teacher-trainers in Korea, for example, a Korean professor would be an excellent source of information about specific activities and expectations related to the proposed functions of the trainees as well as information about general aspects of Korean life. Similarly, if students will be teachers in a bilingual school in the United States, principals from schools like those in which they might serve and other members of the bilingual community can be invited to provide their perspectives on the teachers' probable responsibilities. In using this approach, instructors should endeavor to find good informants, persons recognized for their ability to offer pertinent comments and answer questions honestly, not simply persons who have spent a great deal of time in one place.

b. *Personal observations* carried out by the teacher trainees in their own culture or in others can be an invaluable source of information on cultural practices and attitudes. If carried out in one's own culture, such observations can document the great range of variation that exists, as well as the regularities that appear. If carried out in the culture of another group, such observations can help make language teachers aware of the cultural expectations students might bring into the classroom. Some excellent guidelines for conducting systematic personal observations of any cultural scene appear in Spradley and McCurdy (1972) and Spradley (1979, 1980). Trainees particularly concerned with uses of language in any community will find outstanding discussions of the rationale for observations and methodological instructions in the guides written by Slobin et al. (1967) and Heath (1982). Innovative use of observation and participation in the local cultures of San Antonio, Texas, carried out as part of a bilingual teacher training program, is mentioned in Clark and Milk (1983, pp. 42–43).

3. Media Approaches.   a. *Films and videotapes* can provide vivid illustrations of cultural patterns to enhance and expand any related lectures or readings or introduce new kinds of information into a culture course. There are many fine documentary films which include a wealth of cultural information of interest to language teachers. (See Appendix C for complete information.) Among those we have enjoyed using are "To Be a Man" (1979), which describes changing sex roles in the United States; "Chulas Fronteras" (1976), which provides a portrait of the unique traditions associated with Mexican-American music in Texas; "Yanomamo" (1974), which depicts a tribe living in Venezuelan jungles; "Zerda's Children" (1978), which chronicles the life of an impoverished Argentinian woodcutter; "Kypseli" (1972), which illustrates the strict separation of women and men on a Greek island; "Four Families" (1959), which compares rural family life in four disparate cultures; "The Colonel Comes to Japan" (1981), which describes the way Colonel Sanders' Kentucky Fried Chicken business was adapted for the Japanese market; and "Colliding Worlds" (1978), which details the tensions in the lives of Mono Indians of California, who wish to maintain their traditions despite the attractions of modern, technologically based ways of life. Some of the videotapes that have also stimulated fine discussions are "Crosstalk" (1979), which illustrates some of the sociolinguistic differences between British and Indian speakers of English; "Manwatcher" (1980), which provides a lively illustration of varieties of nonverbal behavior; and "Ben Da" (1981), which documents some of the changes in a small Southern city brought about by the arrival of Indochinese refugees. Nearly any good documentary can serve as a point of departure for comments regarding cultural issues. As long as the instructor's purpose in using such materials is clear and specific, the use of media can add an important dimension to any culture class. Several useful observations on the use of films in studying culture can

be found in Shapiro (1977).

b. *Other artifacts* from a particular culture can be used to study cultural patterns as well. Implements associated with eating, different types of musical instruments, and different articles of clothing that are typical of a particular culture may illustrate behavior patterns that language students and teachers should know. Seelye (1974) gives many good examples.

4. Experiential Approaches. a. *Role plays* can help language teachers and students find out what it means to act like members of another culture in various situations. Some good suggestions for the use of role play in assisting students to adjust to life in the United States are offered in Donahue and Parsons (1982). In our work, we have found that asking teacher-trainees to present a short "reverse role play" (in which they must act out a classroom scene from another culture they have experienced) is quite effective. Frequently the behavior patterns depicted in the role play are more dramatic examples of differences than any of the comments made. The participants can often act out differences they have felt even if they are unable to articulate them, a phenomenon consistent with findings in social psychology (Bandura, 1977; Rosenthal and Bandura, 1978).

b. *Simulation games* like Ba-Fa Ba-Fa (Shirts, 1977), in which participants create artificial cultures and must then "live" according to unusual new cultural rules of gesture, gaze, language, and rewards for short periods of time, help to reveal how arbitrary, and yet how deeply ingrained, many cultural patterns are.

c. *Cross-cultural exercises* in which participants modify various aspects of customary behavior such as interpersonal distance in conversation or manner of address can also help teacher trainees identify cultural patterns and respond to them appropriately. Many useful exercises can be found in Batchelder and Warner (1977).

5. Cognitive Approaches. Some of the most recent approaches to the teaching of culture derive from work in cognitive psychology which seeks to provide a rational basis for choice among alternative behaviors. Many of the techniques used are quite useful and readily adaptable in the second language classroom.

a. *Culture assimilators* consist of a short description of a situation requiring participants to make a choice among potentially reasonable methods of resolving a problem situation: the participants then match their choices against the behavior deemed most appropriate by the natives of the culture, and discuss the cues they used in making correct or incorrect choices. As developed by psychologist Harry Triandis and colleagues (see Fiedler et al., 1971; Hartung, 1983; Chen, 1984), culture assimilators have been used for many groups of persons preparing to undertake special missions such as foreign study, technical assistance, or international commerce. They are a powerful, concise means of illustrating cultural contrasts in relevant behavioral terms and can thus help participants understand why choices which seem acceptable to them are not always appropriate in a cross-cultural situation. The technique has been adapted for use with ESL students in the United States in Ford and Silverman's *American Cultural Encounters* (1981) and Olsen's *American Business Encounters* (1982), aimed specifically at adults who will work in the United States.

b. *Culture capsules* are short descriptions of a minimal difference between two cultures, with illustrations or real objects used to demonstrate the difference. Some good examples of these and of *culture clusters*, which are groups of related culture capsules, appear in Seelye (1974), pp. 111–119.

c. *Culturgrams* are very short descriptions of major aspects of a culture; like telegrams, they are simplified and concise in their summary of differences. Developed at Brigham Young University, they also include some essential vocabulary and suggestions for further reading about a country (Center for International and Area Studies, Brigham Young University).

d. *Culture asides* are spontaneous responses to cross-cultural items of interest that arise in the classroom; the teacher simply suspends the planned lesson for a moment to comment on the cross-cultural meanings of what the students have said or done, and then resumes the lesson.

From this brief overview, it is clear that a variety of approaches are available to the teacher wishing to incorporate explicit cultural information into language instruction. These approaches can provide excellent opportunities for practice of the language being learned; so they need not be viewed as instructional frills; they can further the students' linguistic skills as well as their understanding of the target culture.

Even if second language teachers elect not to include teaching about the target culture in their language classes, training in cross-cultural communication is still an essential part of their professional preparation. Because such a course can make teachers aware of the expectations they and their students bring to the language classroom, it can help them view their work more accurately. Cross-cultural training can also help second language teachers modify their instructional methods according to the settings in which they teach. Hence knowledge of the many cultural influences on language learning, teaching, and use increases a language teacher's ability to offer students appropriate, interesting, and relevant language instruction.

DISCUSSION QUESTIONS

1. (a) What do you mean when you use the term "culture"? How many possible definitions can you think of? (b) Look at the list of definitions of culture that you have compiled. What does each of these views of culture imply for education? Should education in school be expected to supply students with information on every aspect of their culture or the cultures which they are studying? Why or why not?

2. What are some of the stereotypes of various cultural groups or age groups that you have observed on radio or television? Why do you think these stereotyped characterizations are used? If you were a member of a group portrayed in a certain way—as stupid, generally elegant, perpetually late, typically thrifty, typically inebriated, or unusually pompous—how would you react? Do the stereotypes you have observed have any basis in your observations of members of your own cultural group or age group?

3. Why is it difficult to become aware of oneself as a culture bearer? Have you had any specific experiences when unconscious cultural expectations were suddenly challenged? If so, think about the experience: What was your first reaction? How did you come to realize that there might be differing interpretations of the situation?

4. Have you ever been a participant, either as a teacher or as a student, in a culturally diverse classroom? If so, try to identify situations in which you had an indication of cultural differences operating: In what areas of classroom life were these differences apparent? How did the teacher handle these differences? As a teacher, would you follow suit, or would you take another approach?

5. To what extent is a second-language classroom also a second-culture classroom? Should second language teachers endeavor to provide cultural information related to the language they are teaching? Why or why not?

6. How would you go about selecting aspects of a particular culture for presentation in a second-language classroom? How would the language proficiency, age, and goals of the students you teach affect your choice of materials and methods to use?

SUGGESTED ACTIVITIES

1.   *Content Analysis of an ESL Lesson.*
Examine one lesson from an ESL text that you
have used or expect to use. What is the topic
of the lesson—an activity like going to the
store, enrolling in university classes, being
interviewed for a job? Does the lesson imply
that this activity is important in English-
speaking cultures? What kind of speakers are
portrayed, and how are they portrayed? What
are the roles of the men and women, adults
and children, teachers and students depicted
in the lesson? Are these depictions accurate
according to your experience of the English-
speaking culture portrayed? Why or why not?
Is the use of language embodied in the lesson
—formal or informal, grammatically accurate
or hypercorrect or possibly incorrect from a
formal point of view but colloquially
acceptable—natural according to your perceptions? What additional cultural information, perhaps implicit, does this lesson
convey?

2.   *Social Rituals in an English-Speaking
Culture.* Observe members of an English-
speaking culture as they greet each other, say
good-bye, participate in a telephone conversation, ask questions of an instructor in a class,
or perform any other act of communication
involving social ritual. What are the elements,
both verbal and nonverbal, that constitute
successful performance in such situations?
Now compare these rituals with their
functional equivalents in other cultures which
you have experienced. What are the similar
elements? What are the differences? Have you
ever experienced difficulties in such situations when you tried to perform a routine
social ritual in another culture? What happened? How might such differences affect the
teaching of English as a second language?
Argyle (1982, pp. 67–70) describes several
other areas of social life where rituals differ
across cultures; this list could also be used in
formulating activities.

3.   *Gestures across Cultures.* Draw up a list
of common situations which are frequently
expressed in gestures as well as in words.
Some likely candidates are gestures for "I
forgot," "I'm hungry," "I'm broke," "He's
crazy," "No," "Wait a minute," "Be quiet."
(See Levine and Adelman, 1982, pp. 53–56 for
a similar exercise related to American culture.)
Discuss these gestures with other members of
your culture. When, and with whom, can they
be used? Is it considered polite to use these
gestures in all situations? Why or why not?
Now find members of another culture and ask
them to show you the gestures to convey
these meanings in their culture. Are the gestures the same? Do they use other, different
gestures to convey any common meanings
that English speakers would not recognize?
What difficulties, if any, might gestural differences create in cross-cultural situations? Have
you ever experienced such difficulties?

4.   *The Cultural Connotations of Intonation.* Say the same sentence (preferably a
sentence neutral in content, such as "She
wasn't here last Monday" or "Excuse me,
where is the main office?") with several different intonation patterns that correspond to
different affective states like happiness, impa-
tience, confidence, fatigue, uncertainty. Is it
easy for you to do this? Why? Find another
member of your culture and compare the
intonation patterns you used to signal these
conditions. Now ask a nonnative speaker of
English, or an ESL class as a group, to comment
on the intonation cues you distinguished. Do
the nonnative speakers respond in the same
way as you and the other member of your
culture? Have you noticed that, because of
differing intonation patterns, communication
in any situation was impeded in any way? If so,
how did you eventually determine the "true"
message being conveyed? What does this
suggest about cross-cultural difference in
intonation cues? (Note: this activity can be
very profitably carried out in conjunction with
discussion of the videotape "Crosstalk,"
which provides good examples of different
interpretations of intonational cues.)

5.   *Time Boundaries: "Early, Late and On
the Dot Are Not the Same in Every Spot."* Make
up a list of situations common to persons in

your social and occupational situation. Some possibilities might be: university classes, family gatherings, meetings at work, social events like dinner parties or receptions, appointments with professionals like doctors or dentists. In your culture, when should you arrive for all these events? How late can you arrive without apologizing? What should you do if you cannot come? How long should you stay? Compare your answers with those of a colleague in the same situation. Are your answers the same? How much variation do you notice? Have you ever experienced a culture where time boundaries are very different from your own? Do you remember any specific instances of great differences in interpretation of time-related events? What happened as a result of these differences? In ESL teaching, have you ever noticed that differences in definitions of time may puzzle your students? Give some examples, and explain what you might do if you realized this pertained to some of your students. (See Argyle, 1982, p. 68 for other related examples.)

SUGGESTIONS FOR FURTHER READING

For recent comprehensive discussions of the many roles of language in education, see

Children In and Out of School.
1982. P. Gilmore and A. A. Glatthorn (eds.). Washington, D.C.: Center for Applied Linguistics.

Schooling in the Cultural Context:
Anthropological Studies of Education.
1976. J. I. Roberts and S. K. Akinsanya (eds.). New York: David McKay Company, Inc.

Education and Cultural Process:
Anthropology of Education.
1974. G. D. Spindler (ed.). New York: Holt, Rinehart, and Winston, Inc.

For current information on methodology and research in nonverbal communication, see

Handbook of Methods in Non-verbal Behavior Research.
1982. K. R. Scherer and P. Ekman (eds.). Cambridge University Press.

Non-verbal Communication: Survey, Theory, and Research.
1982. D. Druckman, R. M. Rozelle, and J. C. Baxter. Beverly Hills: Sage Publications.

For additional examples of cross-cultural communication issues, see

Language and Social Identity.
1982. J. Gumperz (ed.). Cambridge and New York: Cambridge University Press.

Cultures in Contact: Studies in Cross-Cultural Interaction.
1982. S. Bochner (ed.). Oxford: Pergamon Press.

Communicating with Strangers.
1984. W. B. Gudykunst and Y. Y. Kim. Reading, Mass.: Addison-Wesley.

Research in Culture Learning.
1980. M. P. Hamnett and R. W. Brislin (eds.). University Press of Hawaii: East-West Center.

Behaving Brazilian.
1983. P. A. Harrison. Rowley, Mass.: Newbury House.

REFERENCES

Althen, G. (ed.). 1981. *Learning across Cultures*. Washington, D.C.: National Association for Foreign Student Affairs.

Altman, H. B. 1981. What is second language teaching? In J. E. Alatis, H. B. Altman, and P. M. Alatis (eds.), *The Second Language Classroom: Directions for the '80s.* New York: Oxford University Press, 5–19.

Argyle, M. 1982. Intercultural communication. In S. Bochner (ed.), *Cultures in Contact*. Oxford: Pergamon Press, 61–79.

Arvizu, S. F., W. A. Snyder, and P. Espinoza. 1980. Demystifying the concept of culture: Theoretical and conceptual tools. *Bilingual Education Paper Series*, Vol. 3, No. 11. Los Angeles: Evaluation, Dissemination, and Assessment Center, California State University.

Bandura, A. 1977. *Social Learning Theory*. Englewood Cliffs, N.J.: Prentice-Hall.

Batchelder, D., and E. G. Warner (eds.). 1977. *Beyond Experience: The Experiential Approach to Cross-Cultural Education*. Brattleboro, Vermont: The Experiment Press.

Bauman, R., and J. Sherzer (eds.). 1974. *Explorations in the Ethnography of Speaking*. New York: Cambridge University Press.

Baxter, J., and D. Levine. 1982. Crosstalk. (Review of film "Crosstalk" by J. Twitchin and accompanying background material and notes by J. J. Gumperz, T. C. Jupp, and C. Roberts.) *TESOL Quarterly*, 16, 245–253.

Black, A. J. 1978. A rationale for including a course in culture in an ESL teacher-training program. Unpublished M.A. thesis in TESL, UCLA.

Blount, B. G., and M. Sanches (eds.). 1977. *Sociocultural Dimensions of Language Change*. New York: Academic Press.

Bochner, S. 1981. The social psychology of cultural mediation. In S. Bochner (ed.). *The Mediating Person: Bridges between Cultures*. Boston, Mass.: Schenkman Publishing Co., 6–36.

Brown, H. D. 1980. *Principles of Language Learning and Teaching.* Englewood Cliffs, N.J.: Prentice-Hall.

Cazden, C., V. John, and D. Hymes (eds.). 1972. *Functions of Language in the Classroom.* New York: Teachers College Press, xi–lviii.

Center for International and Area Studies, Brigham Young University. *Culturgrams.* Individual culturgrams available for nearly every country in the world. Provo, Utah.

Chen, A. M. 1984. Developing an American cultural assimilator for students and scholars from the People's Republic of China. Unpublished M.A. thesis in TESL, University of California, Los Angeles.

Clark, E. R., and R. D. Milk. 1983. Training bilingual teachers: A look at the Title VII graduate in the field. *NABE Journal, 8,* 41–53.

Condon, J. C., and F. Yousef. 1975, 1981. *An Introduction to Intercultural Communication.* Indianapolis: Bobbs-Merrill Educational Publishing.

Cook-Gumperz, J., and J. J. Gumperz. 1982. Communicative competence in educational perspective. In L. C. Wilkinson (ed.). *Communicating in the Classroom.* New York: Academic Press, 101–129.

Dodd, C. H. 1982. *Dynamics of Intercultural Communication.* Dubuque, Iowa: William C. Brown Co.

Donahue, M., and A. H. Parsons. 1982. The use of roleplay to overcome cultural fatigue. *TESOL Quarterly, 16,* 359–365.

Dunnett, S., F. Dubin, and A. Lezburg. 1981. English language teaching from an intercultural perspective. In G. Althen (ed.). *Learning across Cultures.* Washington, D.C.: National Association for Foreign Student Affairs, 51–71.

Fiedler, F., T. Mitchell, and H. Triandis. 1971. The culture assimilator: An approach to cross-cultural training. *Journal of Applied Psychology, 55,* 95–102.

Fillmore, L. W. 1981. Cultural perspectives on second language learning. *TESL Reporter, 14* (2), 23–31, winter.

Finocchiaro, M. 1958, 1969. *Teaching English as a Second Language.* Rev. ed. New York: Harper and Row.

Ford, C. K., and A. M. Silverman. 1981. *American Cultural Encounters.* San Francisco: The Alemany Press.

Gavin, C. J. 1981. Television viewing and non-native speakers of English: patterns and preferences. Unpublished M.A. thesis in TESL, UCLA.

Gumperz, J. J., and D. Hymes (eds.). 1972. *Directions in Sociolinguistics: The Ethnography of Communication.* New York: Holt, Rinehart, and Winston.

Hartung, E A. 1983. Difficulties in cultural adjustment and implications for orientation of Japanese high-school students living in America. Unpublished M.A. thesis in TESL, University of California, Los Angeles.

Heath, S. B. 1982. Ethnography in education: Toward defining the essentials. In P. Gilmore and A. A. Glatthorn (eds.). *Children In and Out of School.* Washington, D.C.: Center for Applied Linguistics, pp. 33–35.

Heath, S. B. 1983. *Ways with Words.* Cambridge and New York: Cambridge University Press.

Jaspars, J., and M. Hewstone. 1982. Cross-cultural interaction, social attribution, and inter-group relations. In S. Bochner (ed.). *Cultures in Contact: Studies in Cross-cultural Interaction.* Oxford: Pergamon Press, 127–156.

Klassen, B. R. 1981. Communicative competence and second language learning. In V. Froese and S. B. Straw (eds.). *Research in the Language Arts.* Baltimore: University Park Press, pp. 27–40.

Landes, R. 1976. Teachers and their family cultures. In J. Roberts and S. Akinsanya (eds.). *Schooling in the Cultural Context.* New York: David McKay Co., 401–418.

Levine, D. R., and M. B. Adelman. 1982. *Beyond Language: Intercultural Communication for English as a Second Language.* Englewood Cliffs, N.J.: Prentice-Hall.

Lortie, D. C. 1975. *Schoolteacher: A Sociological Study.* Chicago: University of Chicago Press.

Los Angeles City Schools, Division of Career and Continuing Education. 1975. *ESL: For Adults Only.* (Experimental publication.) Los Angeles.

Mehan, H. 1979. *Learning Lessons.* Cambridge University Press.

Morain, G. 1977. The cultural component of the methods course. In J. F. Fanselow and R. L. Light (eds.). *Bilingual, ESOL, and Foreign Language Teacher Preparation: Models, Practices, Issues.* Washington, D.C.: Teachers of English to Speakers of Other Languages, 82–101.

Morain, G. 1983. Commitment to the teaching of foreign cultures. *Modern Language Journal, 67,* 403–412.

Nine-Curt, C. 1975. *Non-verbal Communication.* Bronx, New York: National Center for Curriculum Development.

Nine-Curt, C. 1976. *Teacher-Training Pack for a Course on Cultural Awareness.* Bronx, New York: National Center for Curriculum Development.

Olsen, R. E. W. -B. 1982. *American Business Encounters.* San Francisco: The Alemany Press.

Pick, A. D., and H. L. Pick, Jr. 1978. Culture and perception. In E. C. Carterette and M. Friedman (eds.). *Handbook of Perception, Vol. X., Perceptual Ecology.* New York: Academic Press, 19–39.

Radford, A. E. 1980. Outstanding teacher characteristics as perceived by Saudi Arabian ESL students and American college students. Unpublished M.A. thesis in TESL, UCLA.

Rosenthal, T. L., and A. Bandura. 1978. Psychological modeling: theory and practice. In S. L. Garfield and A. Z. Bergin (eds.). *Handbook of Psychotherapy and Behavior Change.* (2d ed.) New York: Wiley, 621–658.

Seelye, H. N. 1974. *Teaching Culture: Strategies for Foreign Language Educators.* Skokie, Ill.: National Textbook Co.

Shapiro, H. Suggestions for improving film discussions. In Batchelder and Warner (1977), pp. 75–77.

Shirts, R. G. 1977. *Ba Fa Ba Fa.* Del Mar, Calif.: Simile II.

Slobin, D. I. (ed.). 1967. *A Field Manual for Cross-Cultural Study of the Acquisition of Communicative Competence.* Berkeley, Calif.: Institute of Human Learning, University of California, Berkeley (2d draft).

Smith, E. C., and L. F. Luce (eds.). 1979. *Toward Internationalism.* Rowley, Mass.: Newbury House.

Spindler, G. D. 1974. Beth Anne—a case study of culturally-defined adjustment and teacher perceptions. In G. D. Spindler (ed.). *Education and Cultural Process.* New York: Holt, Rinehart and Winston, 139–153.

Spradley, J. P. 1979. *The Ethnographic Interview.* New York: Holt, Rinehart and Winston.

Spradley, J. P. 1980. *Participant Observation.* New York: Holt, Rinehart and Winston.

Spradley, J. P., and D. W. McCurdy. 1972. *The Cultural Experience: Ethnography in Complex Society.* Chicago: Science Research Associates.

Walmsley, J. B. 1982. Teacher value systems. *TESOL Quarterly, 16,* 79–89.

Wei, H. 1982. Determining the socio-cultural survival skills needed by Chinese science majors at UCLA: A needs analysis. Unpublished M.A. thesis in TESL, UCLA.

Wilkinson, L. C. 1982. Introduction: A sociolinguistic approach to communicating in the classroom. In L. C. Wilkinson (ed.). *Communicating in the Classroom.* New York: Academic Press, 3–11.

APPENDIX A

A sample outline for a course on culture for ESL teachers

Ideally, a course in culture for ESL teachers should provide not only an introduction to the field of cross-cultural communications but also an emphasis on methods for teaching culture in the ESL/EFL classroom. This section presents a sample outline of what a course in culture for ESL teachers should contain.

Statement of Purpose. A course in culture for student teachers should have three main purposes. First, it should develop in its participants an awareness of *their own* culture in addition to an awareness of other cultures and subcultures within their own. Second, it should provide them with the theoretical framework needed to understand how their own culture relates to other cultures. Third, it should guide participants to discover ways of applying their awareness to the actual teaching of ESL/EFL.

Methods. The methods used in the course are, by necessity, varied. Students should view and discuss films and videotapes; they should read and discuss relevant articles; they should analyze actual ESL lessons from a cross-cultural perspective; they should research aspects of their own culture or the culture of a group of students with whom they expect to work; and they should develop a teaching unit based on that research. In addition, teacher trainees should participate in a number of experiential activities designed to

focus on intercultural communication. The activities described in Appendix C can be incorporated into nearly any course format.

Readings. There are many possible texts that could be used as readings for the course. At least one of these should be an introductory test on intercultural communication (such as Condon and Yousef, 1975; or Dodd, 1982). Depending on the emphasis of the class, other readings can be assigned from the references given in Appendix B.

Course Topics. The specific topics covered in the course will vary according to the instructor's preferences and the texts used. However, at a minimum, the course should cover the following: observational skills, verbal versus nonverbal communication, proxemics, cultural assumptions and value orientation, cross-cultural communication/miscommunication, sex-specific behavior, and sociolinguistic/sociocultural variation.

APPENDIX B

Information about specific cultures

(The following sample entries are reprinted from *NAFSA Newsletter,* Vol. 32, No. 4, by permission of the National Association for Foreign Student Affairs, 1860 19th St., N.W. Washington, D.C. 20009. 4. This is not an exhaustive list, but it does provide a good starting point.)

Brazil
Roberta C. Widger. *Brazil Rediscovered.* Dorrance and Co. Philadelphia. 1977. The author of this book is half Brazilian and half American and has lived for a considerable length of time in both countries. The book is full of information on everything from food to the life of a typical middle-class family.

Hong Kong
Paul Thomas Welty. *The Asians.* J. P. Lippincott Co. New York, 3rd edition. 1970. Welty covers Asia from Pakistan to Japan: how people live and work, ideas,

ideologies, economic and political problems and social life.

India

Clark Blaise and Bharati Mukherjee. *Days and Nights in Calcutta*. Doubleday and Co. New York. 1977. Indian wife and Canadian husband write separate journals about their reactions to a long visit with wife's family.

Iran

George W. Braswell, Jr. *To Ride a Magic Carpet*. Broadman Press, Nashville, Tenn. 1977. Description of Iran and travel throughout the country, religious life, and customs.

Japan

Edwin O. Reischauer. *The Japanese*. Belknap Press of Harvard University, Cambridge, Mass. 1977. In-depth study of Japanese by an American who has known them well for a long time. Good bibliography.

Malaysia

John Lent (ed.). *Cultural Pluralism in Malaysia: Policy, Mass Media, Education, Religion, and Social Class*. Northern Illinois University, DeKalb, Ill. Distributed by the Cellar Book Shop, Detroit, Mich. 1977.

Mexico

Oscar Lewis. *Five Families*. A Mentor Book. The New American Library. New York. 1971. Novel-type reading about Mexican life and cultural tradition.

People's Republic of China

Keith L. Pratt. *Visitors to China: Eyewitness Accounts of Chinese History*. Praeger Publishers. New York. 1970. A short interestingly written history of China. Complete with appendices of the chronology of China, list of rulers, early literature, geography, names, and a glossary.

Saudi Arabia

Raphael Patai. *The Arab Mind*. Charles Scribner's Sons. New York. 1973. The author examines the Arab society from many viewpoints: language, religion, the Bedouin ethos. The chapter on child rearing practices is especially helpful.

Vietnam

David C. Cooke. *Vietnam, the Country, the People*. W. W. Norton Co., Inc. New York. 1968. A very readable treatise on how the Vietnamese people differ from the people of the Western world through the eyes of a Vietnamese village family. Includes discussion of the Catholic missionary, Father Alexander of Rhodes, who in 1650 recast the Vietnamese language in the Roman alphabet. Of special interest to ESL teachers.

APPENDIX C

Classroom materials

1. Books suitable for use in ESL and culture classes.

    Ford, C. K., and A. M. Silverman. 1981. *American Cultural Encounters*. San Francisco: The Alemany Press.

    Gregg, J. Y. 1981. *Communication and Culture*. New York: D. Van Nostrand Company.

    Kearny, E. N., M. A. Kearny, and J. A. Crandall. 1984. *The American Way: An Introduction to American Culture*. Englewood Cliffs, N.J.: Prentice-Hall.

    Olsen, R. E. W.-B. 1982. *American Business Encounters*. San Francisco: Alemany Press.

2. Films useful in teaching culture classes.

    "Chulas Fronteras." Produced and directed by Les Blank. El Cerrito, Calif.: Flower Films. 1976.

    "Colliding Worlds." Produced and directed by Orrie Sherman. Los Angeles: Hugaitha Productions, 1978.

    "Four Families." Produced by the National Film Board of Canada. 1959.

    "Kypseli." Produced by the University of California at Berkeley. 1976.

"The Colonel Comes to Japan." Part of the Enterprises Series. New York: Learning Corporation of America. 1981.

"Yanomamo." Produced by Brandeis University; distributed by the U.S. Energy Research and Development Agency. 1971.

"Zerda's Children." Produced and directed by Jorge Preloran. Phoenix Films. 1978.

3. Videotapes useful in teaching culture classes.

"Ben Da, USA." Directed by David Hogoboom. 1981.

"Crosstalk." Produced by Twitchin for the British Broadcasting Corporation; distributed in the United States by Films, Inc., Wilmette, Ill. 1979.

"Manwatcher." Produced by Desmond Morris for the British Broadcasting Corporation; distributed in the United States by Films, Inc., Wilmette, Ill. 1980.

CLASSROOM-CENTERED RESEARCH
ON LANGUAGE TEACHING AND LEARNING[1]

Kathleen M. Bailey

Research into classroom processes and their effects on learning is an interesting and varied field. Much has been done in this area in general education (see, for example, Brophy and Good, 1974 or Dunkin and Biddle, 1974), and recently classroom-centered research has gained a foothold in the field of language teaching as well. The purpose of this chapter is to discuss some of the studies on language learning processes in formal instructional settings. The chapter does not by any means include an exhaustive review of the literature in this field, but hopefully it will provide those who teach English or other languages with a general introduction to classroom-centered research.[2]

The following definition of classroom-centered research is borrowed from Long (1980). He says,

Investigation of classroom language learning may be defined as research on second language learning and teaching, *all or part of whose data are derived from the observation or measurement of the classroom performance of teachers and students* (p. 3).

Thus even though there are many types of research that bear on the teaching and learning which occur in language classrooms, this discussion will be limited to research which includes the observational component Long refers to; that is, all or part of the data in these studies were obtained by observing or measuring what the subjects (both teachers and students) actually did or said in class. To illustrate this view of classroom-centered research, a small number of studies have been chosen which involve a variety of subjects, methods, and research foci.

The type of observational component involved in classroom-centered research depends on the purpose of the research and the sorts of data being collected. For example, in research involving "real time" coding systems, the observer codes behaviors as they occur, typically on an observation form (called a "schedule"), using a set of symbols to record information about the live interaction of the language classroom. The observational coding systems provide quantifiable data which can be tabulated and catalogued for analysis of teacher and student behaviors.[3] In contrast, mechanized data collection, including audio and video recording, permits repeated retrospective analysis of classroom processes. Like live classroom lessons, audio and video recordings may be analyzed with coding instruments. In addition, mechanically recorded data may also be transcribed and utterances from the transcripts can be examined in depth for detailed linguistic analyses. Classroom data are collected either through observational coding systems, through noncoding human recording (e.g., extensive note taking by a participant observer or diarist), or through the use of mechanized observation with audio or video recording equipment. Frequently different data-collection systems are used simultaneously. For instance, it is not uncommon for observers to take extensive notes at the same time a language lesson is being tape recorded.

A fundamental question to be asked about classroom-centered research regards the focus of a given study. Does the research examine teacher behaviors or learner behaviors, or the interaction of the two? If language students are the subjects, are they children or adults, learning a second or a foreign language? Is the research solely concerned with actual formal instruction, or are the subjects acquiring language through exposure by being immersed in the target culture as well as receiving classroom instruction? Or does the study examine some interaction of formal instruction and exposure? (See Long, 1983, for a review of the research on exposure and formal instruction in second language learning.) When students are the subjects and the research focuses on their degree of success in learning the language, what definition of success constitutes the dependent variable in the study? In other words, is learning assessed in terms of linguistic accuracy, quantity and/or quality of verbal output in interviews or compositions, standardized test scores, or some measure of communicative competence? Finally, what student characteristics (e.g., motivation, field dependence/independence, cognitive style, etc.) are considered to be important in the students' language learning? Given the great number of factors operating in language teaching and learning, the variables which can be considered are legion. For this reason, the classroom-centered research that has been done in the field of language learning is highly diversified. (See Gaies, 1983, for further discussion of this point.)

The areas which have received the most attention in classroom-centered research to date are (1) patterns of participation, (2) the speech and behavior of teachers, (3) the treatment of learners' errors, and (4) individual student (or teacher) variables in the classroom. The studies discussed in this chapter will be grouped thematically in these four areas. (See Gaies, 1983, for a similar approach to this body of literature, which he terms "classroom process research.") The sample studies reviewed here have been chosen for their accessibility (all are published) and the variety they represent. Each summary will attempt to characterize both the findings and the methods of classroom-centered research.

PATTERNS OF PARTICIPATION IN LANGUAGE CLASSROOMS

Seliger (1977) reports on a language classroom participation study. In this pioneering research on language learners' interaction patterns, Seliger used a combination of questionnaires, criterion measures (such as a cloze test), and classroom observation with a coding instrument to examine the relationship between practice and language learning. In this study, practice is defined as "any verbal interaction between the learner and others in his environment" (p. 265). Practice in formal instructional settings was quantitatively measured by observers using a coding system developed to record the gross number of interactions, as well as who spoke to whom in what language and whether each utterance was a response or an initiation. In this particular study, such interactions were utterances which could consist of one word or several sentences.

During the classroom observation phase of Seliger's research, Seliger identified two types of language learners. Those who practice "by initiating interactions, and thereby cause a concomitant input from others" are called *high-input generators* (HIGs). In contrast, those apparently passive language learners who react to input but "do little to initiate situations which cause more input to be directed to them" are called *low-input generators* (LIGs). Seliger's first hypothesis is that the HIGs would have higher scores for interaction and achievement than would LIGs.

The subjects in the study were adult ESL students enrolled in an intensive English program in New York. Observers using a coding system studied a class of 12 students for 4 hours. At the end of this period three HIGs and three LIGs were identified for further study. These six students were then interviewed.

The experimenter administered a language contract and motivation questionnaire, as well as an embedded figures test, which is a measure of field independence. These six subjects and the other students had also taken a placement examination, and at the end of the semester they took a final examination. The questionnaire used in this study, the Language Contact Profile, is a self-report instrument which "quantifies the learner's motivation and the extent of contact with the second language (potential practice opportunities) outside of regular language classes"

(p. 269). This questionnaire was used to gather data regarding Seliger's second hypothesis, which stated that HIGs would have more out-of-class language activity in the target language than would the LIGs, as reflected in their Language Contact Profile scores.

At the end of the semester all the students were tested on a 50-item cloze passage. Seliger's third hypothesis was that the HIG subjects would score higher on the integrative cloze test than would the subjects who had been identified as low-input generators.

In addition to the cloze test, Seliger used two other criterion measures. A discrete point of English structure and an integrative aural comprehension instrument were both used as pre- and posttest measures, with achievement defined as the difference between a subject's score on the placement examination (pretest) and his score on the final examination (posttest), which was given 15 weeks later. Operating on the assumption that "HIGs would be field independent, less fearful of experimenting with language, less afraid to make mistakes, and less afraid to speak out" (p. 271), Seliger further hypothesized that HIGs would score higher than LIGs on a measure of field independence. In order to test the fourth hypothesis, the Group Embedded Figures Test (a measure of field independence which involves finding a picture, a symbol or shape within a larger figure) was administered to the six subjects.

The results of the data analysis supported the first two hypotheses. The HIGs outperformed the LIGs on interaction and achievement as well as on the Language Contact Profile scores. The third hypothesis, regarding the cloze test scores, was not supported (i.e., the correlations did not reach statistical significance), although the results indicated a trend toward a positive relationship. The fourth hypothesis, which dealt with field independence, was partially supported. Although the correlations between the number of interactions *initiated* by the subjects and the scores on the embedded figures test did not reach statistical significance, there was

a positive correlation between the *total* number of interactions and the measure of field independence. However, Seliger is careful to point out that these results are limited to the particular group he studied. Six is a relatively small number of subjects, especially when the sample is divided into HIGs and LIGs with three students in each group.

Seliger also notes that the study involved a somewhat narrow means of quantifying interactions. As he points out,

Any speech act by a student in the class was counted as an interaction. Speech acts considered as one interaction might be a single word or several sentences in a discourse (p. 268).

Thus the coding system used a limited number of possibilities: who spoke and to whom, whether the interaction represented a response or an initiation, and what language was used. The data collected with this observational system provide frequency counts, but no information is available about the length, function, or quality (either linguistic correctness or communicative success) of the language generated by the learners. Within the stated definition of practice ("any verbal interaction between the learner and others in his environment," p. 265), Seliger's coding system does provide appropriate data for identifying HIGs and LIGs. In future research on high- and low-input generators as types of language learners, it will be worthwhile to consider the length and function of utterances as well. Linguistic accuracy could also be considered. Such a focus would necessitate the use of a more complex coding system or of recorded data and transcripts of classroom interaction.

Allwright investigated such participation patterns using both quantitative and qualitative analyses. He used a case study approach to investigate the turns, topics, and tasks negotiated in a language lesson. The study (1980) is based on the transcript of a lower-intermediate ESL class of adult students. The hour-long class was audio recorded in stereo to facilitate the identification of speakers. In addition, an independent observer took notes on the nonverbal activity in the classroom.

Allwright notes that the learners' active participation in a language lesson is typically believed to be a key variable in second language learning. However, such involvement "is not a straightforward quantitative measure, but a highly complex qualitative one" (p. 250). He also argues that the management of participation is an interactive negotiated process, not entirely under the teacher's control. Throughout the paper Allwright analyzes the utterances of both teacher and students without assuming that the teacher controls the classroom discourse or that the teacher's speech is necessarily unique when compared with that of the students.

Allwright first establishes the framework for a macroanalysis of language teaching and learning which consists of three basic categories:

(i) SAMPLES, instances of the target language, in isolation or in use.

(ii) GUIDANCE, instances of communication concerning the nature of the target language.

(iii) MANAGEMENT ACTIVITIES, aimed at ensuring the profitable occurrence of (i) and (ii) (p. 251).

Allwright discusses these elements and notes that they may vary in terms of relative proportion, distribution, sequence, and the language used.

At a more specific level, Allwright categorizes the transcribed data with a turn-taking analysis. This numerical analysis reveals a class period which was both teacher-centered and conversational in tone. The teacher and students were found to participate in the turn-taking process by both turn-getting activities (including the accepting, stealing, taking, making, and missing of turns) and turn-giving activities. The latter category includes making either a general or a personal solicit (i.e., in spoken discourse, when one speaker addresses another), fading out or giving way to an interruption, or simply concluding an utterance. Using these categories, Allwright provides frequency counts of the turns taken by the teacher and the students. Not surprisingly, the teacher had the greatest number of turns overall, but one student, Igor, was found to

have "a wholly disproportionate share of the identified turns" (p. 258).

Allwright suggests a number of hypotheses about how Igor got so many turns. Although the types of turns he took were not substantively different from those of the other students, he got more turns by managing to be called on more often, by responding more frequently to general solicits, and by taking advantage more often of opportunities for discourse maintenance (pp. 262–263).

After analyzing the turn-taking system to determine *how* Igor got so many turns, Allwright attempts a topic analysis to explain *why* he did so. This facet of the study also involves a quantitative analysis. It showed that Igor was "probably more interested in contributing whenever the topic got away from the target language or the pedagogy itself" (p. 267). The topic analysis raised still more questions about Igor's participation patterns and led to the task analysis, in which the interactive nature of classroom discourse is examined. In this phase of the research, Allwright was concerned with

how what people do in discourse sets a task for other participants . . . how simply stopping sets a task, implicitly, for someone to do some "discourse maintenance," for example, also how setting a task often involves making a personal solicit, but how the receiver of such a solicit can choose to either accept or reject the turn itself, and, in the case of "accept," choose separately to accept or reject the task involved (pp. 270–271).

To illustrate the task analysis, Allwright provides the transcript of a classroom episode involving Igor and the teacher. Each line of the conversation is considered in terms of the task the speakers set for one another. This part of the study is based on discourse analysis rather than the more straightforward numerical analyses described above.

Several interesting interpretations of the episode arise. For example, based on the transcribed data, it becomes apparent that Igor frequently negotiated a subtle change of topic during the language lesson—including changes of the actual topic category away from the intended focus of the language lesson. The teacher tried to encourage Igor to communicate, yet at the same time she hoped to keep the lesson moving ahead. However, the analysis of the transcript reveals that Igor's utterances caused the teacher to politely seek clarification; that is, "Igor's success at getting turns is indeed largely due to a lack rather than an abundance of communicative competence" (pp. 279–280).

In Seliger's terms, Igor is a high-input generator in this class. He gets people (at least his teacher) to address language to him and to provide him with practice opportunities. Allwright speculates that the presence of such learners in classrooms may contribute to the progress made by other learners who may be low-input generators.

These papers by Seliger (1977) and Allwright (1980) illustrate the variety of possibilities in classroom-centered research on participation patterns. Although the focus of the research in both studies is very similar, the methodologies are quite different. In Seliger's study the classroom observation component served simply to identify the HIGs and LIGs, while in Allwright's study the transcriptions of the recorded classroom sessions provided the bulk of the data. Whereas Seliger used criterion measures and statistical analyses to investigate participation patterns in language classrooms, Allwright's case study approach combines transcription, frequency counts, and discourse analysis. Working in the tradition of experimental research, Seliger operationally defined his terms and collected data to test stated hypotheses against preset levels of statistical significance. Allwright, on the other hand, derived the hypotheses from the data: his category system and analytical framework were progressively modified to accommodate the complexities of a negotiated language lesson. Both studies reveal insights about the behavior of adult learners and both were conducted in teacher-led classrooms.

Another study of participation patterns compared students' classroom discourse with and without the teacher's guidance. This research project, which is reported in Long, Adams, McLean, and Castaños (1976), is concerned with the quantity and function of students' language. The study discussed in this article was conducted in intermediate English classes in a Mexican university. The purpose of the research was to compare the verbal interaction of students in small groups (in this case, pairs) with that of students in a lockstep classroom situation. By "lockstep" the authors mean the style of classroom management in which all the learners are doing the same thing at the same time (e.g., listening to the teacher). This approach is typically teacher-centered and involves only one "conversation" occurring at any given time.

One assumption of the study is that lockstep classroom organization limits the *quality* of the potential discourse in student-student as well as teacher-student interaction because of the pace maintained by the teacher and the inhibitions students may experience (particularly in a second or foreign language) in trying to speak in front of their classmates and the teacher. Small group work, on the other hand, is characterized as providing a less inhibiting environment, a situation which is thought to promote more verbal exploration. Furthermore, in terms of potential discourse, in small group work "roles open to students are more varied, the very absence of the teacher automatically delegating to them responsibilities which result in language use of kinds not open to them in lockstep work" (p. 138).

This study was designed to examine these claims and to compare the quantity and quality of students' language in lockstep classrooms and in pair interaction. Although the hypotheses were not formally stated, the assumption is that students have more opportunity to talk in small groups and will therefore produce greater quantity and quality of language. Here the term *quality* refers to "the varieties of things students *did* with language under the two conditions, i.e., what communicative acts of one kind or another they performed with the language they produced" (Long et al., 1976). Thus the definition of quality is based on communication skills rather than linguistic competence since the research was not concerned with the number of errors of correct forms produced by the students in either situation.

The researchers made audio recordings of intermediate classroom lessons which involved discussions of differences between humans and animals. After 10 minutes of discussion, students chose the partners with whom they wished to work. Students were grouped according to their preferences because the experimenters believed that "it is the ability to work with chosen classmates which provides the intimacy upon which student confidence in small group work is based" (p. 139). One pair of students from each class was randomly selected to continue the discussion in an adjoining room while the remaining students in the class proceeded to discuss the topic with the teacher in a lockstep situation. Both of these segments of discussion were also recorded, and afterward the pairs returned to the large groups where the continuing discussion was recorded for 10 more minutes. The researchers then transcribed the recordings and analyzed the transcripts, using two existing systems first and then a coding system developed by the authors themselves.

The researchers first analyzed portions of the data using Bellack's system (Bellack, Kliebard, Hyman, and Smith, 1966), which describes and codes four pedagogical moves (*structuring, soliciting, responding,* and *reacting*) occurring in classroom interaction. The second existing system used in the study was the FLint system (Moskowitz, 1976), which is discussed below. However, both of these systems are limited in terms of what they can say about the various functions performed by the students' utterances. Before the authors describe the coding system they developed to examine such rhetorical functions, they briefly discuss three other coding systems: (1) FOCUS—foci for observing communications used in settings (Fanselow, 1977a), which has been used in analyzing interaction in language classrooms; (2) the system of analysis developed at Birmingham by Sinclair and Coulthard (1975), which was not designed to investigate student-student interac-

tion; and (3) a system used by Barnes at Leeds, which had been specifically designed to investigate the interaction in small groups of students (Barnes, 1969). The authors then discuss the embryonic category system (ECS), which they developed to categorize and quantify their own data. They also provide a sample transcript to show the reader how the system works.

The embryonic category system was designed by the researchers specifically for the purpose of examining types of communicative uses students make of language, in either small group or classroom interaction. The system includes categories of pedagogical moves (e.g., student initiates discussion, student provides an example, student asks for information about the target language), social skills (e.g., student interrupts, contradicts, jokes, encourages others), and rhetorical acts (student predicts, deduces, negates, identifies, etc.). Multiple coding is permitted in ECS since a given utterance may perform a number of communicative functions.

The ECS was used to analyze the middle 10-minute segments of the simultaneous lockstep and pair interactions from two of the four classes recorded. In analyzing their data, the researchers chose to look at the two least teacher-centered of the four classes. This decision, it was felt, would put the hypothesis to the most severe test since the students would probably talk more in such classes than would students in teacher-dominated classes.

Eight scores were used in the statistical analysis. These scores represented speech acts generated in the small group and large group situations. The eight categories involved both the *quantity* and *variety* of pedagogical moves, social skills, rhetorical acts, and the total number of moves (i.e., the sum of the first three scores). In all of these categories the scores were higher for quantity and variety of speech acts produced in the dyads than for those produced in the lockstep condition. Except for the category of variety of rhetorical acts, these differences all achieved statistical significance. The authors cautiously interpret these findings as providing support for their hypothesis "as to the positive effects on quantity and quality of language production of having students work in small groups as opposed to a lockstep classroom" (p. 149). They point out that further testing should be done with small groups larger than the pair unit examined in this study, and with students at higher and lower proficiency levels.

These three studies reveal several interesting facts about the patterns of participation in language classrooms. Allwright and Seliger both found that some students participate verbally to a much greater extent than others. Seliger found such practice to correlate with various measures of language achievement. Allwright's analysis showed that the teacher gets far more turns than other participants. And, not surprisingly, Long et al. found that when students work in pairs—in the teacher's absence—those students use more language in greater variety than they do in lockstep classrooms. Yet, although the teacher strongly influences and in some cases dominates the classroom discourse, the interactions examined in these studies were not entirely under the teacher's control. Different students use the classroom experience quite differently.

Recent studies on classroom interaction have considered ethnicity as a factor in turn taking (Sato, 1981) and the participation opportunities of limited English proficiency students in fifth and sixth grade content classrooms (Schinke-Llano, 1983). Seliger (1983) has conducted follow-up studies on high- and low-input generators. Beebe (1983) has reviewed the psychological literature on risk taking and discussed second language learners' involvement in the target language as it relates to risk taking. Still more research is needed to explain the complex relationship of classroom participation (the process) to language learning (the product).

INVESTIGATIONS OF LANGUAGE TEACHERS' CLASSROOM BEHAVIOR

Another area of investigation in language classrooms involves the teacher's behavior. Since this behavior is a key factor in the negotiation of classroom lessons, language teachers have often been the focus of classroom-centered research.

In some ways it is easier to study teachers, methodologically speaking, than it is to study learners. For instance, there is usually only one teacher in a classroom with several students. A researcher will have little trouble identifying and transcribing the teacher's voice in a recorded language lesson. In addition, language teachers are typically communicative and linguistically sophisticated subjects. They can often answer questions about why they chose a particular course of action, thus adding their insights to the researcher's observations.

On the other hand, some teachers are intimidated by the presence of observers or recording equipment in their classrooms. Some feel threatened by investigators' questions or think the research will detract from the lesson. Fortunately, in several of the studies discussed below (e.g., Cathcart and Olsen, 1976; Fanselow, 1977b; Nystrom, 1983), teachers collaborated with the researchers. Hopefully, as classroom-centered research gains wider acceptance in the language teaching field, and as teachers become more aware of the issues under investigation, they will be less hesitant to participate in such studies. In the long run, examining and understanding what happens in language classrooms can only serve to advance the profession.

Many studies of teacher behavior in content classes have tried to describe good teaching. This already complex issue is further complicated in language classsrooms, where often the medium of instruction is also the content. Until more is known about what factors contribute to successful second language learning in formal instructional settings, the description of "the good language teacher" will continue to be problematic.

In early research on the classroom behavior of language teachers, Politzer (1970) used videotape recordings in analyzing the behavior of 17 high school teachers of French. For this study measures of the students' achievement on several different French tests were correlated with the various behaviors exhibited by the teachers. Theoretically, a strong positive correlation between a given teaching behavior and student achievement would indicate that the particular teaching behavior was "good" or "effective."

Politzer's study is interesting for a number of reasons. First, it involved a large number of students and teachers, but all these students were studying a foreign language and were therefore not immersed in the target culture. Hence, out-of-class exposure to French input was limited if not nonexistent. All the students were at the same proficiency level—first semester high school French. All 17 classes were taught with the same materials and the teachers all used the audio-lingual method. In addition, the Modern Language Aptitude Test (MLAT, Carroll and Sapon, 1959) was administered to the students. Subsequently their achievement scores were adjusted for the aptitude shown by the various classes. Thus in the final correlations, Politzer controlled for the possibility that some classes might have had more gifted language learners than others. In all of these factors, the researcher took precautions to ensure the comparability of the data.

The data were collected throughout the semester by videotaping four 15-minute segments of lessons in each classroom. The teaching behaviors in these videotaped segments were analyzed according to time, frequency, and category of drills. Six different types of drills were coded: (1) repetition drills, (2) substitution drills, (3) dialogue drills, (4) translation drills, (5) conversion drills, and (6) a free response. The raters also recorded whether four other behaviors occurred *frequently*, *occasionally*, or *never* in a given 15-minute segment. The four behaviors were (1) the teacher's direct reference to the book or cue cards, (2) the use of audiovisual aids, (3) student-student interaction, and (4) varia-

tion in the grammatical structures presented. From these various factors 14 variables were identified on the basis of proportions or ratios of one behavior to another—for example, average substitution drills per drill minute (pdm).

The dependent variable in this research was the students' performance on the French tests. These criterion measures were specifically related to the material covered by all 17 teachers in the first semester. There were seven different tests: Listening, Reading (a cloze test), Grammar, Base Writing, Free Writing, Base Speaking and Free Speaking. In the writing and speaking tests "base" refers to controlled questions based on the audio-lingual materials, while the "free" component was considered supplemental—a means for more advanced students to demonstrate their proficiency in French. Of these tests Politzer says,

The validity of the instruments used derives from the fact that they were based directly on the materials taught. Obviously, equally rated tests of different nature and different emphasis could have been devised. Scores on such tests would quite possibly have related to teaching behaviours quite differently from the test scores used in this study (1970, p. 37).

Thus Politzer identifies the choice of criterion measures as an important issue in assessing the effectiveness of various language teaching behaviors.

The results of these tests were correlated with the teachers' observed classroom behavior. That is, for every class the students' average score on each of the seven subtests was correlated with the quantification of the individual teacher's behaviors. As might be expected, some behaviors had positive correlations with the measures of student achievement in French. These included free response (pdm), the ratio of switched to exclusive drill, and the use of visual aids, with conversion drill (pdm) and variation of structure showing trends toward a positive correlation. A negative correlation emerged between student achievement and other teaching behaviors, including dialogue drill (pdm), translation drill (pdm), reference to book, and student-student interaction. Other teacher behaviors showed no significant correlation with student achievement.

Probably the most interesting part of this article is the interpretation of these results. In fact, Politzer's main point is that there is no simple linear relationship between teaching behavior and student achievement:

With most teaching behaviors measured it is quite obvious that the correlations cannot possibly indicate "the more the better," "the more the worse" (p. 38).

Instead, Politzer concludes that there is a curvilinear relationship between student achievement and the incidence of specific teaching behaviors. That is, a given teaching behavior may be more or less effective based on the frequency with which it is used in comparison with all other options. Politzer suggests that there is an optimum range (somewhere between too much and too little) for the use of various teaching behaviors. In this perspective, what different teachers do in language classrooms cannot be easily characterized as "good" or "bad" teaching:

... there are probably very few teaching behaviors or devices which can be classified as intrinsically "bad" or "good." Ultimately, most teaching activities undertaken by a language teacher in a language class have probably some value; but each activity is subject to what might be called a principle of economics. Each activity consumes a limited resource—namely time. Thus the value of each activity depends on the value of other activities which might be substituted for it at a given moment (p. 41).

Politzer is also careful to point out that "good" teaching is determined in part by individual student differences and the specific teaching setting. Given this interpretation, "the 'good' teacher is the one who can make the right judgment as to what teaching device is the most valuable at any given moment" (p. 43).

Moskowitz (1976) has approached the "good teacher" issue from a different perspective. The purpose of this research was

to gather observational data on outstanding foreign language teachers and to find out what differences might exist between their teaching patterns and those of a comparison group of foreign language teachers (1976, p. 4).

A basic premise of this study, indeed an underlying philosophy in much of Mosko-

witz's work on observing teaching behavior, is that

in the end, it's the teacher who makes the difference. Good teachers seem to know how to make students like learning a foreign language and want to continue this study. The search then becomes one of finding out what it is that makes "good" teachers "good" (1976, p. 1).

This study, which used an observational coding system for data collection, took two years to complete. It involved four major steps: (1) the identification of "outstanding" foreign language teachers, (2) the observation of the classroom behaviors of those teachers, (3) the observation of the classroom behaviors of a comparison group of "typical" teachers, and (4) a comparison of the behaviors of these two groups of teachers.

In order to identify outstanding foreign language teachers, several thousand students at Temple University were given a questionnaire asking them to name any outstanding foreign language teachers they had had in high school or had worked with in a student-teaching situation. These students included "a number of preservice and inservice foreign language teachers" (p. 3). The questionnaire elicited the teacher's name, the school, and the foreign language taught. Thus student evaluation of teaching (SET) was used to identify good teachers rather than any criterion measure of student achievement in the subject area. A frequency count of teachers' names on the returned questionnaires enabled the researcher to identify 11 teachers of high school French and Spanish who were willing to participate in the study.

The 11 teachers identified as outstanding by these means were observed with a coding instrument called FLint (foreign language interaction), Moskowitz's adaptation of the Flanders interaction analysis model (Flanders, 1970). The IA system includes two main categories of teacher behavior, *direct influence* (in which, for example, the teacher gives information, gives directions, criticizes student behavior, etc.), and *indirect influence* (e.g., teacher uses students' ideas, jokes, praises or encourages, deals with feelings, etc.). Three types of student responses are also recorded: responses by specific students, choral responses, and student-initiated responses.

FLint includes all of the IA categories as well as categories for coding nonverbal behavior and verbal behavior in both English and the target language. As with IA, behaviors are coded as they occur, and these data are then tabulated in a matrix which provides a composite picture of the behaviors recorded in a given observational period. The use of such coding systems to collect observational data in classroom-centered research produces quantifiable information in a limited number of categories. The FLint system and the Flanders IA system upon which it is modeled are two of the most frequently used observational coding systems.

In order to ensure comparability of the data, each teacher was observed during three lessons based on goals specified in advance by the researcher. For each teacher one lesson dealt with grammar, another with new material presented orally, and a third with some aspect of reading. A fourth observation was conducted for each subject, during which the teacher was free to choose the lesson content, the only restrictions being that the students not be taking a test, doing group work, giving reports, or conducting the class. In other words, Moskowitz was concerned with the behavior of teachers in teacher-fronted classrooms. These guidelines as to the content of the observed lesson ensured that the focus on the teacher was maintained and that the data were comparable. In addition, all the teachers were observed while teaching two lessons to first or second year classes and two lessons to more advanced language students. The observers had been trained to use FLint, and they also spoke the target language of the classroom.

The same observational procedures were followed with the 11 subjects in the comparison group. These "typical" teachers were matched with the outstanding teachers according to years of teaching experience, sex, and school locale (i.e., they were drawn from the same school or from a school in a similar socioeconomic area).

Throughout the study the comparison subjects are described as "typical" foreign language teachers. Moskowitz makes a distinction between *average* and *typical* since the comparison group was intended to represent a heterogeneous cross section of language teachers whose classroom behaviors might be expected to be classified at any point along an imaginary continuum of poor to excellent teaching. Moskowitz notes that there could have been some "outstanding" teachers in the comparison group even though none of their names appeared on the frequency count of the questionnaires. Following the data collection, the observers were asked to rate the 22 teachers they had observed:

Every teacher in Group 1 was viewed by the observers as "excellent" or "exceptionally good" while the teachers in Group 2 had varied ratings along the continuum. If these impressions can be considered, then the make-up of the groups was in the hoped-for direction with Group 1 consisting of outstanding foreign language teachers and Group 2 being a heterogeneous cross section of foreign language teachers (p. 4).

The observers also informally rated the subjects on their proficiency in the target language. The ratings for the outstanding teachers were consistently higher than those for the typical foreign language teachers.

In the data analysis the coded behaviors of the outstanding teachers were compared with those of the typical teachers. In all, 85 differences in the behavior of the two groups were found to be statistically significant. These behavioral differences are discussed at length in the Moskowitz article; here a summary will suffice. The data revealed that in at least three out of four lessons, the outstanding teachers' lessons involved:

1. More total use of the foreign language by the teacher and the students combined.
2. More teacher talk in the foreign language.
3. More student talk in the foreign language.
4. Less student talk which is off the task.
5. More indirect behaviors in the total lesson.

6. More indirect behaviors in the foreign language.
7. More nonverbal indirect behaviors.
8. More use of praise and joking.
9. More use of personalized questions.
10. More nonverbal information giving (i.e., gesturing to convey meaning).

The findings of the study indicate that the teachers who had been identified as outstanding did exhibit these behaviors to a statistically greater extent than did the typical teachers. However, it would be an oversimplification to assume that these 10 behaviors are what constitute good teaching, since no cause-and-effect relationship can be established, given the research design. For example, one cannot say that more student talk in the foreign language is what makes a good language teacher. Indeed, it may be that there is more talk in the target language because of the teacher's expertise in explaining grammar to the students. At any rate, Moskowitz's classroom-centered research, like Politzer's, has contributed to efforts to describe "the good language teacher." (For a discussion of the teacher effectiveness issue in classroom-centered research, see Allwright, 1983.)

In a different type of study which focused on teacher behaviors, Townsend and Zamora (1975) reported on the verbal and nonverbal interaction patterns of teachers and teacher aides in bilingual classrooms. Actually this article summarizes the findings of two studies, the authors' doctoral dissertations. These studies were designed to answer two broad research questions:

1. Do verbal and/or nonverbal behaviors of bilingual teachers differ from those of assistant teachers?

2. Do bilingual teachers and assistant teachers exhibit different interaction patterns verbally or nonverbally as they teach similar subject matter in two languages (1975, p. 198)?

The 56 teachers and assistant teachers who were the subjects in these studies taught in elementary classes in a Spanish-English bilingual program in Texas. Some background information is presented on the education of these subjects.

The classroom observation component in these studies involved live coding with the system for coding interaction with multiple phases (SCIMP), which was developed by Townsend (1974). As with Moskowitz's FLint system, parts of this instrument are based on Flanders's interaction analysis model. SCIMP was designed for coding both verbal and nonverbal behaviors, including behaviors designated as affective. In addition, the instrument can accommodate verbal interaction in two or more languages. The authors point out that the encoder must be:

proficient in both languages of instruction. It is obvious that if a recorder does not sufficiently understand part of the interaction, the data obtained would be of no use. The person, then, must both know the system and be bilingual (Townsend, 1976, p. 216).

The researchers used SCIMP in observing each subject four times for an average of 10 minutes per observation session. As in Flanders' and Moskowitz's studies, coding for the verbal interactions was tallied every 3 seconds. Nonverbal behaviors were recorded every 5 seconds. These tallies produced quantifiable data which were statistically analyzed along two dimensions: (1) verbal behavior was compared for the Spanish and English interactions of all subjects, and (2) the teachers' behaviors (both verbal and nonverbal) were compared with those of the teacher aides.

Significant differences in behavior were found between the teachers and assistant teachers. The four main differences in verbal interaction were that (1) the teachers were more "indirect" than the aides; (2) there was a greater percentage of "teacher talk" for aides than for teachers; (3) teachers allowed more student responses than teacher aides did; and (4) the assistant teachers switched languages more often than did the teachers during lessons.

In nonverbal behaviors there were five statistically significant differences between the teachers and the assistant teachers. The assistants demonstrated (1) more "void" behaviors (defined as "the absence of nonverbal behavior" by Townsend and Zamora, 1975, p. 198), (2) more negative head nodding, (3) more "negative use of the eyes," and (4) more combined negative nonverbal behavior. Finally, the teachers had a higher percentage of combined positive nonverbal behaviors than did the teacher aides. According to the SCIMP categories, the teachers generally tended to interact with the children more positively than the aides did.

In the other half of the research, the comparison of interactions in Spanish and English, no significant differences were found in the nonverbal behaviors of teachers and aides. That is to say, the subjects' nonverbal behavior was consistent across both languages.

Significant differences did emerge, however, in the subjects' verbal behaviors in Spanish and English. While teaching in English the teachers and assistant teachers had more direction-giving behaviors, more student responses followed by praise from the adult, and a higher percentage of consecutive reinforcing behaviors. While teaching in Spanish the subjects exhibited greater percentages of questions asked, students' responses, rejecting students' answers, and responding to students' comments with acceptance.

The rest of the article is devoted to possible implications of these findings for teacher training and bilingual education. The classroom-centered research reported in Townsend and Zamora's paper is illustrative of the type of information gained through the use of IA-type observation schedules. The portrait of teaching behaviors revealed here is a sketch rather than a detailed picture, but such coding systems provide useful information about classroom interaction at the global level.

Some research in language classrooms has dealt specifically with teacher speech as opposed to the broader aspects of teacher behavior. In a study involving the syntactic analysis of ESL teachers' classroom language, Gaies recorded three lessons taught by each of eight ESL teacher trainees (five native and

three nonnative speakers of English). The lessons were recorded at the beginning, middle, and end of a semester in four different levels of adult ESL classes. Gaies also obtained samples comparing the subjects' speech with that of their linguistic peers by recording one hour on each subject participating in a course on teaching ESL. Thus each subject was recorded once with his peers and three times with his students. Five hundred words of each sample were transcribed and T-units were counted as a measure of syntactic complexity. The data were then examined in order to answer questions about language learning in formal instructional settings.

In one paper Gaies (1977) characterizes the linguistic input to which first language learners are exposed as involving (1) short, grammatical sentences which are transformationally simpler than those normally found in adult-adult discourse, (2) a restricted lexicon, and (3) a reduced rate of speech, clearer articulation, and exaggerated stress and intonation patterns. Gaies states that these are the characteristics of a "situational register deemed appropriate for use when the interlocuter is a young child in the process of acquiring a language" (1977, p. 205). Gaies also reviews some of the literature on "communicative and/or language training strategies," including repetition, prodding, prompting, and modeling. After discussing these behaviors, he poses the following research question:

Does the input to which formal second language learners are exposed through the oral classroom language of their teachers involve linguistic and communicative adjustments analogous to those which are characteristic of much of the adult input in first language acquisition? (p. 207).

In answering this question, Gaies found the subjects' speech to linguistic peers to be syntactically more complex than their classroom speech to students. He also found that "at any level the syntax of the teachers' oral classroom language is more complex than at the level immediately below it and less complex than at the level above it" (1977, p. 209). In addition, he found that the classroom speech of the teacher trainees exhibited "the very training strategies characteristic of adult input to children," particularly at the lower levels of instruction. Gaies feels that these findings provide "evidence, however preliminary, that the organization and presentation of the input with which second language learners work is not unlike the primary linguistic input which children hear" (1977, p. 211). (See Hatch, 1983, pp. 183–184, for a summary of the research on simplified input to second language learners.)

In another paper, Gaies (1976) looks at the same data and asks what the relationship is between the target language adjustments made by second language teachers (for both communicating and teaching purposes) and the development of interlanguage in classroom language learners. Here Gaies' hypothesis is that the second language learner's

transitional grammar—the interlanguage system, which can be characterized as the product of the hypotheses formed by the learner on the basis of the primary linguistic data—will at any point correctly generate at the maximum the total number of structures and transformational processes which the learner has had the opportunity to hear or see used in the target language (1976, p. 6.)

Gaies returns to the transcripts and focuses on examples of passivization, relativization and question embedding in the teacher trainees' classroom speech to ESL students. In analyzing these data, he found that the frequency of each transformational process in the teachers' speech increased with the proficiency level of the students. Clearly these findings are related to Krashen's (1977) "i+1 hypothesis" —the notion that second language acquisition occurs when the input to the learner is one stage beyond his current interlanguage ("i") development. Long (1983), in reviewing the research literature on second language acquisition with and without formal instruction, notes that for many second language learners, the classroom may be the only place where "i+1" input is available.

In considering teacher speech and its implications for second language learners' interlanguage development, Gaies discusses two sources of error: first, the misapplication of rules the learner has had the opportunity to deduce, and second, "ignorance" or gaps in the second language training, which lead to attempts to fill in with information regarding the target language or the native language. Gaies concludes that the development of the second language learner's interlanguage

can be viewed as a process paralleling and in part resulting from his/her exposure to target language data which itself increasingly incorporates and illustrates the transformational operations which characterize the target language as it is used among fully proficient speakers (p. 8.)

This type of detailed syntactic analysis of ESL teachers' speech would not have been possible without mechanized recording and careful transcription of the speech samples. These two papers by Gaies, when compared with the studies of teacher behaviors which used coding instruments, illustrate the variety possible in classroom-centered research which focuses on the language teacher.

TEACHER TREATMENT OF LEARNER ERROR

One particular facet of teacher behavior which has prompted a great deal of recent classroom-centered research involves teachers' reactions to language learners' errors. The studies discussed below deal specifically with the treatment of language learners' errors in verbal classroom interaction. (The correction of second language learners' errors in written discourse is an entirely different—though equally complex—topic for investigation.) During the 1970s, trends in theories of language teaching, particularly in the areas of contrastive analysis and error analysis, focused attention on the errors produced by second language learners. (See Richards, 1974, and Schumann and Stenson, 1974, for discussions of these issues.) The appropriate interpretations and effective treatment of those errors is typically seen as central to the language teacher's role.

Some of the earliest classroom-centered research on language teachers' treatment of learners' errors was conducted by Fanselow (1977b). In this study 11 experienced ESL teachers each taught a lesson based on English adjective order and the verbs *holding* and *wearing*. All the teachers used the same materials and the same lesson plan. The lessons, which averaged 21 minutes in length, were videotaped and transcribed. The transcripts included both verbal and nonverbal behaviors, permitting quantitative and descriptive analyses.

In this study error was defined in two ways: (1) by the teachers' behavior and (2) by the researcher's criteria in the absence of a reaction from the teacher involved. In analyzing the data from all 11 classes, Fanselow found that there was an average of 16 responses per minute and that 27 percent of those utterances were judged to be incorrect. An error occurred every 15 seconds on the average. Fanselow grouped these errors as follows:

	Percent
Function word errors	27
Pronunciation errors	28
Word form errors	19
Word order errors	7
Factual content errors	12
Performance of a task other than the one set by the teacher	7

Fanselow also describes four major types of tasks found in the data: (1) question-answer drills with WH-questions, (2) repetition of words or patterns, (3) substitution drills, and (4) question-answer drills with *yes/no* or *either/or* questions. Nearly half the errors occurred with question-answer drills involving WH-questions. This finding led Fanselow to conclude that "asking students WH-questions that require identification of objects or the recall of sentences practiced earlier seems to be one sure way to elicit errors" (1977b, p. 585).

In analyzing teachers' reactions to the students' errors, Fanselow found 16 types of error treatment in his data. These treatment types are listed along with examples, frequency counts, and percentages. He also compared the treatment types with instances of errors and found that grammar errors were the least likely to be treated. In contrast, "If a student did a task different from the one the teacher had set or produced an incorrect

content word, there was a 94 percent chance that treatment of some kind would follow." Thus the quantitative analysis compares types of errors, types of tasks, and types of error treatment.

In the descriptive analysis, Fanselow points out that the figures obscure some of the facts. For instance, teachers often used two or more error treatments simultaneously—and some of these combinations of treatments conveyed potentially ambiguous messages to the students. There was also a lack of consistency in the treatment types, which was not revealed by the numerical analysis. One behavior that was common to all the teachers involved presenting the right answer (or part of it) after an error. Fanselow deduces that the teachers' goal was for the students to

answer questions and use patterns in a way the teacher had planned—with *no* variation allowed. . . . Hypothesis testing, experimenting with language rules, seemed absent; congruence with the teachers' expectations seemed to be the rule (p. 586).

In addition, the transcripts showed that pronunciation errors were often followed by brief repetition cycles. Finally, because all the data were lumped together, the quantitative analysis did not reveal the differences among the 11 teachers' reacting patterns.

This article includes a number of practical suggestions for language teachers. For example, Fanselow discusses the importance of "wait-time," the length of time a teacher will wait for a student to respond to a question before making another move (e.g., prompting, turning to another student, or simply providing the desired response). (See Holley and King, 1974, for a brief discussion of wait-time in language lessons.) Fanselow also considers the "learning value" of various error types and suggests ways for teachers to minimize the production of less valuable errors. He points out that in many cases what the teachers expected of students was implicit—and was made only slightly more explicit after an error had occurred. He also discusses the issue of repeated errors and suggests several possible error treatments.

Fanselow distinguishes between two different goals in the use of error treatment types: immediate correction of an error (potentially only a short-term measure) and the ultimate teaching and learning of the correct form (the long-range objective). To help teachers achieve this second goal, Fanselow describes error treatments which involve analyzing, categorizing, and manipulating correct forms. He also emphasizes the need for both teachers and students to listen carefully during language lessons and points out that presenting information about the language in different media can provide language learners with much needed redundancy. He also discusses two philosophical perspectives that have influenced his work on error treatment. The first is the idea that errors are a normal part of language learning. (For a discussion of this point of view, see Corder, 1974, or Holley and King, 1974.) The second is the view that errors should be corrected only when they impair communication (as in George, 1972). Fanselow considers this selective correction approach as parallel to what happens in the real world beyond the classroom.

In his conclusion, Fanselow discusses the effect this research project had on the 11 teachers who participated:

After viewing the tapes and discussing the issues presented here, the teachers saw how what they had done in their classes differed from what they thought they had done. Seeing what they had done and abstracting what they had done through coding gave them a clearer perception of their treatment of error as well as the way they and the students used language. Options appeared to them that might otherwise not have without systematic coding and analysis (Fanselow, 1977b, p. 692).

Fanselow gives several suggestions for further research, some of which have since been acted upon by others investigating teachers' classroom treatment of language learners' errors.

One person who was influenced by Fanselow's work is Allwright, the British researcher whose study of classroom turn taking was discussed above. In research on teachers' reactions to ESL students' errors, Allwright studies the interaction of four teachers with Venezuelan students in Britain. These four teachers collaborated on preparing a single lesson plan, which each teacher then presented to his own students. The lessons were videotaped and transcribed, and the teachers used the data in examining their responses to the learners' errors. (See Allwright, 1975a, for the teachers' reports of their findings.) However, Allwright also used these data in writing an influential paper (1975b).

In this paper Allwright discusses the role of error in second language learning and points out that occurrences of errors in a language lesson are potential crisis points for the learner-speaker and for other learner-hearers in the classroom. Errors may also be considered as crisis points for the teacher because "the teacher's reaction to learner error will be the major factor in determining what the learners actually learn" (Allwright, 1975b, p. 98). Previous research on the topic had shown that teachers are often imprecise (Fanselow, 1977b) and inconsistent (Mehan, 1974) in their handling of learners' errors. Allwright notes, however, that inconsistency in this situation is not necessarily a shortcoming:

Teachers have a duty, perhaps, to be inconsistent, in the sense that they must adjust their treatment of any error to the needs of the moment. At the very least the teacher must reserve the right to adapt to the individual differences among learners (Allwright, 1975b, pp. 98–99).

He cautions that teachers should be aware of the potential problems such impreciseness and apparent inconsistency may cause for language learners.

Allwright discusses another serious issue in classroom-centered research on the treatment of language learners' errors: the definition and subsequent identification of error. One possibility is to define error in terms of the teacher's behavior. Here Allwright borrows from George (1972), who defined errors as "a form unwanted by the teacher or course designer" (cited in Allwright, 1975b, p. 101), a definition which parallels Fanselow's observation that the teachers' goal was for the students to respond "in a way the teacher had planned—with no variation allowed" (1977b, p. 586). (This definition of error was also used in Nystrom's (1983) research on student-teacher interaction in bilingual first-grade classrooms, in which teachers identified student errors while viewing videotapes of their classes.) Allwright further points out that errors could be identified in terms of the learner's perspective on the target language or on the basis of judgments by an independent expert (typically the native-speaking researcher).

The categorization of errors is another complicated issue. Allwright suggests four major ways of categorizing errors: (1) according to their linguistic description (content area versus skill area), (2) according to their present and future importance, (3) according to their source (including intralingual and interlingual inference, learning strategies, communication strategies, teaching, carelessness, stress, and factual ignorance), and (4) according to their ease of correction (including both the time and resources available as well as the teacher's competence). Allwright is careful to note that these means of categorizing errors are not mutually exclusive: in fact, "the teacher's behavior may need to be based on a categorization in all four ways at once" (1975b, p. 102).

It is apparent that the teacher's position in classroom error treatment is complicated: "the teacher's error analysis has to be 'instant' ... and any treatment given, typically, is public, a fact that has consequences for the researcher as well as for the teacher" (p. 103). Allwright summarizes the teacher's role at the crisis point when an error is made during verbal classroom interaction:

The key task for the teacher, then, is firstly to sum up the whole situation on the spot, and then to react appropriately, in public, conscious of the need to treat the problems of the individual without misleading or confusing the other learners.

Allwright also describes the error treatment options from which a language teacher may select the appropriate response to a particular student at a particular point in time. Again, the tentative list of options reveals the complexity of the language teacher's job:

A. Basic Options:
    1. To treat or to ignore completely.
    2. To treat immediately or delay.
    3. To transfer treatment or not.
    4. To transfer to another individual, a subgroup, or the whole class.
    5. To return, or not, to original error maker after treatment.
    6. To call upon, or permit another learner (or learners) to provide treatment.
    7. To test for efficacy of treatment.

B. Possible Features:
    8. Fact of error indicated.
    9. Blame indicated.
    10. Location indicated.
    11. Opportunity for new attempt given.
    12. Model provided.
    13. Error type indicated.
    14. Remedy indicated.
    15. Improvement indicated.
    16. Praise indicated (p. 104).

Allwright discusses these options with illustrative data from the transcripts and with constructed samples of possible classroom discourse.

In closing, Allwright considers the language learner's interpretation of the teacher's behavior in dealing with errors. Seen from the learner's perspective, understanding the treatment of error in classroom discourse is a highly complex task. Allwright states that

teachers need a way of predicting the interpretations their behavior will give rise to. The effectiveness of their treatment will depend on how it is perceived rather than on what it is intended to be (Allwright, 1975b, p. 108).

Error treatment options, such as those discussed above, have been examined further by Long (1977), who built on Allwright's work in constructing a "model of the decision-making process prior to the teacher feedback move" (Long, 1977, p. 289).

Teachers' and students' ideas about error treatment were compared by Cathcart and Olsen (1976). The authors acknowledge that the main purpose of research on error correction is to find out what types of feedback actually help people learn languages.

However, their rationale for this study is based on the importance of attitude in language learning:

We believe it is important to ascertain what students and teachers assume to be the most effective methods for correcting errors. What teachers and students think is helpful may not turn out to be so, but on the other hand, bias and attitude may prove to have a strong influence on effectiveness of corrections (Cathcart and Olsen, 1976, p. 41).

In fact, this line of investigation was prompted by Fanselow, who suggested that researchers "ask teachers and students the types of (error) treatments they prefer and why they prefer them" (1977b, p. 593).

Cathcart and Olsen's study is based primarily on data from questionnaires, but it did include a classroom observation component. Twenty-one teachers of adult and university ESL classes each tape-recorded one of their classroom lessons. The correcting moves found in these lessons were transcribed and then classified. Twelve types of correcting moves were identified. Following the taping sessions, several of the teachers responded to questionnaires regarding their use of various correcting moves, including their preferences and the frequency with which they employed those moves. In addition, 188 students responded to a similar questionnaire, which gave examples and elicited the students' preferred correction types.

The teachers' responses on the questionnaire were compared with the recordings of their classroom correcting behavior. Cathcart and Olsen found that most of the teachers gave accurate descriptions of their correcting strategies—that is, they did in fact use the correcting moves they preferred. However, some teachers did use correcting strategies they thought they never used (e.g., overt location of the error plus provision of the correct form, such as "Don't say go. Say went.").

On the students' questionnaire the subjects rated sample correcting moves as *very good, good, not very good,* and *bad*. The analysis of the students' responses to the questionnaires showed that:

1. All the students wanted to be corrected when they made oral errors.

2. Seventy-four percent of the respondents preferred to be corrected all the time; another 17 percent preferred to be corrected most of the time.

3. Students at all levels thought pronunciation and grammar errors were the most important to correct (with grammar errors considered slightly less important than pronunciation errors).

4. A majority of the students thought teachers corrected more grammar than pronunciation, and that both of these areas were corrected more than word order and vocabulary.

Of the various types of possible grammar corrections, students preferred, in order, correct model, comparison of error and model, grammar explanation, repetition of cue and, finally, partial model locating error. The students said they did not like teacher responses which did not correct the error, merely indicated disapproval, asked for repetition (e.g., "What's the second word?" or "What?"), or gave the correct model embedded in a request for further information.

In addition, students' assessment of the correcting moves their teachers actually used in class corresponded fairly well to the students' preferences. In other words, the students felt the teachers used helpful feedback moves, although they would have preferred more correction of pronunciation—especially at the more advanced levels. The students' responses were also analyzed according to nationality and class levels, but no strong differences among students emerged.

In general, the students wanted to be corrected more than the teachers felt they should be. One teacher in the study did agree to correct all the errors in a class discussion. However, in spite of their stated preference for rigorous correction, the students found that "it was impossible to think coherently or produce more than fragmented sentences

when they were interrupted constantly"
(Cathcart and Olsen, 1976, p. 50).

The authors also report that this study was "valuable as a consciousness raising tool" (p. 52):

Teachers and students who participated became more interested in the subject of error correction, and in so doing, took the first step towards understanding and improving correction techniques (pp. 52–53).

Perhaps such awareness is just as useful a contribution to the language teaching field as are the actual findings of classroom-centered research.

The studies by Fanselow, Allwright, and Cathcart and Olsen describe fairly concrete results of classroom-centered research on teacher treatment of learner errors. The last paper to be discussed in this section is somewhat more theoretical in nature, but it too is based on classroom-centered research.

Building on the findings of the three studies discussed above, as well as other research in language and content classrooms, Chaudron (1977) has proposed "a descriptive model of discourse in the corrective treatment of learners' errors." The observational component of this research involved tape recording the lessons of three teachers in an eighth and ninth grade French immersion program for English-speaking students. Six lessons were recorded early in the academic year and then again later. The tape recordings were transcribed and coded for teachers' corrective reactions to linguistic errors and subject matter error (i.e., Allwright's distinction between skill areas and content areas), as well as other discourse errors. The model Chaudron proposes was "derived through analysis of the coded transcripts" (Chaudron, 1977, p. 31). Thus, like Long in his 1977 paper, Chaudron has used observational data from classrooms in building a testable model.

Chaudron describes three functions of feedback, or "knowledge of results" (Annett, 1969):

(1) incentive—stimulating increased effort (motivating), (2) reinforcement—promoting maintenance of the learner's responses, and (3) information—contributing to changes in responses (Chaudron, 1977, p. 30).

Chaudron points out that corrective feedback will often fulfill more than one of these functions. He feels that a detailed description of the treatment options available would help teachers determine which treatment types "are most likely to be motivating, reinforcing, and/or informative."

Chaudron discusses the criteria needed to identify both errors and teachers' corrective reactions to those errors. He describes four different possible concepts of correction. The first is to "consider as corrections only those treatments which, after correction of a given item, succeed in establishing the learner's consistent correct performance and his autonomous ability to correct himself on the item" (p. 31). This interpretation of correction corresponds to Fanselow's long-range goal of error treatment, as discussed above. Chaudron notes that such a criterion cannot be used to identify successful corrective moves within a given class period. For this reason, he turns to a second definition of correction, which is related to Fanselow's short-term goal of error treatment:

A correction occurs when the teacher is able to elicit a corrected response from the committer of the error or from one or more of his classmates. This conception is henceforth named "successful correction."

Chaudron's third conception of correction parallels the criterion of teacher-defined error treatment discussed by Fanselow and Allwright. It involves "any reaction of the teacher which clearly transforms, disapprovingly refers to, or demands improvement of the learner's utterance." Chaudron feels that this third notion of correction "allows the most inclusive study of teachers' reactions, while the second conception, 'successful correction,' can be used to isolate apparently effective corrective treatments." A fourth definition of correction as positive or negative reinforcement is rejected as being too narrow to develop an adequate description of corrective classroom discourse.

Having accepted the second and third criteria for locating teachers' corrective reactions, Chaudron identifies errors by (1) the teachers' reactions in the transcripts, (2) the retrospective location of errors by the teachers while listening to the tape-recorded lessons, and (3) "objective linguistic judgments" (p. 32), i.e., Fanselow's and Allwright's criterion of the researcher's independent observation.

Chaudron's work reemphasizes the idea that teacher treatment of learner error is a complex phenomenon. He reports that "a given error is rarely corrected all the time." Teachers may ignore learners' errors, fail to notice them, and even occasionally repeat them. Additionally, in this immersion situation, classifying error types is a complicated issue:

Categories of errors range from the strictly "linguistic" (phonological, morphological, syntactic), to subject matter "content" (factual and conceptual knowledge) and lexical items, to errors of classroom interaction and discouse—insofar as these last ones are orally manifested, as in speaking out of turn, taking up the wrong question in the lesson, using English in the immersion context, on occasion failing to speak, and not speaking in complete sentences.

Chaudron states that earlier researchers have used broad terms to discuss these possibilities and that his model will help describe "simultaneous correction of different errors, as well as combinations of types of reaction and recursive corrective interaction" (p. 33). He then proceeds to construct a model based on Allwright's (1975b) options (discussed above) and work in discourse analysis by Sinclair and Coulthard (1975).

Chaudron's model of corrective discourse is too complex to discuss in detail here. (Interested readers are referred to his article and to Salica's 1980 master's thesis, which sought to test Chaudron's model by applying it to ESL classroom data.) Essentially the model is a detailed flow chart that depicts series of opening moves, answering moves, and follow-up moves (Sinclair and Coulthard, 1975), which constitute a correcting exchange in classroom discourse. Chaudron illustrates the model with hypothetical examples of a teacher's reactions to one error made by a student of French.

In analyzing the transcribed data, Chaudron discovered that the teachers used a number of regular patterns in their responses to learners' errors. Within these reaction patterns he distinguishes between *features* and *types*:

Features are those linguistic or discursive markers which are either "bound" to larger utterances (e.g., stress and some attention-getters, like 'mais'), or which exist *only* by the fact that two adjacent utterances bear a relation to each other... *Types*, on the other hand, are self-standing, unbound utterances; their relationship to surrounding utterances will, however, determine their specific nature and information potential. Often, certain features serve to distinguish between the common types (Chaudron, 1977, p. 35).

Chaudron states that the identifiable types and features together comprise the "acts" of corrective discourse. He feels that some of the "expressive components" of such acts probably help language learners to interpret teachers' reactions to errors, but this idea remains to be tested.

Using the concept of corrective acts and the data from the tape-recorded lessons, Chaudron develops a long list of corrective reactions which can be plotted on his flow chart. This list provides the feature or type of act, a description of each feature and type, and examples of many of the corrective acts identified in the data.

Chaudron illustrates one use of his model by discussing several possible examples of repetition. The various uses of repetition are analyzed in terms of error type, frequency and success of correction, and the success ratio of the various types of repetition. The analysis demonstrates ways in which Chaudron's model could be used in future classroom-centered research to compare teachers' input to students with the students' subsequent output of target language forms.

INDIVIDUAL STUDENT (OR TEACHER) VARIABLES

The first three sections of this chapter have dealt with student participation in language classrooms, the language teacher's speech and behavior, and teacher treatment of learner error. In each of these areas of investigation, researchers have considered observable facets of language classroom behavior. But much of the substance of the language learning and teaching process is essentially unobservable. For instance, how do learners utilize the input they receive? How do they process feedback from teachers and peers? How does the teacher's behavior influence their language learning and their attitudes? What causes some to participate more actively (apparently) than others? More importantly, why are some learners so much more successful than others? Or, if one focuses on the teacher, how and why do language teachers, given all the complexities of language classroom interaction discussed above, *decide* to do just what they do in language classrooms? None of these key questions can be answered through external observation (mechanized data collection, real-time coding systems, or non-participant observers).

To get at these issues, some researchers have tried a different approach to classroom-centered research. In order to better understand what happens to language learners (or teachers) some researchers have *become* learners (or teachers) and conducted diary studies. A diary study is a first-person case study: the researcher investigates his or her own language learning (or teaching). On an imaginary continuum of self-involvement in the research process, the diary studies fall just beyond participant observation in terms of focus. A participant observer enters a society (here a language classroom) to study the behavior and motives of its members. A diarist enters the learning or teaching situation to study his or her *own* behavior and motives. In this way the diary studies can address otherwise unobservable facets of the individual learner's (or teacher's) experience.

In general, the process of conducting a diary study involves five major "steps" (Bailey and Ochsner, 1983, p. 189), although they may not occur in this exact sequence:

1.   The diarist provides an account of his personal language learning (or teaching) history

2.   The diarist systematically records events, details, and feelings about the current

language experience in a confidential and candid diary.

3.   The diarist revises the journal entries (i.e., names are changed and information damaging to others or extremely embarrassing for the diarist is omitted) for the public version of the diary.

4.   The diarist studies the journal entries looking for significant patterns and events. (*Significance* here refers to frequency of occurrence or the salience of an event.)

5.   The factors identified as important to the language learning (or teaching) experience are interpreted and discussed in the finished diary study.

The retrospective language learning history and the introspective language learning (or teaching) diary constitute the data for such a study. It is the second point, the recording of events, details, and feelings regarding the current language experience, that meshes with Long's (1980) definition of classroom-centered research cited above. The diary is, in fact, derived from (self) observation of the classroom performance of one student or teacher (the diarist-researcher).

To date relatively few language learning or teaching diary studies have been published. The studies are typically very long (if the rewritten diary is included) and the methodology is new and unpolished. However, a few diary studies are accessible to the professional reading public, and each of these includes a classroom-centered research component.

The first language learning diary study to be published was conducted by Schumann and Schumann (1977). They examined their own language learning in three different settings: studying Farsi in Iran (without formal instruction), studying Arabic in Tunisia (via both exposure and instruction), and studying Farsi in a university language course (instruction only) in the United States. The research is based on the diaries of both authors. Their results are summarized in a paper (1977). Each author discusses three factors which influenced the language learning process.

One is struck by the fact that although the "subjects" were undergoing essentially the same language learning experience, their individual reactions to those situations were quite different.

For example, Francine Schumann found that her language learning was affected by her "nesting patterns" (the powerful need to feel comfortable with her surroundings before devoting time and energy to language study) and by the choice of language learning materials. With regard to the latter, she found that her motivation to read and study Farsi was higher when she used brightly illustrated children's books rather than more traditional language textbooks. She also reacted very strongly to the pedagogical techniques used in one classroom. In fact, to a certain extent, she rejected the language learning situation—or at least she made less than optimal use of the input she received in that class—because she reacted so negatively to the teaching method. (In a further analysis of these data F. Schumann, 1980, later discusses the role of the expatriot community, her situation as a woman learning a second language in Iran, and the difficulty of getting practice in Farsi, given her background as an English speaker.)

John Schumann, on the other hand, found that it was important for him to maintain his own language learning agenda. He preferred a flexible teacher who would let him pursue his own goals as a learner. He also discovered that his way of coping with transition anxiety en route to the target culture was to throw himself into language study. Finally, he found that he preferred eavesdropping to speaking as a language learning strategy. This last finding has implications for the participation studies, such as those by Seliger (1977) and Allwright (1980), discussed above. It may be that Seliger's low-input generators, like John Schumann, prefer to learn by listening rather than by speaking in class. (See Tarone, 1981, for further discussion of this point.) The actual *effect* of such a preference has not yet been investigated.

Jones also kept a diary in a combined instruction-immersion setting. She studied Indonesian in an intensive program in the target culture. Her diary focuses on the social and psychological factors (J. Schumann, 1976) influencing her language learning. The research is reported on in Jones' master's thesis (1977a), which includes the rewritten diary, but it is also summarized in a shorter paper (1977b).

One striking aspect of Jones' experience, as depicted in her diary study, is the contrast between the tense, competitive Indonesian program and the friendly, supportive environment of her host family's home. This study illustrates many of the ways in which an instructional program can undermine the language learner's effort—in effect, sabotaging its own mission. Jones was so unhappy with the tone of the classroom environment that she ultimately abandoned her attempts to succeed in the program, though she continued to learn Indonesian through exposure. Like Francine Schumann (Schumann and Schumann, 1977), Jones found the teaching method and the affective tone of the formal instructional setting to be counterproductive—in fact, damaging—to her language learning. She relates her findings to the issues of psychological and social distance (Schumann, 1976), but like the Schumanns, she concludes that personal variables must also be taken into account in second language learning research.

Bailey investigated her language learning in a college French class. In this case, French was being studied as a foreign language with input provided almost exclusively by the classroom interaction. In one paper based on the diary kept during this French instruction, Bailey (1980) discusses her response to the language learning environment (both physical and social) as influencing her efforts to learn. In particular, the behavior of her classmates affected her self-esteem and attitude toward the French class. She also found that she preferred a democratic teaching style, a conclusion which may parallel John Schumann's desire to maintain a personal agenda in language learning (Schumann and Schumann, 1977). Bailey also discusses her need for success and positive feedback in language learning. This last area clearly has implications for the research on teacher treatment of learner error. Bailey's attitude toward and use of feedback was more emotional than cognitive or linguistic. (Vigil and Oller's 1976 discussion of the difference between affective and cognitive feedback is related to this issue.) Bailey relates the themes that emerged in her personal diary to trends in the French classroom, specifically the levels of (1) student-student interaction, (2) interpersonal tension, and (3) her own enthusiasm for studying French.

Most of the diary studies conducted to date are guided by the (implicit) research question, "What factors are important in *my* language learning?" However, one paper (Bailey, 1983) has compared several diary studies to investigate a more specific problem: the relationship of competitiveness and anxiety in adult second language learning.

In the first section of that article, Bailey discusses the problems associated with research on affective factors in second language acquisition, using research on anxiety as an illustration. The diary studies are proposed as a research methodology for investigating hidden affective factors in adult second language learning.

By examining her own language learning diary (again, the diary of the French class discussed above), Bailey found that she was both highly anxious and highly competitive initially, with anxiety decreasing somewhat as she became more proficient (in comparison with her classmates). The review of this diary produced a list of seven characteristics of the journal entries which reveal competitiveness. The author posits a cyclic relationship between competitiveness and anxiety in the language classroom.

Bailey then compares 10 similar diary studies to see if any other language learning diarists deal with the issues of competitiveness and anxiety. The detailed accounts of these journals and that of the author are used to develop a description and then a definition of competitiveness in adult second language learners. Bailey discusses the concept of language classroom anxiety, a term borrowed and expanded from work on French classroom

anxiety by Gardner, Smythe, Clement, and Gliksman (1976). She advanced the hypothesis that language classroom anxiety can be caused and/or aggravated by a learner's competitiveness if (1) he perceives himself as less proficient than his classmates, and (2) the comparison entails ego involvement.

Finally Bailey addresses the issue of the generalizability of the diary studies. Like other case studies, the diary studies by definition are not based on a random sample (i.e., the researcher does not randomly select himself from among the entire universe of language learners or teachers). Hence, their findings cannot be generalized to the wider population. As Long (1980) has pointed out, such findings may be relevant to any or all language learners, or they may be completely idiosyncratic. Bailey argues that whether or not the diary studies can be generalized, they (like other case studies) can be compared. She also discusses some possible contributions the diary study metholodology may make to our understanding of second language learning and acquisition. (For further discussion of the diary study as an approach to language learning research, see Bailey and Ochsner, 1983.)

In general, the diary studies are relatively new compared with the other types of classroom-centered research discussed in earlier sections of this chapter. At the present time they show more promise as hypothesis-generating rather than hypothesis-testing research (Gaies, 1983; Long, 1980). As the methodology is refined and means for aggregating qualitative data are developed, the diary studies may provide access to the underlying cognitive and affective processes of second language learning and teaching.

CONCLUSION

Even though this is a long chapter, this discussion has reviewed only a small portion of the classroom-centered research conducted to date. Because the field is relatively new, much interesting work remains unpublished. Access to advanced technology, on the one hand, and a better understanding of qualitative research methods, on the other, will undoubtedly lead to many exciting developments in classroom-centered research in the years ahead. As a setting for investigating language learning, the classroom provides researchers with numerous challenges and possibilities, only a few of which have been dealt with here. Its potential fruitfulness alone suggests that classroom-centered research will receive more attention in the future, and that criteria for judging classroom-centered research will be utilized (Gaies, 1980).

But such research has value beyond the fertile opportunities it offers investigators. Indeed, classroom-centered research should provide one means of bridging the gap between teachers and researchers (Hatch, 1981), because both groups are concerned with the same issue: how people learn and teach languages in formal instructional settings. Furthermore, in some studies cited above (e.g., Cathcart and Olsen, 1976, and Fanselow, 1977b) the teachers who participated in the research projects gained new insights into their teaching behavior. Finally, the findings of classroom-centered research may be more directly applicable to teachers' needs than other types of second language research. Ultimately these findings will help teachers and researchers alike to better understand the teaching and learning process, thereby facilitating that process in all its complexities.

NOTES

1. This chapter is an expanded version of a paper presented at the 1979 CATESOL State Conference, Los Angeles, April 8, 1979. The author wishes to acknowledge the help of José L. Galvan, Michael H. Long, and Marianne Celce-Murcia, who critiqued various stages of the manuscript and shared their knowledge and insights on the complexities of classroom-centered research. The chapter has also benefited from the reactions of the TESOL students at the Monterey Institute of International Studies, and the capable editorial assistance of Jennifer Love Costanza.

2. For a history of classroom-centered research in language teaching and learning, see Allwright (1983). For a collection of recent empirical studies in what is becoming the classroom-centered research tradition, see Seliger and Long (1983).

3. See Long (1980) for a discussion of the various types of observational coding systems that have been used in classroom-centered research on language learning.

DISCUSSION QUESTIONS

1. What are the characteristics of an outstanding language teacher? How can "good teaching" be defined by classroom-centered research?

2. In what way(s), if any, can the findings of classroom-centered research be used in teacher training programs?

3. Specify a problem or research question of interest to you as a language teacher. Which of the classroom-centered research methods discussed in this chapter could be used to investigate this particular issue?

4. How is *error* defined in classroom-centered research? Does the definition change if a researcher focuses on *teacher error,* as opposed to *learner error*?

5. What are the strengths and limitations of the diary studies for investigating classroom language learning and teaching?

6. How and to what extent can the teacher determine or control the turn-taking patterns in a language classroom? Should the teacher attempt to control the students' turn-taking behavior?

7. What sort of information is communicated to students by a language teacher's nonverbal behavior?

SUGGESTED ACTIVITIES

1. If you are teaching a language class, tape record two class periods—one in which you try to distribute turns evenly among all the students and one in which you do not purposefully alter your "turn-giving" behavior. What quantitative and qualitative differences

emerge in the two lessons? Are there identifiable high- and low-input generators in the two sessions? How does the discourse change when you try to distribute turns evenly?

2. Keep a daily journal of a language class you are teaching or taking for one week. Record your impressions of the experience as soon as possible each day after class. At the end of one week, reread your diary. What patterns emerge? What factors seem to promote or hinder your success as a language teacher or learner?

3. Observe a language class taught by a colleague or tape record a language class in which you are the teacher or a learner. How many different types of reacting moves does the teacher make? What types of errors are treated? What apparent effect do the teacher's reacting moves have on the students' production of the target language?

4. Present one lesson to your class in a teacher-fronted mode and then present a similar topic using small group interaction instead. Tape record both lessons and compare the results. What are the strengths and limitations of small group work? What are the strengths and limitations of the teacher-centered "lockstep" approach?

5. Ask a colleague to observe you teaching, noting especially your nonverbal behaviors. As an alternative, arrange to have your class period videotaped. What nonverbal behaviors do you use (consciously or subconsciously) in your teaching?

6. Describe an outstanding language teacher you have known. What characteristics of that teacher have you incorporated in your own repertoire of teaching behaviors?

7. If you are a teacher, ask your students about their preferences regarding error correction. What techniques do they think are useful and not so useful? How closely do the students' ideas on error correction match your own?

SUGGESTIONS FOR FURTHER READING

For a thorough treatment of classroom-centered research methods on language teaching, including a description of several different observation instruments, see M. Long (1980).

For a rationale for the use of a variety of approaches in second language research on acquisition and learning, see R. Ochsner (1979), A poetics of second language learning, *Language Learning* 29. 1, 53–80.

For a discussion of how students' evaluations of teaching can be used to improve teaching, see K. Jacoby (1976), Behavioral prescriptions for faculty based on students' evaluations of teaching, *American Journal of Pharmaceutical Education, 40*:8–13.

For a collection of recent studies involving classroom-centered research on language teaching and learning, see H. W. Seliger and M. H. Long (eds.), 1983.

For an overview of a great deal of classroom-centered research in content subjects, see Brophy and Good (1974).

REFERENCES

Allwright, R. L. (ed.) 1975a. *Working Papers: Language Teaching Classroom Research.* Colchester: University of Essex, Department of Language and Linguistics.

Allwright, R. L. 1975b. Problems in the study of teachers' treatment of learner error. In M. K. Burt and H. C. Dulay (eds.), *On TESOL '75: New Directions in Second Language Learning, Teaching and Bilingual Education.* Washington, D.C.: TESOL.

Allwright, R. L. 1980. Turns, topics and tasks: patterns of participation in language learning and teaching. In D. Larsen-Freeman (ed.), *Discourse Analysis in Second Language Research.* Rowley, Mass.: Newbury House.

Allwright, R. L. 1983. Classroom-centered research on language teaching and learning: a brief historial overview. *TESOL Quarterly, 17,* 2, 191–204.

Annett, John. 1969. *Feedback and Human Behaviour.* Harmondsworth, England: Penguin Books, Ltd.

Bailey, K. M. 1980. An introspective analysis of an individual's language learning experience. In S. Krashen and R. Scarcella (eds.), *Research in Second Language Acquisition: Selected Papers of the Los Angeles Second Language Research Forum.* Rowley, Mass.: Newbury House.

Bailey, K. M. 1983. Competitiveness and anxiety in adult second language learning: looking *at* and *through* the diary studies. In Seliger and Long (1983).

Bailey, K. M., and R. Ochsner. 1983. A methodological review of the diary studies: windmill tilting or social science? In K. M. Bailey, M. H. Long, and S. Peck (eds.), *Second Language Acquisition Studies.* Rowley, Mass.: Newbury House.

Barnes, D. 1969. Language in the secondary classroom. In D. Barnes (ed.), *Language, the Learner and the School*. London: Penguin Books.

Beebe, L. M. 1983. Risk-taking and the language learner. In Seliger and Long (1983).

Bellack, A., H. Kliebard, R. T. Hyman, and F. L. Smith. 1966. *The Language of the Classroom*. New York: Teachers College Press.

Brophy, J. E., and T. L. Good. 1974. *Teacher-Student Relationships: Causes and Consequences*. New York: Holt, Rinehart and Winston, Inc.

Carroll, J. B. and S. M. Sapon. 1959. *Modern Language Aptitude Test, Form A*. New York: The Psychological Corporation.

Cathcart, R. L., and J. Olsen. 1976. Teachers' and students' preferences for correction of classroom conversation errors. In J. Fanselow and R. Crymes (eds.), *On TESOL '76*. Washington, D.C.: TESOL.

Chaudron, C. 1977. A descriptive model of discourse in the corrective treatment of learners' errors. *Language Learning, 27*, 29–46.

Corder, S. P. 1974. The significance of learners' errors. In *J. H. Schumann and N. Stenson (eds.), *New Frontiers in Second Language Learning*. Rowley, Mass.: Newbury House.

Dunkin, M. J., and B. J. Biddle. 1974. *The Study of Teaching*. New York: Holt, Rinehart and Winston, Inc.

Fanselow, J. 1977a. Beyond Rashomon—conceptualizing and describing the teaching act. *TESOL Quarterly, 11, 1*, 17–39.

Fanselow, J. 1977b. The treatment of error in oral work. *Foreign Language Annals, 10, 5*, 583–593.

Flanders, N. A. 1970. *Analyzing Teaching Behavior*. Reading, Mass.: Addison-Wesley.

Gaies, S. J. 1976. Gradation in formal second language instruction as a factor in the development of interlanguage. In R. St. Clair and B. Hartfold (eds.), *LEKTOS: Interdisciplinary Working Papers in Language Sciences (Special Issue: Error Analysis and Language Testing)*, Louisville, Ky.: University of Louisville.

Gaies, S. J. 1977. The nature of linguistic input in formal second language learning: linguistic and communication strategies in ESL teachers' classroom language. In H. D. Brown, C. A. Yorio, and R. H. Crymes (eds.), *On TESOL '77, Teaching and Learning English as a Second Language: Trends in Research and Practice*. Washington, D.C.: TESOL.

Gaies, S. J. 1980. Classroom-centered research: some consumer guidelines. Paper presented at the Second Annual TESOL Summer Meeting, Albuquerque, N.M.

Gaies, S. J. 1983. The investigation of language classroom processes. *TESOL Quarterly, 17, 2*, 205–217.

Gardner, R. C., P. C. Smythe, R. Clement, and L. Gliksman. 1976. Second-language learning: a social psychological perspective. *Canadian Modern Language Journal, 32*, 198–213.

*George, H. V. 1972. *Common Errors in Learning English*. Rowley, Mass.: Newbury House.

*Presently out of print.

Hatch, E. M. 1981. TESOL and second language acquisition. In J. C. Fisher, M. A. Clarke, and J. Schachter (eds.), *On TESOL '80: Building Bridges: Research and Practice in Teaching English as a Second Language*. Washington, D.C.: TESOL.

Hatch, E. M. 1983. *Psycholinguistics: A Second Language Perspective*. Rowley, Mass.: Newbury House.

Holley, F., and J. K. King. 1974. Imitation and correction in foreign language learning. In *J. H. Schumann and N. Stenson (eds.), *New Frontiers in Second Language Learning*. Rowley, Mass.: Newbury House.

Jones, R. A. 1977a. Psychological, social and personal factors in second language acquisition. Unpublished M.A. thesis, University of California, Los Angeles.

Jones, R. A. 1977b. Social and psychological factors in second language acquisition: a study of an individual. In C. A. Henning (ed.), *Proceedings of the Los Angeles Second Language Research Forum*, University of California, Los Angeles.

Krashen, S. 1977. Some issues relating to the monitor model. In H. D. Brown, C. A. Yorio, and R. Crymes (eds.), *On TESOL '77*. Washington, D.C.: TESOL.

Long, M. H. 1977. Teacher feedback on learner error: mapping cognitions. In H. D. Brown, C. A. Yorio, and R. H. Crymes (eds.), *On TESOL '77, Teaching and Learning English as a Second Language: Trends in Research and Practice*. Washington, D.C.: TESOL.

Long, M. H. 1980. Inside the "black box": methodological issues in classroom research on language learning. *Language Learning, 29, 1*. Reprinted in Seliger and Long (1983).

Long, M. H. 1983. Does second language instruction make a difference? A review of research. *TESOL Quarterly, 17, 3*, 359–382.

Long, M. H., L. Adams, M. McLean, and F. Castaños. 1976. Doing things with words—verbal interaction in lockstep and small group classroom situations. In J. Fanselow and R. Crymes (eds.), *On TESOL '76*. Washington, D.C.: TESOL.

Mehan, H. 1974. Accomplishing classroom lessons. In A. V. Cicourel (ed.), *Language Use and School Performance*. New York: Academic Press.

Moskowitz, G. 1976. The classroom interaction of outstanding foreign language teachers. *Foreign Language Annals, 9, 2*, 135–143, 146–157.

Nystrom, N. J. 1983. Teacher-student interaction in bilingual classrooms: four approaches to error feedback. In Seliger and Long (1983).

Politzer, R. L. 1970. Some reflections on "good" and "bad" language teaching behaviors. *Language Learning, 20, 31*, 31–43.

Richards, J. C. 1974. *Error Analysis: Perspectives on Second Language Learning*. London: Longman.

Salica, C. 1980. Testing a model of corrective discourse. Unpublished M.A. thesis, University of California, Los Angeles.

Sato, C. 1981. Ethnic styles in classroom discourse. In M. Hines and W. Rutherford (eds.), *On TESOL '81*. Washington, D.C.: TESOL.

Schinke-Llano, L. A. 1983. Foreigner talk in content classrooms. In Seliger and Long (1983).

Schumann, F. E. 1980. Diary of a language learner: a further analysis. In S. Krashen and R. Scarcella (eds.), *Research in Second Language Acquisition: Selected Papers of the Los Angeles Second Language Research Forum.* Rowley, Mass.: Newbury House.

Schumann, F. E., and J. H. Schumann. 1977. Diary of a language learner: an introspective study of second language learning. In H. D. Brown, C. A. Yorio, and R. H. Crymes (eds.), *On TESOL '77, Teaching and Learning English as a Second Language: Trends in Research and Practice.* Washington, D.C.: TESOL.

Schumann, J. H. 1976. Social distance as a factor in second language acquisition. *Language Learning, 26,* 1, 135–143.

*Schumann, J. H., and N. Stenson. 1974. *New Frontiers in Second Language Learning.* Rowley, Mass.: Newbury House.

Seliger, H. W. 1977. Does practice make perfect? A study of interaction patterns and L2 competence. *Language Learning, 27,* 2, 263–278.

*Presently out of print.

Seliger, H. W. 1983. Learner interaction in the classroom and its effect on language acquisition. In Seliger and Long (1983).

Seliger, H. W., and M. H. Long. (eds.) 1983. *Classroom Oriented Research in Second Language Acquisition.* Rowley, Mass.: Newbury House.

Sinclair, J. M., and R. M. Coulthard. 1975. *Towards an Analysis of Discourse: The English Used by Teachers and Pupils.* London: Oxford University Press.

Tarone, E. 1981. Some thoughts on the notion of communication strategy. *TESOL Quarterly, 15,* 3, 285–295.

Townsend, D. R. 1974. A comparison of the classroom interaction patterns of bilingual early childhood teachers. Unpublished doctoral dissertation, University of Texas, Austin.

Townsend, D. R. 1976. Bilingual interaction analysis: the development and status. In A. Simoes, Jr. (ed.), *The Bilingual Child: Research and Analysis of Existing Educational Themes.* New York: Academic Press.

Townsend, D. R., and G. L. Zamora. 1975. Differing interaction patterns in bilingual classrooms. *Contemporary Education, 41,* 3, 196–202.

Vigil, N. A., and J. W. Oller. 1976. Rule fossilization: a tentative model. *Language Learning, 26,* 2, 281–295.

PART IV
THE RESEARCH PROCESS

INTRODUCTION

This section of the anthology introduces us to current methods and concerns in two important research areas: second language acquisition in the chapter by Larsen-Freeman and language testing in the chapter by Davidson, Hudson, and Lynch. These two chapters have been included since, as teachers of ESOL, it is essesntial that we become familiar with the two most important research tools available for influencing program or course development as well as assessing the strengths and weaknesses of language programs or courses, the proficiency of language learners, and (indirectly) the effectiveness of language teachers.

By understanding what the major research considerations are and how such research is conducted, we will be better prepared to critically read and evaluate the research reported to us at our conferences and in our journals. We will also be better equipped to carry out research projects of our own in the future.

CONSIDERATIONS IN RESEARCH DESIGN IN SECOND LANGUAGE ACQUISITION[1]

Diane Larsen-Freeman

The word "research" sometimes intimidates teachers. They imagine forbidding jargon and unfathomable numbers. They avoid reading research articles and instead depend upon others to interpret research findings for them. Although I understand such teachers' feelings, it is my contention that reading research reports and even conducting research need not be intimidating. In fact, in many ways teaching classes and conducting research are similar processes.

In both processes an objective must be established. The teacher's objective might be to teach second language students to form conditionals in the language they are studying and the researcher's to investigate how such students acquire these conditionals. In order to accomplish the objectives, both teacher and researcher must make a number of choices. For example, the teacher has to decide whether to present the formation of conditionals inductively or deductively. The researcher must decide whether to study the acquisition of conditionals longitudinally or cross-sectionally (see below). The alternatives from which each chooses are neither right nor wrong. What the teacher and the researcher strive to do is to make the best possible choices given their experience, the situation, and the objective they want to achieve. Both, however, have criteria to satisfy, i.e., things they *should* do to see that the objective is properly met. For instance, teachers should assess what their students have learned; researchers should design studies which produce *valid* results.

In addition, both teachers and researchers often find that they have in common a curiosity about the nature of the teaching/learning process. If research can be defined as "a systematic approach to finding answers to

questions" (Hatch and Farhady, 1982, p. 1), it is entirely possible that teachers would want to join researchers in the quest for answers, provided that conducting research was not perceived as so formidable a task.

The following considerations were compiled to give those who seek to conduct research some sense of the choices they must make and the criteria they must satisfy in designing a second language acquisition (SLA) research project. Many of these considerations will need amplification before a study can be responsibly fashioned. A course in research design, books such as those recommended in Allwright (1983), or a review of numerous research articles such as those published in the journal *Language Learning* will help provide the necessary background. The considerations offered here, however, will lead readers to a greater understanding of what is involved in conducting research and thereby hopefully demystify the process. It is also my hope that these considerations will support critical reading of the research done by others. The SLA field would derive enormous benefit from teachers' doing so. Then, too, an extensive reading of the research literature is the way to begin a research project of one's own.

The second language acquisition field currently embraces several different approaches to conducting research: interaction analysis (see Long, 1980, for discussion), ethnographic observation, self-reported introspective studies, and studies of a pre, true, quasiexperimental and ex post facto design (see Hatch and Farhady, 1982, for a discussion of the distinction among these last four). Not all the considerations which follow are appropriate for each of these approaches. The focus of these considerations is on the type of study in which it is the researcher's intention to describe the second language learner's interlanguage from a linguistic perspective. The researcher examines the learner's linguistic performance to analyze specific phonological, morphological, syntactic, semantic, or discourse features. Alternatively, the researcher looks for salient performance patterns in the data he or she has collected without establishing any a priori hypotheses. Thus the considerations are more applicable to certain of the above approaches (ethnographic observation, preexperimental), than to others (introspective studies, true and quasi experimental and ex post facto). Still, some of the considerations (e.g., subject selection) apply to all the approaches.

The reader will note that some of the considerations require the researcher to make a choice among two or more acceptable alternatives (e.g., the choice between a longitudinal and a cross-sectional design), depending on the objective of the study. The other type of consideration involves a criterion that a researcher strives to meet (e.g., obtaining valid results). Failing to meet the criterion results in an unacceptable study. I will discuss each of these major categories of considerations in turn.

CHOICES

Longitudinal or cross-sectional

Will the general design of the study be longitudinal or cross-sectional: The longitudinal approach involves studying the development of linguistic performance, usually the speech, of a small sample of subjects when the speech is collected at periodic intervals over a span of time. In the alternative, the cross-sectional design, the linguistic performance of a larger number of subjects is studied, but data are collected at only one or two sessions. Theoretically, the developmental view the longitudinal paradigm affords can be preserved in the cross-sectional study if the subjects are at various levels of L2 proficiency. (See how this is actualized in Adams' study, 1978, using a "pseudo-longitudinal" design.)

It should be noted that it is a point of contention among researchers today as to whether both designs yield identical results. First language acquisition researchers Jill and Peter de Villiers (1973) using a cross-sectional design were able to corroborate the order of acquisition of certain grammatical morphemes established by Brown's (1973) longitudinal study of three children learning English as a first language. In the area of child SLA, however, Hakuta (1975), using a longitudinal design to study the acquisition of English morphemes by a 5-year-old Japanese girl, obtained a different order than Dulay and Burt (1973, 1974), who had opted for a cross-sectional design in their studies of morpheme acquisition by large numbers of Spanish- and Chinese-speaking children.

Subjects

How are the subjects to be recruited? How many subjects are needed for the general design chosen? Are they to be selected randomly or expressly to meet certain criteria? As Schachter and Celce-Murcia (1977, p. 449) point out, the sampling of subjects "is rarely random in the statistical sense of the word since researchers work with available subjects, do research with existing classes of students, etc." Nevertheless, how important is representation? Are there to be variables in terms of age, sex, socioeconomic status, native language background, target language proficiency, years in an English-speaking country, years of language instruction, etc.? Research (Taylor, 1975; Larsen-Freeman, 1975) has shown that factors affecting the SLA process vary in the degree to which they apply depending upon the level of proficiency of the subjects. It would certainly be advisable, therefore, to adopt a proficiency measure that enables one to make an assessment and a report of the level or range of proficiency of the population being studied.

Is compensation of the subjects in order? Is funding available for such payment? Compensation, of course, does not always have to be monetary; the provision of extra tutorial sessions in the second language, for instance, might be a fair exchange for the subjects' time and cooperation.

Does permission from the subjects' parents or a participating institution need to be sought? How much about the study will subjects be told in advance of the data collection?

Task

What are the features to be studied, i.e., phonological, morphological, lexical, syntactic, semantic, pragmatic, or discourse features? Will the subjects' performance on these be observed naturalistically, or will subjects be asked to perform a particular task? If there is a task, are the subjects to be asked to demonstrate their ability to recognize, to comprehend, or to produce the chosen features? Or are they to perform a task which involves more than one of these, for example, to imitate a stimulus sentence, which according to Naiman (1974) requires subjects to both comprehend and produce the target language?[2]

Is the task to involve a graphic or phonic medium or a combination of both? This would have to be specified both for the task format presentation and for the medium that the subject uses to respond. The preeminent consideration, of course, is to choose the medium which best elicits the structures[3] selected for study or which best determines the subjects' comprehension of them. But practical matters like the time involved in administering and following up the task must also be weighed. For instance, it is generally acknowledged that using videotape to record a subject's performance in a given task is superior to simply audiotaping a subject's response, since the researcher gains access to all the nonverbal behavior of both the researcher and the subject. However, if videotape is used, the researcher should be prepared to have many working hours consumed by transcription.[4]

Is the task one where the subject is to read, write, speak, or listen to the target language? This question is not redundant because the researcher might have already decided that he or she wants to test the subject's production through a phonic medium but still must choose a particular skill, e.g., translating, imitating, or speaking. Of course, even these skills require further definition, since there is mounting evidence (e.g., Larsen-Freeman, 1975; Beebe, 1980) that the learner's performance varies depending on whether, for example, the subject is being asked to speak by answering questions in an interview or to speak by engaging in a spontaneous conversation with the researcher. Tarone (1979) suggests that it is the latter, i.e., the use of the vernacular where the subject is paying the least attention to his or her speech, which will give researchers the most systematic sample of second language learner speech. The dilemma is that the mere presence of the researcher encourages subjects to pay attention to their speech.

Is the format to be discrete-point or integrative? In the former case, with an item such as a minimal pair discrimination item, "it is never necessary for a student to understand a context longer than a sentence" in order to respond to an item (Oller, 1973, p. 190). In the case of the latter, using a dictation passage, for instance, the subject's ability to understand the language as a whole is being examined. Of course, as Oller (1973, p. 190) points out, the relationship between the two is probably better characterized as "a continuum ranging from discrete-point items on one end to full-scale language use at the other."

Thus, designing a task to obtain a sample of language performance is very critical in affecting whether or not the objective of the study will be met. A researcher must be clear on the content, medium, skill, and format of the task and make sure that all are consistent with the objective. These considerations are ones that also concern test designers. Elaboration of these points can be found in the following chapter on language testing by Davidson, Hudson, and Lynch.

Time

There are many diverse questions under this heading, their only commonality being the consideration of time: How much time will the entire study take? If a longitudinal design is to be used, will there be some degree of assurance that the subjects will be in the area until the completion of the study? How much time is required for each data-collection session? How much time should elapse between sessions? How much time can the researchers commit to the entire project? If a structured task is used, how much response time will the subjects be given? Krashen (1977), for example, has claimed that subjects' performance with regard to the suppliance of certain morphemes will vary depending upon the amount of response time subjects are given.

Equipment/materials

Is the students' performance to be audiotaped? Is it to be videotaped? As was indicated earlier, the latter is sometimes preferred, but the transcription time is greatly increased.

Is the plan to use pictures or props as stimuli? What will be the effect of these on the results? Researchers should bear in mind the finding of Klapper and Birch (1969), who discovered that children behaved differently when presented with actual props versus pictures of the same props. They write that for children up to 7 years, "photographs of objects were not equivalent to the objects they pictorially represented as directive stimuli for appropriate action" (p. 763).

The nature of any pictures used should also be considered. As Plaister (1968, p. 104) comments on the trying experience he had in getting pictures drawn for a test he was constructing:

It is difficult to get picture tests of any type drawn satisfactorily unless the test writer himself happens to be an artist. On the earlier versions of this test I worked with a very intelligent girl who, I thought, had grasped what I wanted: straight-forward, plain drawings. I found that I had to return many of the drawings time and again to have the humor, silly facial expressions, etc. removed. I was not entirely successful. The version of the test we are still using contains pictures which can be easily criticized, but the old story of pressures of time and money made us settle for something less than we wanted.

Hatch (personal communication) suggests that the use of color slides is a good compromise between real items and line drawings.

Environment

Is the study to take place in a classroom, in the subject's home, outside, etc.? What will be the conditions for recording? Is it important to vary the environment, thereby varying the interlocutors the subject interacts with? (See Cazden, Cancino, Rosansky, and Schumann, 1975, who attempt to do this.)

Is it important that the environment be conducive to relaxing the subjects as much as possible? Can the subjects be segregated if individual responses are to be recorded?

Context

What is the nature of the context to accompany the task? It is very clear that the verbal context supplied by a conversational interlocutor will affect the subject's response. (See Hatch, 1978 and the introduction to Larsen-Freeman, 1980 for an elaboration of this point.) As such, the input to the subject will have to be considered in the analysis of the subject's speech.

What is the effect of a nonverbal context? Following Rodd and Braine's (1971) suggestion that a context be supplied for an elicited imitation task, I chose to use a different picture for each stimulus sentence I presented to a subject (Larsen-Freeman, 1975). This helped to avoid problems the subjects might have encountered if they had misconstrued the vocabulary. However, as with so many other of these considerations, one should be aware that one might obtain different results depending on which alternative is chosen.

As Spurling (1979) discovered in his study involving contextualized and decontextualized cloze passages, students perform differently "depending on whether the test format is contextualized. ... Decontextualized tests seem to be testing a different skill from contextualized tests."

Then, too, Spurling also acknowledges that in a given test (or task) the tester (or researcher) must often resort to supplying highly contrived contexts, affecting the "naturalness" of the language product elicited. He notes (1979, p. 597):

In order for the tester to make up for the lack of real context, he must supply an artificial context. For example, he must supply an artificial cue like "last week" to elicit the past tense or "now" to elicit the present continuous tense. In real discourse this type of stimulus-response sequence is rarely used. Instead, other cues are used in a more fully contextualized setting.

Length

How many tasks will the study contain? How many items per task will there be? How many of these will be distractors, i.e., items designed to conceal the purpose of the task from the subjects? How many items will be included for each linguistic structure the researcher intends to examine? As Hatch and Wagner Gough (1976) have pointed out, second language acquisition researchers will have to account for variable performances not only among subjects but also by individual subjects, who sometimes supply a structure in a given context and other times do not. In order to comply, researchers would have to include a sufficient number of items or occasions for a subject to demonstrate ability to use or understand a given structure if any nonrandom variation pattern is to be detected.

Then, too, Rosansky (1976) has shown that a task must provide enough opportunities for individual subjects to attempt to use a given structure, in order to avoid having to aggregate the data from a number of subjects to detect any pattern. Rosansky argues that by grouping the data, individual subject deviances from general patterns can be obscured; thus, a spurious acquisition pattern emerges. (See, however, Andersen, 1978, who claims that Rosansky's data do not really challenge the acquisition pattern reported by other researchers.)

Scoring

How are the data to be quantified once they have been collected? How will the structures which are the object of the study be objectively scored?

Roger Brown (1973), a first language acquisition researcher, addressed these questions by awarding a point to a subject's score every time the subject correctly supplied a structure in a context in which the structure was required. When the correct structure was omitted, the subject received no points. Dulay and Burt (1974), second language acquisition researchers, in a refinement of this procedure, increased a subject's score by two points for a structure correctly supplied and by one point for a misformed structure, reasoning that the subject knew something belonged in the context but had not yet fully developed control of the form of the structure. Thus, in a context calling for suppliance of the past tense of the verb "to walk," a subject would gain two points for "walked" and one point for "walks." This refinement promised to provide a more sensitive measure of a subject's degree of competence for manipulating a given structure.

What this scoring schema does not take into account, however, is that subjects are not penalized for using -ed in unnecessary contexts. Subjects might overgeneralize and say something like, "He did walked." Utterances of this sort would provide evidence about the subjects' acquisition of this particular morpheme and should therefore also be scored. Researchers such as Stauble and Schumann (1983) have done just this, calculating the frequency with which a particular morpheme was used in a targetlike manner as well as the subjects' correct or incorrect suppliance of a structure in obligatory contexts.

As may be obvious, both of the above scoring schemata view the learner's interlanguage from the perspective of the target language; the learner's performance is scored in terms of its conformity to and deviance from native speaker norms. Adjemian (1976), Heubner (1979), and Bley-Vroman (1983) have argued persuasively that researchers should aim to describe what learners are actually doing, not what the learners should be doing. In other words, learners' interlanguage should be seen as a natural language in its own right and not viewed (or scored) by comparing it with the target language (Bley-Vroman's "comparative fallacy").

Another question which may need addressing when making decisions about scoring schemata is how to score responses which show that a subject did not understand the question. Dulay and Burt (1974) decided to ignore such responses because in order for them to determine if a structure had been supplied correctly in an obligatory context, it was necessary that they comprehend what the subject was saying. However, by disposing of these responses, Dulay and Burt might have been risking the loss of valuable data.

In his study, Naiman (1974) was able to incorporate the use of a "correction factor" which he subtracted from a subject's score when he had reason to believe a subject was guessing at an answer. In Naiman's task a subject had to point to the appropriate picture following a given stimulus. Since such a task would be vulnerable to the influence of a subject's guessing, Naiman's innovation provided a more accurate picture of a subject's true score.

This ends my discussion of the considerations I have categorized as requiring choices. I turn next to the considerations involving the satisfaction of criteria. Choices have to be made in this category, too. More importantly, however, for each of the following, the researcher must endeavor to meet the criterion in order to design the best possible research study.

CRITERIA
Validity
How faithfully does the task measure what it's supposed to? Is the behavior brought about by a subject's response to a particular task representative of the behavior the research is purporting to assess?

To take just one example of a dispute concerning validity, Kessel (1970) faulted Carol Chomsky's (1969) experimental design, arguing the task demands operating in Chomsky's study were restrictive and thus forced the results. Chomsky studied children acquiring English as a first language to see if the children could correctly assign an NP in a stimulus sentence as the subject of an infinitive complement. Testing her hypothesis with the verbs "ask" and "tell," Chomsky said to one of two children present in the room

with her, "Ask X what to feed the doll." Chomsky reported that the child she had addressed interpreted the "ask" directive as "tell" and supplied an answer rather than redirecting the question.

Kessel asserts that since Chomsky presented the sentences to the child in the form of a command, there were "task demands other than those of a linguistic nature [which] may have been operating," to wit:

1.   The child was not asked simply to interpret a sentence, but rather he was required to carry out an instruction by saying something to his partner. "Tell" with a one word answer would seem to require "less effort than the grammatical work of generating a question."

2.   Given the interview situation, it is likely that one expects to give out information, not to ask for it.

3.   With "ask" there is role-switching from addressee to addressor to addressee. "Role-taking may thus be more demanding for 'ask' than 'tell' " (p. 10).

Kessel used pictures to test the same construction as Chomsky and found that many 7-year-olds and most 8-year-olds correctly distinguished subject assignment for "ask" and "tell," the ages of his subjects being young in relation to those of Chomsky. Thus, if Kessel is correct, and Chomsky's results were an artifact of her research design, we would be justified in questioning the validity of her claims.

Reliability
If the procedure were to be repeated under similar conditions, is it likely that similar results will be obtained? If two or more researchers are to score the same data, how will high interscorer reliability be assured (i.e., will researchers agree with the way a particular item is to be scored)?

Jill de Villiers (1974) provides an example of the challenge confronting two different researchers who attempt to score the same data looking for evidence that a subject has acquired the rules of English morphology.

A cardinal number followed by a noun requires a plural ending; this is a more elementary example. Compare it to the example: "Every day my wife drive over to see me." Clearly there is something missing on the verb, but which tense marking? In a case as complicated as this, the whole verbal and non-verbal context must be examined for clues. If the sentence is prefaced by: "When I was in hospital last year . . . ," then some form of the past tense is appropriate, probably *drove*. If the person instead continues: ". . . even though it's difficult for her at the moment with the kids," then the strongest possibility is the third person regular ending *drives*. Such judgements can be made quite *reliably* [italics mine] among different judges though they are certainly not absolute. It is assumed here that the error rate will be constant enough across subjects and across morphemes that differences between them will not be due to scoring inconsistencies (p. 38).

Of course, no researchers can guarantee in advance the validity or reliability of their studies, but researchers should keep these two criteria foremost in their minds and be continually asking themselves what evidence there is that they have designed a valid and reliable study.

Naturalness

How natural will the task be? In a listening comprehension task, for example, will the subject receive feedback on whether or not he or she has comprehended what was intended? Rarely is this the case; most tasks have artificial features.

Although it is desirable to strive for naturalness in a task, without the imposition of constraints in terms of the range of possible responses the subject is likely to produce, it might be impossible to focus on one grammatical structure or to achieve any comparability with other studies. A researcher would have to wait a long time, for example, for subjects to produce enough infinitive complements for the researcher to be able to say anything about the subjects' acquisition of the complements. Another problem with natural communicative situations is that it is possible that subjects will avoid using troublesome structures. If subjects circumlocute aspects of the language which cause them difficulty, the researcher will not be able to adduce evidence of any sort.

The elicited translation task was thought to be a solution to this problem. Elicited translation involves giving subjects a sentence in their L1 and asking them to say the same thing in their L2. Although the task can successfully elicit specific structures it does so at the expense of naturalness. Swain, Naiman, and Dumas (1974) admit that there is no context and no natural reason for the subject to repeat the same thing in another language "when it serves no communication purposes." They continue: "so perhaps it would be worth complementing the task with another type of translation task, where the subject would be made to play the role of an interpreter— thereby providing him with an opportunity for a 'more natural communication situation'" (p. 74).

Use of an elicited imitation task does not guarantee that subjects will produce the structure under study either. When I was interested in studying ESL learners' ability to produce the possessive construction in English (NPs), one of the tasks I administered was an elicited imitation test. I showed the subjects some pictures, provided them with a model sentence, and asked them to repeat the sentence. To my chagrin, sometimes the subjects would substitute a possessive pronoun for the NPs construction I was seeking. The subjects demonstrated an obvious comprehension of the structure under examination, but my initial efforts to study their production of the structure were thwarted.

Comparability

If the study contains more than one task focusing on the same structure, how will comparability be achieved? One solution for my study of L2 morpheme acquisition (Larsen-Freeman, 1975), for example, was to deliberately construct five different tasks which could all be scored using the same schema.

Are the procedures of the study to be sufficiently similar as to allow comparability with the results of other studies? (See Brown, 1983, for a discussion of variegation among different acquisition studies.) Given the infancy of our field, and our rather tenuous findings, many have acknowledged (e.g., Tarone, Swain, and Fathman, 1976, p. 21) the need for study replication and result validation. Not only should researchers consider designing studies to be comparable with those conducted prior to their own, but also they should fully disclose their own procedures so as to enable researchers of subsequent studies to replicate their design.

Function as well as form

Will the task be such that the researcher will be able to evaluate not only the subject's ability to manipulate the form of a structure but also his or her knowledge of the semantic and pragmatic functions of the structure?

As Wagner Gough (1975) observed since her 5-year-old Persian- and Assyrian-speaking subject was able to correctly supply the English present progressive when necessary, at first one would be tempted to conclude that the subject had acquired that tense. Upon further examination of the data, however, it would be apparent that the subject had not yet acquired the semantic function of the form, since he overgeneralized the use of the present progressive tense to inappropriate contexts. To conclude that a subject has truly acquired a structure, therefore, a researcher should be able to attest to the subject's ability to supply the form correctly while observing all the relevant semantic and pragmatic constraints as well.

Avoidance of a task-ordering effect

If the study includes more than one task, will these tasks be presented to individual subjects in different sequences to avoid any task-ordering effect? It is possible that if tasks (or items within a task) are administered to all subjects in an identical order, the subject's having an opportunity to adjust to the situation would result in consistently superior performances on late-occurring items or tasks. Unless there is a good reason to do otherwise, then, a researcher should strive to present tasks in a scheduled order so that no one task is always administered first. Rather, each task should appear an equal number of times at each rank in the order.

Adequate sampling

Will the sampling procedure take into consideration the "language-as-fixed-effect fallacy"[5] (Clark, 1973)? Clark contends,

"Current investigators of words, sentences and other language materials almost never provide statistical evidence that their findings generalize beyond the specific sample of language materials they have chosen. Nevertheless, these same investigators do not hesitate to conclude that their findings are true for language in general" (p. 335). In so doing, Clark maintains, they are committing the "language-as-fixed-effect fallacy."

The lesson to be drawn from Clark's observation is that researchers have to be more realistic about their findings. They cannot imply that their findings for the language sample chosen can be generalized to all instances of that structure within the language unless the proper precautions are taken. Among them Clark lists the use of the right statistics, the appropriate research design, sampling language by systematic, repeatable procedures "or alternatively, by proceeding according to the so-called method of single cases."

A possible compromise between an elaborate research design and the method of single cases is to aggregate the findings of many case studies, as Schumann (1979) has done with regard to negation, for instance.

Clear and consistent administration

Are the instructions to be given the subjects simple and clear enough so that the results will not be confounded by the subjects' misunderstanding the task demands? How will consistency in adminstration be assured for different subjects? This is particularly relevant if more than one researcher is involved in collecting the data. Tarone (1974a) suggests discrepancies between Dulay and Burt's 1973 and 1974 studies might possibly be due to differences in the test instruments used or to the fact that there might have been different experimenters administering the instrument.

Appropriate statistics

What will be the best statistical procedure to use given the research question, the data-collection procedure, and the sample size? What will be the most conservative test of the results? Are the necessary assumptions for using a particular test met?

Some related questions, although not necessarily contingent upon a criterion, could be subsumed in this area: What is the best form in which to collect the data so that they can be analyzed easily? Will there be access to a computer to aid in the calculating? If so, are there computer programs available or will it be necessary to write a new one for the analysis chosen?

Pilot study

Is there to be a pilot study so that the researcher will have had an opportunity to eliminate unforeseeable problems in the administration before the actual study? Will there be an item analysis conducted in order to rid the task of weak items? Will more items be included in the pilot than are necessary for the actual study, so that eliminating items will not result in a shortage of items for the study?

Adherence to guidelines for ethical research

Has the study been designed to conform to the Guidelines for Ethical Research drawn up by the TESOL Research Committee? The guidelines were prepared to safeguard the right of subjects in SLA research studies. The guidelines were published in the *TESOL Quarterly* (1980), volume 14, number 3, pp. 383–388.

CONCLUSION

Although the SLA field is still young, interest in it is growing rapidly. As Hatch (1978, pp. 3–10) has observed, prior to the early 1970s, only a few notable SLA studies were conducted. Since 1970, however, there has been an incredible proliferation of studies. For those with an interest in the field, these are truly exciting times. It is my assumption that teachers reading this book do have an interest in the field; it is my hope that reading this chapter has made the prospect of reading and conducting research more real.

Making responsible decisions based on the considerations discussed here may appear to readers to be a formidable feat. I believe that committed individuals, however, will view the considerations as a challenge to design the best possible study in accordance with the objective of the study, the resources and limitations of the situation, and their own particular predilection for qualitative (e.g., ethnographic observation) or quantitative (e.g., preexperimental) research.

Merely following these procedures does not guarantee that good research will result; however, it is my hope that they will heighten the consciousness of researchers and encourage the kind of quality research the field deserves.

NOTES

1. I wish to thank Robert Cooper and Evelyn Hatch for their helpful comments on an earlier version of this chapter.

2. Of course, from Tarone's (1974b) discussion of Neisser's (1967) model of speech perception, it can be seen that it may not make any difference whether researchers tap comprehension or production, since they do not have to be concerned about the writing of two separate interlanguage grammars to account for each. If the model is accurate, researchers can probe either comprehension or production in order to elicit data upon which to base a single interlanguage grammar.

3. I will use the word "structures" for simplicity's sake, but I do not mean to restrict the reference of this term to syntactic forms. It is true, however, that far fewer studies have been conducted in the areas of phonology, lexical development, and discourse analysis than in the realm of morphology and syntax. With the increasing awareness of the importance of exploring discourse analysis vis-à-vis SLA, we may see a shift in the concentration of studies to this area. Most of the examples provided here do, however, deal with syntactic and morphological structures.

4. It has been estimated that, depending upon the detail and precision desired, one could spend anywhere up to 20 hours transcribing a single hour of videotape.

5. I am grateful to Jack Upshur for bringing this consideration to my attention.

DISCUSSION QUESTIONS

1. What is "the observer's paradox" about which Tarone (1979) writes? What are some ways in which SLA researchers might minimize the effect of the researcher's presence?

2. Can you think of any reasons why elicitation of a structure in written form might reveal differences in learner performance from elicitation of the same structure in speech?

3. What value might there be in avoiding the comparative fallacy, i.e., in describing what the learner is doing without reference to the target language?

4. Why must the researcher attend to acquisition of function as well as acquisition of form?

5. Are there some reasons why it might be desirable for the ESL classroom teacher to be an SLA researcher?

SUGGESTED ACTIVITIES

1. Carol Chomsky (1969) reports on the acquisition of some syntactic structures in children aged 5 to 10. Frank Kessel (1970) comments extensively on Chomsky's research design. Read about Chomsky's methodology and Kessel's comments. Do you agree with Kessel's criticism?

2. Read Jean Berko's morpheme acquisition study (1958). Then look at Roger Brown's comments (1973, pp. 282–293) regarding his study of the same morphemes. To what does he attribute the differences in their findings?

3. Read about Rosansky's criticism (1976) of the L2 acquisition morpheme studies. Do you agree with her arguments?

4. Read Larsen-Freeman (1978). Do you agree with her contention that a global proficiency assessment is necessary?

5. Plan an SLA study as a group project. Reflect on the considerations listed in this chapter in deciding upon the most suitable design.

SUGGESTIONS FOR FURTHER READING

Illustrations of Murphy's Law Abound in Classroom Research on Language Use.
1983. K. M. Bailey. *TESOL Newsletter, 17* (4), August.

Bailey provides a first-hand account of pitfalls she encountered when conducting classroom research and she advises readers on how to avoid these as much as possible.

A Methodological Review of the Diary Studies: Windmill Tilting or Social Science?
1983. K. M. Bailey, and R. Ochsner. In K. M. Bailey, M. Long, and S. Peck (eds.), *Second Language Acquisition Studies.* Rowley, Mass.: Newbury House.

The authors provide guidelines for researchers interested in journal-keeping as a tool in second language research.

Research on Metalinguistic Judgments: A Review of Theory, Methods, and Results.
1983. C. Chaudron. *Language Learning, 33,* 3, 343–377.

Chaudron offers a comprehensive review of research studies in which subjects were asked to exercise metalinguistic judgments.

Second Language Acquisition: Getting the Whole Picture.
1983. D. Larsen-Freeman. In K. M. Bailey, M. Long, and S. Peck (eds.), *Second Language Acquisition Studies.* Rowley, Mass.: Newbury House.

Larsen-Freeman recommends viewing the contributions of researchers and theorists from both doubting and believing perspectives.

Inside the "Black Box": Methodological Issues in Classroom Research on Language Learning.
1980. M. Long. *Language Learning, 30,* 1, 1–42.

Long discusses the strengths and weaknesses of basic methods that have been employed in conducting classroom research.

A Poetics of Second Language Acquisition.
1979. R. Ochsner. *Language Learning, 29,* 53–82.

Ochsner distinguishes two basic research traditions (the nomothetic and the hermeneutic) and discusses the questions each addresses and the assumptions each makes.

REFERENCES

Adams, M. 1978. Methodology for examining second language acquisition. In E. Hatch (ed.), *Second Language Acquisition.* Rowley, Mass.: Newbury House.

Adjemian, C. 1976. On the nature of interlanguage systems. *Language Learning, 26,* 2, 297–320.

Allwright, R. 1983. TESOL researchers: What do they read? What do they recommend? *TESOL Newsletter, 17* (1), February.

Andersen, R. 1978. An implicational model for second language research. *Language Learning, 28,* 2, 221–282.

Bailey, K. M. 1983. Illustrations of Murphy's law abound in classroom research on language use. *TESOL Newsletter, 17* (4), August.

Bailey, K. M., and R. Ochsner. 1983. A methodological review of the diary studies: windmill tilting or social science. In K. M. Bailey, M. Long, and S. Peck (eds.), *Second Language Acquisition Studies*. Rowley, Mass.: Newbury House.

Beebe, L. 1980. Sociolinguistic variation and style shifting in second language acquisition. *Language Learning, 30, 2,* 433–448.

Berko, J. 1958. The child's learning of English morphology. *Word, 14,* 150–177.

Bley-Vroman, R. 1983. The comparative fallacy in interlanguage studies: the case for systematicity. *Language Learning, 33,* 1, 1–18.

Brown, J. D. 1983. An exploration of morpheme-group interactions. In K. M. Bailey, M. Long, and S. Peck (eds.), *Second Language Acquisition Studies*. Rowley, Mass.: Newbury House.

Brown, R. 1973. *A First Language*. Cambridge, Mass.: Harvard University Press.

Cazden, C., H. Cancino, E. Rosansky, and J. Schumann. 1975. Second language acquisition sequences in children, adolescents and adults. Final Report, United States Department of Health, Education and Welfare.

Chaudron, C. 1983. Research on metalinguistic judgments: a review of theory, ,methods and results. *Language Learning, 33,* 3, 343–377.

Chomsky, C. 1969. *The Acquisition of Syntax in Children from 5 to 10*. Research Monograph No. 57. Cambridge, Mass.: MIT Press.

Clark, H. 1973. The language-as-fixed-effect fallacy: a critique of language statistics in psychological research. *Journal of Verbal Learning and Verbal Behavior, 12,* 335–359.

de Villiers, J. 1974. Quantitative aspects of agrammatism in aphasia. *Cortex, 10,* 36–54.

de Villiers, J., and F. de Villiers. 1973. A cross-sectional study of the acquisition of grammatical morphemes in child language. *Journal of Psycholinguistic Research, 2,* 267–278.

Dulay, H., and M. Burt. 1974. Natural sequences in child second language acquisition. *Language Learning, 24,* 37–53.

Dulay, H., and M. Burt. 1983. Should we teach children syntax? *Language Learning, 23,* 45–258.

Guidelines for Ethical Research in ESL. 1980. *TESOL Quarterly, 14,* 3, 383–388.

Hakuta, K. 1975. Becoming bilingual at age five: the story of Uguisu. Unpublished thesis, Harvard University.

Hatch, E. 1978. Discourse analysis in second language acquisition. In E. Hatch (ed.), *Second Language Acquisition*. Rowley, Mass.: Newbury House.

Hatch, E., and H. Farhady. 1982. *Research Design and Statistics for Applied Linguistics*. Rowley, Mass.: Newbury House.

Hatch, E., and J. Wagner Gough. 1976. Explaining sequence and variation in second language acquisition. In H. D. Brown (ed.), *Papers in Second Language Acquisition*. Proceedings of the 6th Annual Conference on Applied Linguistics, Ann Arbor, Mich., 39–58.

Heubner, T. 1979. Order-of-acquisition vs. dynamic paradigm: a comparison of method in interlanguage research. *TESOL Quarterly, 13,* 1, 21–28.

Kessel, F. 1970. The role of syntax in children's comprehension from ages six to twelve. *Monograph for the Society for Research in Child Development, 35,* 139, 6.

Klapper, Z., and H. Birch. 1969. Perceptual and action equivalence to objects and photographs in children. *Perceptual and Motor Skills, 29,* 763–771.

Krashen, S. 1977. Some issues relating to the monitor model. In H. D. Brown, C. Yorio, and R. Crymes (eds.), *On TESOL '77*. Washington, D.C.: TESOL.

Larsen-Freeman, D. 1975. The acquisition of grammatical morphemes by adult ESL students. *TESOL Quarterly, 9,* 409–419.

Larsen-Freeman, D. 1978. Evidence of the need for a second language acquisition index of development. In W. Ritchie (ed.), *Second Language Acquisition Research: Issues and Implications*. New York: Academic Press, Inc.

Larsen-Freeman, D. 1980. *Discourse Analysis in Second Language Research*. Rowley, Mass.: Newbury House.

Larsen-Freeman, D. 1983. Second language acquisition: getting the whole picture. In K. M. Bailey, M. Long, and S. Peck (eds.), *Second Language Acquisition Studies*. Rowley, Mass.: Newbury House.

Long, M. 1980. Inside the "black box": Methodological issues in classroom research on language learning. *Language Learning, 30,* 1, 1–42.

Naiman, N. 1974. The use of elicited imitation in second language acquisition research. *Working Papers on Bilingualism, 2,* 1–37.

Neisser, U. 1967. *Cognitive Psychology*. New York: Appleton-Century-Crofts.

Ochsner, R. 1979. A poetics of second language acquisition. *Language Learning, 29,* 53–82.

Oller, J. 1973. Discrete-point tests versus tests of integrative skills. In J. Oller and J. Richards (eds.), *Focus on the Learner*. Rowley, Mass.: Newbury House.

Plaister, R. 1968. Testing and competence. *Language Learning,* Special Issue No. 3, 103–110.

Rodd, L., and M. Braine. 1971. Children's imitations of syntactic constructions as a measure of linguistic competence. *Journal of Verbal Learning and Verbal Behavior, 10,* 430–443.

Rosansky, E. 1976. Morpheme studies and second language acquisition: A question of methods. Paper presented at the 10th Annual TESOL Conference, New York, March 5.

Schachter, J., and M. Celce-Murcia. 1977. Some reservations concerning error analysis. *TESOL Quarterly, 11,* 4, 441–452.

Schumann, J. 1979. The acquisition of English negation by speakers of Spanish: A review of the literature. In R. W. Andersen (ed.), *The Acquisition and Use of Spanish and English as First and Second Languages*. Washington, D.C.: TESOL.

Spurling, S. 1979. Contextualized and decontextualized tests. *TESOL Quarterly, 13,* 4, 597–598.

Stauble, A., and J. Schumann. 1983. Toward a description of the Spanish-English basilang. In K. M. Bailey, M. Long, and S. Peck (eds.), *Second Language Acquisition Studies*. Rowley, Mass.: Newbury House.

Swain, M., N. Naiman, and G. Dumas. 1974. Alternatives to spontaneous speech: Elicited translation and imitation as indicators of second language competence. *Working Papers on Bilingualism, 3*.

Tarone, E. 1974a. A discussion of the Dulay and Burt studies. *Working Papers on Bilingualism, 4*.

Tarone, E. 1974b. Speech perception in second language acquisition: A suggested model. *Language Learning, 24, 2*, 223–233.

Tarone, E. 1979. Interlanguage as chameleon. *Language Learning, 29, 2*.

Tarone, E., M. Swain, and A. Fathman. 1976. Some limitations to the classroom application of current second language acquisition research. *TESOL Quarterly, 10, 1*, 19–32.

Taylor, B. 1975. The use of overgeneralization and transfer learning strategies by elementary and intermediate students in ESL. *Language Learning, 25*, 73–107.

Wagner Gough, J. 1975. Comparative studies in second language learning. CAL-ERIC/CLL Series on Language and Linguistics, 26.

LANGUAGE TESTING: OPERATIONALIZATION
IN CLASSROOM MEASUREMENT AND L2 RESEARCH

Fred Davidson, Thom Hudson,
and Brian Lynch

Teachers at an intensive language institute want to know how many of their students have mastered the course objectives. They develop and hand out a final exam. Students from several countries hover over their test papers. After collecting the tests, the teachers correct them, decide which students have mastered the material well enough to go on to the next level, and then give marks. Similarly, a language researcher wants to determine the extent to which second language learners can process written embedded wh-questions. The researcher develops an instrument to help answer the research question. After the instrument is administered to the subjects, the researcher corrects it, performs appropriate statistical analyses, draws conclusions, and presents the research at a conference.

These two situations are much closer than is often thought. Both the teacher and the researcher must determine the appropriate content for their tests, decide how they will operationalize what they want to test, select an appropriate format for testing, and determine the degree to which their decisions will be influenced by the results. Language testing, then, is a method of operationalizing the inferences of both student assessment and of research. This paper will present examples of how that operationalization takes place, how decisions are made, and how concerns about the process of measurement may be addressed.

However, before discussion of just how this operationalization takes place, a point should be made concerning the nature of language skills or traits. Specifically, the issue of the divisibility of language factors, and how that linguistic divisibility affects assumptions about language testing needs to be addressed.

That is, while the tester may have intuitive concepts about what language is, the conflicting arguments as to just how divisible and definable language skills are will affect the method, mode, form, and interpretation of the language testing which takes place. It is crucial to address this state of affairs, if only briefly, in any consideration of language testing as a tool. Oller (1983) for example, indicates that while it is necessary to determine a priori the type of data to collect and the structures or skills to be tested, our ability and willingness to do so depend upon theoretical assumptions which are not always empirically testable. Thus, while we may assume that a language learner develops a language system which operates in an integrated manner, or more explicitly that there is "a general factor underlying performance on many language processing tasks," we must also recognize that this language factor will be "componentially complex" (p. 353).

The theoretical arguments as to the extent to which these language components are autonomous or are a reflection of some general language factor are outside the purview of this paper (for a review of the arguments see Oller, 1983; Bachman and Palmer, 1982, and their references). However, whether the classroom teacher or language acquisition researcher views language as having a general factor or not, the issue of how discretely to define language traits and skills will be an on-going concern. That is, whether one believes that there is some general language factor or that language is a series of interacting and definable subskills, it will be necessary to carefully delineate the language skill(s)/trait(s) which are to be measured. This is as true for measuring the differential effects of some language program as in measuring a skill such as reading comprehension, which may itself be viewed as a reflection of a set of subskills. As we will see, this is essentially the concern of operationalization, and it is a concern which is ever present in language testing. In short, language testing is tied to the mode of operationalizing the teacher's or researcher's notions of how language operates for people, and each decision in the testing process will be tied to the tester's concepts of language context, language function, and cognition.

OPERATIONALIZATION

NRM and CRM approaches

Operationalization is the process of arriving at what Kerlinger (1973) calls an "operational definition [which is a definition that] ... assigns meaning to a construct or variable by specifying the activities or 'operations' necessary to measure it" (Kerlinger, 1973, p. 31). Language testing is, essentially, an example of this process. After determining the skill or trait which is of concern or interest, the teacher or researcher must decide what the student or subject should be able to do in order to indicate ability on that skill or trait. While this may seem like a fairly straightforward process, it should be pointed out that operationalizing language skills is an extremely difficult task, requiring the operationalization of both the trait or the skill itself and the standard against which it will be judged. As Farhady (1983), p. 261) mentions, the specification of what the language learner will be required to demonstrate, i.e., the operationalization of the standard for evaluating a language skill or trait, is often highly ambiguous, leading to difficulty in the interpretation of test performance. For example, if the standard for the skill to be measured is *successful, efficient communication*, it will be extremely difficult to develop a test which can be scored objectively and interpreted clearly.

Thus, a precondition for language testing is the determination of how the results are to be interpreted or to what the results of the test are to be referenced. As indicated above, the operationalization process includes a specifi-

cation of a standard for evaluating performance as well as the activities or operations being used to measure the language skill or trait. In order to accurately specify that standard, the teacher or researcher must decide whether the decision will be *relative* or *absolute*. Relative decisions involve the comparison or rank ordering of individuals, whereas absolute decisions refer to the estimation of a person's "universe score", i.e., their true ability on a particular trait. This distinction comes from educational measurement theory, and it is not meant to imply that decisions are "absolute" in the sense of being without error or without consideration of other factors. From this perspective, decisions are absolute in a statistical sense in that an error term is calculated which includes the variance associated with the test items. In relative decisions, the effect of test items is considered as a constant in that it will not affect the rank ordering of individuals (for further discussion see Shavelson and Webb, 1981).

This notion may best be seen in the distinctions which are made between norm-referenced measurement (NRM) and criterion-referenced measurement (CRM). With CRM we are interested in tests which are "used to ascertain an individual's status with respect to a well-defined behavioral domain" (Popham, 1978). NRM, on the other hand, is concerned with tests that are "designed to ascertain an examinee's status in relation to the performance of a group of other examinees who have completed the test" (Popham, 1978). If the teacher or researcher is interested in evaluating in an absolute fashion, e.g., mastery versus nonmastery, with respect to a well-defined language skill or trait, CRM would offer the most help. When the interest is primarily in ranking individuals relative to each other or to some normative group, NRM would be the appropriate approach.

It must be noted here that our definition of CRM is not the same as that used by those who define criterion as being a specified score, or standard for determining mastery/nonmastery. For example, see the discussion of *edumetric* and *psychometric* approaches to testing by Cziko (1983)—following Carver (1974). Cziko defines CRM as a *domain-referenced* (where "domain" is a well-defined behavioral domain, as mentioned above) for which a cut score, or standard, has been set. In this sense the cut score is the criterion. Cziko's discussion is extremely helpful in clarifying the different approaches to educational measurement, especially when the focus is on general proficiency testing. However, when the teacher or researcher is focusing on achievement rather than general proficiency, CRM should be viewed in a broader context which incorporates both the model of test construction based on something like Popham's instructional objectives exchange (IOX) specifications (Popham, 1978), and a potential numeric score, or standard, used for making mastery/nonmastery decisions. The definition of *criterion* used here, then, is the behavior or skill to be operationalized, while the cut score for mastery/nonmastery decisions will be referred to as a *standard*.

The items produced in the CRM test, then, will sample a "well defined behavioral domain." This is defined as "a set of skills or dispositions examinees display when called on to do so in a testing situation." This criterion behavior is basically whatever we are actually trying to measure, or test for. It may be a skill or set of skills, or knowledge of a specific sort which is defined and described in detail. For instance, in math, it could be the ability to determine the area of a specified set of geometric figures. Or, in ESL, it could be to identify the correct form for restrictive relative clauses, to produce topic sentences, or to select from among multiple-choice alternatives the best statement of the main idea for a reading passage which has certain specified characteristics.

As mentioned earlier, the operationalization of a standard for evaluating a language skill or trait is extremely difficult. This is obviously true for the operationalization of the criterion behavior itself. One problem is how specific or how small we define a criterion behavior. That is, do we define it as the tense/aspect system in English or as the present perfect in personal narratives? There

are no definite prespecified rules for the decision. This is a programmatic decision that one makes at the beginning of CRM test development, and it becomes a critical part of operationalization. Once the specificity of the criterion skill or behavior has been determined, test specifications are written. This, too, is a critical part of operationalization, perhaps the central part of the process. The writing of the CRM test specifications is the precise delineation of the operations that will define the skill or trait to be measured.

In contrast to the CRM approach, NRM results in an overall estimate of ability in the general field of knowledge or skill in relation to the other students or examinees. This relation is essentially one of rank; students who are more proficient are ranked higher, and vice versa. To the extent that the *rank* based on the test *scale* accurately reflects the reality of the trait being measured, NRM has tested what it set out to. Consequently, NRM scores tell us whether Abdul or Haruko or Juan is behind or ahead of other students in the class on the trait.

NRM test specifications are written in less detail than CRM specifications; that is, NRM operationalization will be more general than CRM. An indication of the major difference appears in Figure 1, if our concern is to evaluate students' reading comprehension (after Popham, 1978).

As indicated in the figure, NRM provides a broad indication of relative standing, while CRM produces information which is more descriptive and addresses absolute decisions with respect to the instructional goal. With CRM, we seek information that will help answer questions such as "Is this person qualified for advancement?" or "Is the program succeeding in reaching its goals?" Furthermore, we are seeking an instrument that is sensitive to instruction and helps make instructional goals more explicit. This will hopefully lead teachers to more directed instruction. In reality, tests tend to fall along a continuum which is defined by the two "poles" of NRM and CRM. That is, most NRM language tests are tests of skills to some extent, and most CRM language tests reflect

NRM	CRM
reading comprehension	reading comprehension = subskills: inferencing, main idea, vocab. in context
A global indication of ability	There could be 5, 7, or 10 subskills, depending upon how specific we want to be.

FIGURE 1 NRM and CRM Criterion Behavior Score Indications

some concern with relative standing. However, a primary distinction remains in terms of the specificity with which items are defined.

Test generation and evaluation

The test writer must select the content and determine the appropriate format for testing, as well as develop and revise the test. These stages are dealt with in detail in the following paragraphs; throughout this discussion it should become clear how the NRM or CRM decisions discussed above color the process of operationalization.

Test Content The first concern of the test writer centers around a determination of the test content. While the test needs to cover the content the students are to be held responsible for having learned, or the particular language skill which is of research interest, the operationalization of test content involves a recognition of the interactions between the examinee and that content. That is, the test writer must consider the extent to which the test content confounds language skill, with culture, background, and intelligence. Oller (personal communication) has indicated the importance in language testing of fixing the facts of either the world or the text (i.e., language). In terms of content, we are concerned with fixing the facts. This is always a particularly relevant concern when testing students or subjects from differing backgrounds and cultures. Work in L1 and L2 schema theory (Adams and Collins, 1977; Anderson, 1977; Carrell, 1983; Carrell and Eisterhold, 1983; Hudson, 1982; Johnson, 1982; Rumelhart and

Ortony, 1977; and others) has indicated the effects of background and culture on comprehension in reading, and it can be assumed that this also carries into other skill areas. Of particular concern here is that the material we select as content on a test may turn out to be a cause of student errors, rather than the errors being due to breakdowns in the specific language skill we are assessing. This is a conundrum in that materials which are sensitive to the background knowledge and culture of the student may have limited application to inferences about real-world tasks in the target language. It is important that the teacher or researcher recognize that the student may perform poorly because of the mismatch of his or her background to the particular material selected as the context of the test (Johnson, 1983; Hall, Reder, and Cole, 1975). That is, the teacher or researcher should be aware of the need to "fix the facts" in determining the content of the test.

Additionally, in the selection of content, serious consideration needs to be given to the levels of language functions which are being tested. For example, on one level the test may measure basic language proficiency in terms of local grammatical skills. That is, the content of the test may be aimed at determining grammatical achievement or proficiency, and as such, the content selected for the test will need to reflect this. On another level, the test may measure communicative tasks in a variety of social and academic settings. That is, the focus of measurement may be the examinee's use of language in defined communicative settings. When this is the case, the test writer will develop contexts for the test content which reflect this goal of the test. On a third level the test may measure the autonomous use of language in problem-solving activities. For example, the researcher may wish to tap the examinee's use of language in what Canale terms "intrapersonal uses of language such as problem solving, monitoring one's thoughts, verbal play, poetry, or creative writing" (1983, p. 340). The content for these uses will differ from the content used in communicative or local grammatical skill contexts. These levels will be determined as the content is specified. In short, there are many methods of outlining the content or "specifications" prior to test writing (cf. Ebel, 1979, pp. 69–71; Gronlund, 1981, pp. 126–135, for varying degrees of specification). However, the content which is specified will require a functional level of processing, and the test writer will want to keep this in mind.

Test Item Format A second concern in test operationalization is that of test format. In selecting a format, the tester is concerned with the degree to which the test is *integrative* or *discrete* (for an in-depth discussion of the distinction see Farhady, 1983; Oller, 1979) or *communicative* versus *structural*, or other such dichotomies. The importance here is that the particular format of the test should produce the level of performance desired. Almost all teachers and researchers have found that they have students and subjects who score well on a paper and pencil grammar test but who cannot write a paragraph which correctly utilizes the same grammar. To a large extent this is a problem of eliciting the level of performance which is of concern. As with other domains of operationalization, in selecting a format for the assessment task it is important that we know exactly what we are asking the student to do in terms of the activities of the test. The particular task and format we select can be measuring a number of different factors. Johnston (1983) has indicated that various assessment tasks may be examined in terms of several factors which are tied to a large extent to the format selected for use.

In order to discuss how test formats may affect performance, however, a brief review of test formats is in order. First, let us assume that we develop a paper-and-pencil test which utilizes several types of items. These may be binary-choice items, for which the examinee selects from one of two choices as in true-false questions. Some of the items may be matching, for which the examinee matches items in one list to appropriate items in a second list. Other subtests may be multiple-choice items, for which the examinee selects from possible answers that answer which best completes an incomplete statement. The test may also utilize short-answer items for which the examinee supplies a word or phrase which completes an incomplete statement, or which answers a question. Further, the test may include an essay topic and the examinee is directed to write an organized composition based on the topic. In addition to these sections of the test, we may include a cloze passage, a passage with every *n*th word deleted, and the student is directed to fill in each blank space with a word which is acceptable, or we may include a dictation section which requires the examinee to re-create in writing what is spoken. Each item type has its advantages and disadvantages. (For detailed discussions of the merits of various item formats in language testing see Cohen, 1980; Madsen, 1983; Oller, 1979; Heaton, 1975; for educational measurement in general see Ebel, 1979; Popham, 1981; Gronlund, 1981). To be sure, we are not limited to paper-and-pencil tests; we may elect to develop an oral test, a computer-adaptive test, or a test with other performance sections, but for the following discussion let us assume we are writing a paper-and-pencil test.

Aside from particular weaknesses of any given format, such as the fact that on a true-false test item the examinee has a 50 percent chance of being correct, the types of items have effects in terms of what we as teachers and researchers learn from the item and how the item format affects the examinee. Johnston (1983) has indicated that item formats may be selected in terms of the student or subject's interaction with the item demands. That is, item format may be considered in terms of cognitive requirements and affective influences.

Cognitive Requirements Item formats require differing levels of language production. This is of concern in that some people have difficulty in expressing ideas and organizing information in their first language. When using item types such as free recall or true-false questions, we are at opposite ends of a production continuum, with short-answer questions falling somewhere between. The levels of performance which are obtained from different test formats due to the student's ability at organizing and producing text independent of second language proficiency should be kept in mind while constructing a test as well as while interpreting the results of a test. Additionally, the differing production requirements of test formats must be considered in that the level of production of a particular skill expected must be established in some rational way prior to administration of the test.

A second concern in terms of item format selection is the fact that the formats have different memory retrieval and reasoning requirements. Multiple-choice or true-false items call on short-term memory and require a comparison of possible answers, while open-ended questions require the use of long-term memory. Whether the tester wishes the examinee to partially base decisions on pairwise comparison of alternatives is a question to be considered in terms of the test's goals. The examinee will need to utilize more or less reasoning in a multiple-choice format depending upon the individual problem-solving style and the plausibility of the distractors.

The test writer and test users need to consider the memory and retrieval requirements in the same terms as they consider organization and production requirements. That is, for each skill or category which is to be tested, the test items will measure differing types of mastery depending upon item format.

Affective Concerns Little attention has traditionally been placed on concerns of the subject's motivation, purpose, or expectations of a test and the test setting. Examinees will find the content of the test or the test formats motivating to differing degrees. That is, the actual information on the test needs to be interesting and motivating. A fairly clear example of this is in the differences of test construction for bilingual children versus adult ESL/EFL learners. Attention spans differ, and the test writer will want to take this into account if an accurate measure is to be obtained. Additionally, the sequential format of a test may lead the examinee to different conclusions about the purpose of manipulating information in a test. That is, if an examinee is presented with several multiple-choice items on a listening or reading passage and is then asked to write a composition on the same general topic, he or she may be led to believe that the examiners want as much detail as possible included in the essay, and may thus include a great deal of information which the grader considers irrelevant to the particular topic assigned (Johnston, 1983).

A final consideration of item format centers around the social interpretations and requirements of the examinee. That is, the testing setting itself requires a particular motivation for use of language. It requires the examinee to perform the metalanguage task of interpretation of the task. Some people are better at this interpretation and inferencing task than others. This is a major factor in the cultural backgrounds of examinees. Some examinees may come from backgrounds which have Western attitudes and methods of testing, while others may come from backgrounds in which a multiple-choice test is a new experience. In testing contexts involving heterogeneous groups this needs to be taken into account when one is selecting an item format.

Test development: item refinement for reliability and validity

As a test development activity, operationalization can be seen as a series of sequential steps:

1. Theory is clarified; skills to be measured are delineated.
2. Specifications are written which follow that delineation.
3. Specification-generated items are written (as outlined above).
4. Specification-generated items are refined (this includes judgmental refinement, item statistics, and item banking).

It can be seen that operationalization *technically* occurs in the writing of the specifications and the item writing is a secondary operationalization. Step 4, item refinement, is an essential tool in *bettering the fit* between the items and the theory. The discussion below focuses on item refinement as a bettering of fit activity aimed at achieving two desirable test characteristics: reliability and validity.

Simply put, reliability is consistency of measurement. In NRM, it refers to the degree to which the test ranks examinees consistently. This consistency of rank can be checked via equivalent test forms, test-retest methodology, or internal consistency measures (for a detailed discussion of NRM reliability, see Ebel, 1979, pp. 274–296). In CRM, reliability uses similar technology, but with a task/decision-based focus. Rather than being concerned with the rank consistency of examinees, a CRM test aims for reliability of decisions regarding the task(s) measured. Hudson and Lynch (1984) offer a summary of CRM reliability methodology.

Validity is measurement truth. A set of test measurements is valid to the extent it measures what it claims to measure; hence validity is a claim-specific concept: by rights, one should say: "the measurements from test A are valid for content field A, but not content field B." In both NRM and CRM, reliability is a precondition for validity. Unless a test is consistent, it cannot measure truthfully. Traditionally, validity is categorized into several different types:

1. Face validity, or apparent validity.
2. Criterion validity, or validity against a well-accepted test of the trait under consideration, or some related trait.

3. Content validity, or measurement of syllabus fit.
4. Construct validity, or measurement of fit with a priori theoretical characteristics.

This breakdown of validity is applicable to both NRM and CRM, but CRM addresses the issue of content validity in greater detail than NRM. Further, within CRM, an additional approach to construct validity has been proposed, one that makes use of "decision validity" (Berk, 1980a). Here, a coefficient is derived which indicates the power of the test to make correct decisions about placement into mastery of nonmastery groups. In terms of construct validity, this decision consistency provides an indication that the test is accurately measuring the construct, i.e., is classifying instructed students as masters and uninstructed as nonmasters.

As will be discussed below, the technical process of ascertaining validity is *validation*. In research, perhaps most critical is construct validation, for which procedures are available. One is factor analysis, in which underlying traits are outlined using clustering tendencies within a correlation matrix (cf. Kerlinger, 1973). Another (used in language testing by Bachman and Palmer, 1981, 1982) has the ponderous name: Multitrait Multimethod Convergent Discriminant (MTMM) Construct Validation. In this procedure, the researcher uses many tests designed to tap many skills, and uses multiple test methods/formats. A priori theorizing states where the tests and methods should converge (agree, correlate) and diverge (disagree, correlate negatively) with other tests and methods (see Campbell and Fiske, 1959). The construct(s) is (are) validated if the convergence and discriminance are as predicted. Recently, language testing has combined these two procedures (Bachman and Palmer, 1982; Purcell, 1983) in structural modeling, where underlying traits are identified by MTMM, and strength and direction of influence between traits/constructs are analyzed using factor analysis and regression techniques (Pedhazur, 1982, pp. 575–682).

Given the above definitions of reliability and validity, how can test items be refined to better achieve these qualities, without which fit to theory is very difficult? Popham (1978, 1981) discusses judgmental analysis as a powerful tool to revise or eliminate items. Certainly in CRM it is a valuable method for judging content validity. Hudson and Lynch (1984) found that a procedure of correlating expert judgments on item-to-instructional objective fit provided useful information in a larger CRM test development framework. Thus, expert judgment is one method of checking item to theory matchup.

In addition to judgmental analysis, both NRM and CRM test development make use of item statistics. In NRM, a desirable item is one of average difficulty; i.e., about 50 percent of the examinees are successful on that item; in addition, it should correlate well with the total score; i.e., the item should tend to rank examinees similar to the total score ranking. In NRM theory, if these two item qualities are maximized, the item is an excellent variance component—it helps to draw out examinee variability on the trait(s) being measured. Such variability is critical to item-to-theory fit in NRM, as well as to production of useful norms.[1] CRM, on the other hand, views its item statistics differently. Rather than seeking items which maximize variability, it selects items that distinguish between mastery and nonmastery groups on the skills being measured.

Regardless of whether one operates from an NRM or CRM perspective, the effect of item refinement is the same. One discards or modifies items that do not fit the theory as it was operationalized in the specifications. The discarding is done via the procedures outlined above; hence those procedures presume to focus on item-to-theory fit. Eventually, especially in large-scale testing, one builds an item bank containing items and their characteristics.[2] To the extent that item refinement is successful, indices of overall test reliability and validity should improve. In bettering the item to theory fit, and indirectly bettering the operationalization, one betters the theoretical focus of the entire test.

So, test development item refinement focuses on bettering the fit of the items to the theory. This process may be clarified through its application to practical examples from language research and classroom language teaching. For example, consider a researcher who wishes to determine if a certain rhetorical support structure is evident in a series of native speaker student essays versus essays by ESL students. After reviewing the literature, the researcher settles on devising a "rhetorical mode judgment questionnaire" to accompany essays given to expert judges. On receiving the essays and completed questionnaires, the researcher consistently finds that a certain questionnaire item received comments which indicated perplexity on the part of the expert judges, and also yielded bizarre item statistics. The researcher discards that item and its results. This researcher has used item refinement to improve the fit of the questionnaire to the theory behind the research.

As another example, imagine an ESL instructor who is designing a vocabulary final exam to be given to eleven sections of a high intermediate ESL course. Results indicate that five items may be odd: the instructor calculates item difficulties and item-total correlations (an NRM activity), and solicits judgments of the fit between items and instructional objectives from colleagues (a CRM activity). Based on the findings, the instructor decides not to count those five items toward the final exam total score, and not to add them to the vocabulary item bank being started. This instructor has also followed item refinement procedures to better the fit of the items to the skills being measured (i.e., the theory).

DECISION MAKING

Relationship to operationalization
In a very practical sense, the primary reason for language testing is decision making. The central thesis of this paper is that language testing is the process of operationalizing language skills or traits. In addition, it involves the operationalization of standards for evaluating performance. However, before

these processes can begin, it is necessary to determine the types of decisions that are to be made, e.g., relative or absolute, as well as the bases and rationale for setting the standards. Thus, decision making is the reason for the need to operationalize. In application, this involves the contexts of program evaluation and student placement into classes, classroom assessment and student advancement, research questions and hypothesis testing, as well as performance and competency testing.

Contexts for decision making

Program Evaluation One important context for decision making involves the level of instructional programs. The concerns here are, basically, the evaluation of the overall program and the placement of students into the levels, or classes, of that program. The types of decisions made in program evaluation tend to be absolute. That is, we are typically not interested in ranking the instructional program of concern with other programs—a relative decision. We are, on the other hand, usually interested in determining whether or not the program has reached its goals—an absolute decision. This does not imply that we are not interested in determining the degree to which these goals have been reached. In this case the decision is still absolute in the sense that it is in reference to preestablished goals rather than being relative to other programs.

Ultimately, the goals for students of an ESL/EFL instructional program are the acquisition of language skills. Ideally, reaching those goals implies that all students master those skills. However, this is not realistic, and standards will need to be set, both in terms of what level of performance on the language skills will be considered as mastery, and what percentage of students attaining mastery will be considered as success for the program. These standards reflect the nature of the decisions being made. They are typically absolute, in the sense discussed above, and do not depend upon the performance of students relative to one another (For an excellent summary of existing models for program evaluation and a specific proposal for ESL, see Robertson, 1982).

Decisions concerning student placement may be relative or absolute. If the program has a fixed quota enrollment, it may be necessary to make relative decisions. For example, it may be necessary to decide, given a particular group of applicants, which ones are in the greatest need of ESL instruction; or which ones are closest to the range of proficiency that the program is designed for. On the other hand, many programs are designed for open enrollment, and the decisions are absolute (e.g., has the student attained a particular level of language proficiency or not?).

Program evaluation will influence decisions concerning the definition of the levels of proficiency that distinguish classes with the program. Decision making concerning standards will be especially critical and will need to examine such factors as student achievement in relation to length of instruction. That is, will there be enough hours of instruction to attain the prescribed level of proficiency at each class level? Thus, with program evaluation and student placement there needs to be a clearly defined interaction between proficiency/placement testing and classroom achievement testing.

Classroom Assessment and Student Advancement In additional to end-of-term achievement testing in the classroom, which can be a part of program evaluation, there are decision-making contexts such as diagnosing individual problems and assigning final grades. Diagnostic testing helps the teacher decide which parts of the curriculum need to be emphasized in a particular classroom by providing student need profiles. These decisions are largely absolute; e.g., does the student need further instruction on a particular skill or not? However, relative decisions may also be appropriate, e.g., when deciding to divide the class into proficiency level work groups. As with achievement testing, the teacher is operationalizing the language skills of concern in order to obtain information that will allow accurate decisions to be made.

The assignment of final grades (or advancement recommendations) concerns decision making in relation to student advancement and makes use of all language testing that has occurred in the classroom. End-of-term achievement testing helps the teacher make decisions concerning the degree of improvement for individual students. Other testing, such as quizzes, compositions, and homework assignments, aid in arriving at an overall decision regarding student achievement. When the concern is whether or not the student has mastered the course objectives and is ready for advancement, these decisions are necessarily absolute. The idea of grading "on the normal curve," or making relative decisions, is inappropriate, since effective instructions can (and should) result in a larger percentage of high achievers than the normal curve would allow. Judging students in relation to each other rather than in relation to the prespecified standards of the program's curriculum also assumes that the range of proficiency will not vary from classroom to classroom or from term to term. Unless student placement to level is consistently accurate and assignment to classrooms entirely random, this assumption will not be met.

Research Questions and Hypothesis Testing Another context for decision making is research. The researcher makes decisions about what questions are important and require answers. Like the classroom teacher, the researcher needs to operationalize the language skill or trait of interest in order to answer the research questions. Answering these questions is a decision-making process traditionally manifested as hypothesis testing. The researcher formulates hypotheses concerning the research question and then operationalizes the language skill or trait of interest in order to provide a test of the hypotheses. The outcome of that test leads to a decision concerning the accuracy of the hypotheses.

Competency Testing Language tests involve decisions in yet another context, one that overlaps with public domain concerns

such as quality education, multilingualism, and professional training: the issue of competency testing. A competency test is a measurement instrument which is intended to determine if an individual or group of individuals is qualified to perform some task(s). Measurement outside of language testing is replete with such tests, e.g., the bar exam, medical boards, and so on. Within language testing, interest is also high regarding such measurement. The professional body of ESL teachers, TESOL, cites "the insights gained from recent movements of competency-based program designs" as worthy of a professional position paper (TESOL, 1979).

Competency testing is not a simple task. Popham (1981) warns "the setting of standards has been a major, but well-camouflaged educational problem for centuries" which, with regard to competency tests, run into problems of setting a competency standard too high (potentially harmful to society). He does support greater trust in professional judgment, and disapproves of using arbitrariness as an argument against competency testing (Popham, 1981, pp. 373–377).

Ebel (1979) also probes the complex difficulty of what he calls "mandated assessment" (1979, pp. 2–3). He discusses competency and remarks:

What these tests of occupational competency primarily measure is an applicant's knowledge of how a job *ought* to be done .... Other factors are undoubtedly involved in success, elements that remain untested and probably untestable" (Ebel, 1979, p. 4; emphasis in the original).

In its statement of competency testing in language, TESOL is also highly aware of the "complex nature of this kind of measurement" (1979, p. 1). They go on to call for considerations affecting competency outside of measurement information, and urge multiple examinee opportunities "to demonstrate what they know; ... decisions regarding competency testing [should] never be made on the basis of a single test" (TESOL, 1979, p. 1). This call is in line with the validity discussion above; the truest (i.e., most valid) measurement may involve many tests. In addition, the TESOL statement reflects the argument for multiple measurement information sources, detailed below.

A recent development in language testing technique is intended to supplement paper-and-pencil tests and hence offer such multiple opportunities: performance testing. A performance test asks the examinee to demonstrate English skills via real world action. For example, with ESL computer operator trainees, a performance test would take place at a terminal. The examiner would give instructions and answer questions, possibly suggesting courses of action—all in English. To the extent that "computer English" exists, it ought to account for some score variance as measured by real world success on the computer. It is clear that such a measurement situation may be testing computer expertise to a large extent. However, it could also be a more valid real world performance measure because it gives the examinee a tangible goal during the test. Perhaps a balance can be struck in this regard. Ultimately, used in conjunction with paper-and-pencil measures, performance tests may offer an additional source of explanation of examinee score variance. (For an in-depth look at performance testing in language measurement, see the abstracts of the Fifth Annual Language Testing Research Colloquium, Carleton University, Ottawa, Canada, 1982. A majority of the papers there focused on this type of test.)

CAVEATS

Construct validation

Validity is a *characteristic* of a test. "Validation" is *the technical process of ascertaining validity*. Because the validity of a test is so critical, it is offered here as the first of four caveats to test users; however, this caveat does not concern validity per se, but rather constitutes a warning about the need for validation in the testing process. Specifically, a test user needs to address the question of construct validation.

Construct validity was defined above as "measurement of fit to a priori theoretical characteristics." Construct *validation* is the technical means to do so. Usually it involves:

(1) a clear statement of theory, (2) an a priori prediction of how the test(s) should behave given that theory, and (3) following administration of the test(s), a check of the fit of the test to the theory. If that fit is good, the test has been *construct validated*.

An underlying theory of some sort (call it a "theory," a "hunch," a "suspicion," etc.) must precede test development; because operationalization is the first step in forming a test instrument, some sort of theoretical stance is presumed. That is, operationalization cannot occur without a theory. Thus, construct validation is a verification of that theory, as it appears in the test.[3]

How then might one construct validate a test? For the classroom tester, it is an umbrella notion: all the effort and time spent in planning, preparing materials, teaching, and testing come together under the question: "Are my underlying beliefs (theories/hunches/suspicions) about what language is and how to teach it being upheld in this test? Did the test tap those beliefs as I predicted it would?" The classroom teacher also has the option to use research construct validation procedures described below, but nonetheless needs to constantly review the fit of the totality of the language teaching and measurement to an underlying theoretical framework. Technical research procedures for construct validation were discussed previously.

The driving purpose behind all construct validation is a caveat of which research and classroom language test users must be aware: the test must be validated against a theory. Unless that is done, the tester operates in a sort of unsupported limbo.

Test affect

Another caveat concerning language testing involves *test affect*, or examinees' reactions and attitudes toward tests. Affective concerns involving item format selection have already been discussed, above. While the cultural backgrounds of examinees may cause differential preference for certain test formats, there is evidence that certain types of tests, e.g., the oral interview, are preferable over others, across different native language groups (Scott and Madsen, 1983; Shohamy, 1983). It also appears that student reactions to tests cannot be directly related to such factors as novelty of format, previous EFL instruction, or test difficulty. On the other hand, there is evidence that "emotional responses generated by some tests may constitute a hidden bias in relation to certain cultural groups" (Scott and Madsen, 1983, p. 271).

The potential for test affect to weaken the performance of certain groups or individuals poses a serious threat to test validity (Scott and Madsen, 1983). In order to accurately interpret test scores, we must know that they represent the examinee's actual level of ability on the skill or trait being measured. Of course, there will always be a certain amount of error in our measurements. However, when we can identify obvious sorts of systematic error, such as that produced by test affect, steps must be taken to eliminate that source of error. There are several ways to attempt a reduction of negative test affect, including the use of humor, arranging the items on a test from easy to difficult, and even the use of relaxation and hypnosis (for a complete listing of references, see Scott and Madsen, 1983). Perhaps the most effective and important approach to reducing test anxiety is providing the opportunity for practice. Increased familiarity with the item format, test directions, and strategies for taking tests should reduce text anxiety and ensure more accurate measurement of student ability. Without serious consideration of test affect, the researcher runs the risk of making inaccurate interpretations of the data and the teacher runs the further risk of creating a negative classroom environment which may seriously impede the learning process.

Multiple information sources

A third caveat affecting language test users states: be aware of multiple sources of information impinging on the advancement decision. The test *alone* is not *all*.[4] Many indications of student ability may be considered. Let us examine some general types, other than a test per se.

First, there are a host of demographic, background information sources. At first blush, these may not appear as critical as a well-operationalized, reliable, valid test. (Indeed, they may not be.) For example, attendance and promptness should not overpower a test result, *but such information can explain many things.* In addition, demographic characteristics of students may not directly impinge on an actual test score but can definitely provide explanations of why some test performance turns out as it does. For example, consider a humanities ESL student who stumbles on a bit of technical test prose, versus one from physics who found a social science essay arduous. Knowledge of each individual's major is a valuable consideration, especially if some critical decision rests on comprehension of those two test prose pieces. In general, the teacher can view a test score against a backdrop of explanatory background information and demographic variables, all of which are alternate measurement information sources, none of which is a test.

Second, an alternate information source is the measurement of individual learner improvement profiles. Such measurement information can indicate attainment against specified, individually tailored student goals. This information is thus more properly a teaching *and* testing tool. For example, one such learner profile device is a learning contract, in which a pattern of needs is set before the student as formal written goals. Such a mechanism permits individualization of student differences in success rates, and accommodates variability in needs; in addition it has a motivational component. (Contract learning has been applied to ESL composition teaching and testing; cf. Davidson, 1984.)

When one considers background/ demographic information and individual learner profile measurement, one realizes that teachers often use such sources of information intuitively. An end-of-term test is, and should be, tempered by a professional judgment that takes into account multiple advancement decision information. Figure 2 formalizes this multiple source framework.

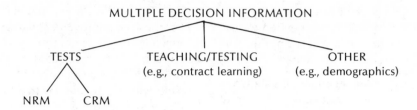

FIGURE 2 Multiple Information Sources in Student Measurement

The terms "NRM" and "CRM" are not used as they are traditionally defined—i.e., as conditions on score interpretation. Rather, they represent differing sources of information. Further, "other" may include many types of information besides demographic/background data. Thus, when a teacher makes an advancement decision, many types of information exert influence. Stated as a caveat, the above diagram advises: "When making an advancement decision, do not rely totally on a test."

The Test User and the Larger World   A final caveat affects the user of language tests. We have already seen how a larger quasi-political domain affects measurement, in the discussion of competency testing above. This can be expanded into the general caveat: do not forget that a measurement instrument operates in a larger sphere of human endeavor. Regarding testing in research, there is Sax's admonition that innovation without empirical evidence is dangerous (Sax, 1979, p. 23). Yet often, "innovation" seems to have been implemented without the evidence provided by a well-operationalized test. Furthermore, Popham, in his educational measurement text, also discusses evidence at great length and perhaps ascribes a certain political power to the tester: "In an evidence-oriented enterprise, those who control the evidence-gathering mechanisms also control the entire enterprise" (Popham, 1981, p. 6).

As applied specifically to language testing in education and research, this caveat emerges as (1) the complex of factors, other than measurement information (cf. Figure 2), which affect language advancement decisions, and (2) conversely, (as Popham's quote implies) any unjustified overconfidence in language test results. Perhaps it is simplest to phrase this caveat as: "test users should be aware of the range of consequences stemming from the power of tests."

NOTES

1.   In large-scale NRM testing development, pretest phases often focus largely on such item refinement procedures. The final revised test form has thus undergone item revision before extensive use.

2.   Recently, educational measurement and language testing have made use of a technique called Rasch modeling. This reduces the need for vast item banks, by using a small set of item calibrators. For a concise description of this procedure, see Popham, 1981, pp. 135–150.

3.   One method of construct validation that has been claimed by some is to check language test results on a native speaker population. Properly, though, NS performance is not a *theory* but a *criterion*, and it may not be appropriate in a construct validation discussion. Construct validation can and should be a concern of research and classroom test use, as outlined below.

4.   It should be noted that this is often urged by testing textbooks and test score manuals.

DISCUSSION QUESTIONS

1.   How divisible is language proficiency? Review the discussion of integrative versus discrete testing. What does your experience indicate should be the role of each test type? How would operationalization have to change to produce an integrative test versus a discrete test?

2.   In the competency testing section of this chapter mention was made of an ESL test for computer programmers. What is the difference between testing competency in a

technical field such as computer programming and testing the English needed to read computer manuals, talk with computer specialists, and interact at a terminal?

3. For each of the situations below, discuss whether a CRM or NRM test would be most appropriate:

> a. An ESL instructor wants to determine whether his students have successfully learned to write topic sentences for one-paragraph compositions.

> b. Another ESL instructor has been asked to divide her class into two equal-sized sections, one of high proficiency and one of low proficiency.

> c. The chief administrator of a large ESL institute is preparing a report to the dean, about ESL student admission quotas. A subsection of that report surveys the past three years' success in student attainment of specific course goals; here the administrator wishes to cite test evidence that each goal was measured.

> d. An ESL administrator is placing students into a four-level instructional program. Each level is defined with a clear set of objectives.

4. How do you know when a student's anxiety level is causing his test performance to decline?

SUGGESTED ACTIVITIES

1. A learning contract is a written agreement between an instructor and a student. It specifies the student's needs and goals, and states the resulting reward for successful attainment. If the student has the option for renegotiation, the contract is actually a teaching/testing instrument aimed at the student's improvement profile across time (see above). Design a contract learning system: prepare a master "communicative attainment learning contract" for ESL students in a basic speaking skills class. Write some sample contracts for students with differing

needs, and include renegotiated contracts for hypothesized improvement during the course term. Outline the method by which those contracts will be integrated into the course syllabus; include a statement of how contract results will be integrated with other measurement information that affects decisions (e.g., grades, promotion).

2. Examine the test(s) currently being used in your ESL program. Evaluate the degree to which they are CRM or NRM measures, with reference to the kind of decisions(s) made based on each test.

3. Select a current theory in language learning/acquisition research, and discuss how it would be operationalized (1) under CRM, and (2) under NRM.

4. Review a test of your choice, in terms of the cognitive requirements and affective concerns of the items (see above).

SUGGESTIONS FOR FURTHER READING

Issues in Language Testing Research.
1983. John W. Oller (ed.) Rowley, Mass.: Newbury House.

This collection of articles covers a wide range of testing concerns, including the divisibility of language proficiency, the evaluation of new instruments, cloze testing, and some new research considerations. The editor provides several interesting introductory comments, and permits the authors to rebut his comments in appendices.

Modern Educational Measurement
1981. W. J. Popham. Englewood Cliffs, N.J.: Prentice-Hall.

This text provides a comprehensive overview of educational measurement; as such it is a valuable reference. Furthermore, it details CRM and NRM approaches to measurement, indicating the situations in which one is more appropriate than the other. Professor Popham is one of the leading proponents of CRM, and lends his expertise to expand the scope of a very solid measurement textbook.

Journal of Personalized Instruction
1976 to 1981.

For ESL teachers and administrators interested in individualized instruction and measurement, e.g., contract learning (see above), this journal provides a good overview of the personalized instruction movement in education. Unfortunately, the journal disappeared in 1981. One might ponder why. (Note: Fred Keller's article in the first volume: "Goodbye, Teacher . . . " is a classic reference in individualized instruction and measurement. It is more accessible, however, as Keller (1974).)

Criterion-Referenced Measurement: State of the Art.
1980. R. A. Berk (ed.) Baltimore Md.: Johns Hopkins University Press.

As the title suggests, this collection of articles will bring the reader up to date on issues related to CRM. It is divided into sections which deal with such topics as item analysis, validity, and reliability from the CRM perspective. The discussion of different CRM approaches to these topics is quite technical at times but provides a comprehensive collection of procedures for CRM test development.

REFERENCES

Adams, M. J., and A. Collins. 1977. A schema-theoretic view of reading comprehension (Tech. Rep. No. 32). Urbana: University of Illinois, Center for the Study of Reading (ED 142 971).

Anderson, R. C. 1977. Schema-directed processes in language comprehension (Tech. Rep. No. 50). Urbana: University of Illinois, Center for the Study of Reading (ED 142 977).

Bachman, L., and A. Palmer. 1981. The construct validation of the FSI oral interview. *Language Learning*, 31, 67–86.

Bachman, L., and A. Palmer. 1982. The construct validation of some components of communicative competence. *TESOL Quarterly*, 16, 4, 449–466.

Berk, R. A. 1980a. A consumer's guide to criterion-referenced test reliability. *Journal of Educational Measurement*, pp. 186–223.

Berk, R. A. (ed.). 1980b. *Criterion-Referenced Measurement: State of the Art*. Baltimore: Johns Hopkins University Press.

Campbell, D. T., and D. W. Fiske. 1959. Convergent and discriminant validation by the multitrait-multimethod matrix. *Psychological Bulletin*, 54, 2, 81–105.

Canale, M. 1983. On some dimensions of language proficiency. In J. W. Oller, Jr. (ed.), *Issues in Language Testing Research*. Rowley, Mass.: Newbury House, 333–342.

Carrell, P. L. 1983. Three components of background knowledge in reading comprehension. *Language Learning*, 33, 2, 183–207.

Carrell, P. L., and Eisterhold. 1983. Schema theory and ESL reading pedagogy, *TESOL Quarterly*, 17, 4, 553–573.

Carver, R. P. 1974. Two dimensions of tests: psychometric and edumetric. *American Psychologist*, 24, 512–518.

Cohen, A. 1980. *Testing Language Ability in the Classroom*. Rowley, Mass.: Newbury House.

Cziko, G. A. 1983. Psychometric and edumetric approaches to language testing. In J. W. Oller, Jr. (ed.), *Issues in Language Testing Research*. Rowley, Mass.: Newbury House., 289–307.

Davidson, F., 1984. Teaching and testing ESL composition through contract learning. Paper presented at the 18th Annual TESOL Convention, Houston, March 1984.

Ebel, R. 1979. *Essentials of Educational Measurement*. Englewood Cliffs N.J.: Prentice-Hall.

Farhady, H. 1983. The disjunctive fallacy between discrete-point and integrative tests. In J. W. Oller, Jr. (ed.), *Issues in Language Testing Research*. Rowley, Mass.: Newbury House.

Fifth Annual Language Testing Research Colloquium. 1982. *Abstracts* Ottawa, Canada, Carleton University and the University of Ottawa.

Gronlund, N. 1981. *Measurement and Evaluation in Teaching*. New York, Macmillan.

Hall, W. S., S. Reder, and M. Cole. 1975. Story recall in young black and white children: Effects of racial group membership, race of experimenter, and dialect. *Developmental Psychology*, 11, 828–834.

Heaton, J. B. 1975. *Writing English Language Tests*. London, Longman.

Hudson, T. 1982. The effects of induced schemata on the "short-circuit" in L2 reading: non-decoding factors in L2 reading performance. *Language Learning*. 32, 1, 1–31.

Hudson and Lynch. 1984. Achievement testing and the ESL curriculum: The UCLA ESL exam project. Paper presented at the 18th annual TESOL Convention, Houston, March 6–11, 1984.

Johnson, P. 1982. Effects on reading comprehension of building background knowledge. *TESOL Quarterly*, 16, 4, 503–516.

Johnston, P. H. 1983. *Reading Comprehension Assessment: A Cognitive Basis*, International Reading Association.

Keller, F. S. 1974. "Goodbye Teacher . . ." In J. G. Sherman (ed.), *PSI: Personalized System of Instruction: 41 Germinal Papers: A Selection of Readings on the Keller Plan*. Menlo Park, Calif.: W. A. Benjamin, Inc.

Kerlinger, F. N. 1973. *Foundations of Behavioral Research*, 2d ed. New York: Holt, Rinehart, and Winston.

Madsen, H. S. 1983. *Techniques in Testing*. New York: Oxford University Press.

Oller, J. W., Jr. 1979. *Language Tests at School*. London: Longman.

Oller, J. W., Jr. (ed.). 1983. *Issues in Language Testing Research*. Rowley, Mass.: Newbury House.

Pedhazur, E. 1982. *Multiple Regression in Behavioral Research: Explanation and Prediction*. New York: Holt, Rinehart and Winston.

Popham, W. J. 1978. *Criterion-Referenced Measurement*. Englewood Cliffs, N.J.: Prentice-Hall.

Popham, W. J. 1981. *Modern Educational Measurement*. Englewood Cliffs, N.J.: Prentice-Hall.

Purcell, E. T. 1983. Models of pronunciation accuracy. In John W. Oller, Jr. (ed.), *Issues in Language Testing Research*. Rowley, Mass.: Newbury House.

Robertson, D. I. 1982. Toward a model for the evaluation of programs in English as a second language. In B. Kachru and R. Cowan (eds.), *TESL Studies Volume 5*. Urbana-Champaign: ESL, University of Illinois, 155–171.

Rumelhart, D., and A. Ortony. 1977. The representation of knowledge in memory. In R. C. Anderson, R. J. Spiro, and W. E. Montague (eds.), *Schooling and the Acquisition of Knowledge*. Hillsdale, N. J.: Erlbaum.

Sax, G. 1979. *Foundations of Educational Research.* Englewood Cliffs, N.J.: Prentice-Hall.

Scott, M., and H. Madsen. 1983. The influence of retesting on test affect. In J. W. Oller, Jr. (ed.), *Issues in Language Testing Research.* Rowley, Mass.: Newbury House, 270–279.

Shavelson, R. J. and N. Webb. 1981. Generalizability theory, 1973–1980. *British Journal of Mathematical and Statistical Psychology, 34,* 133–166.

Shohamy, E. 1983. Interrater and intrarater reliability of the oral interview and concurrent validity with cloze procedure in Hebrew. In John W. Oller, Jr. (ed.), *Issues in Language Testing Research.* Rowley, Mass.: Newbury House, 229–236.

TESOL. 1979. TESOL statement on statewide programs of competency testing. Washington, D.C., Teachers of English to Speakers of Other Languages.

PART V
THE IMPLEMENTATION PROCESS

INTRODUCTION

In the fifth and final section of this anthology we look at two of the areas in which the research reported in the earlier chapters has been integrated and put into practice.

First, in Olshtain's chapter we consider how language policy—given all its complexities—is ideally formulated and implemented at either the national or local level. In the final chapter by Cohen we look at bilingual education, a special language policy—calling for special methods and curricula—which aims at making proficiency in a second language *and* one's native language an integral part of the learner's total educational experience.

LANGUAGE POLICY AND THE CLASSROOM TEACHER[1]

Elite Olshtain

Modern language teaching methodology views the teacher as a multifaceted, central figure in the teaching/learning process, whose primary function has changed considerably from what it used to be in more traditional approaches. In the past, language teachers were expected to know about the language and to be able to use the language itself. They were also teaching primarily to help students learn that language through practice and careful explanation along the way. Today, in addition to these minimal requirements, teachers are expected to act as resource persons, evaluators, facilitators, and classroom managers. Moreover, classroom teachers are expected to be decision makers and policy implementors, adjusting general educational philosophies to the needs of their specific students.

In order to meet societal as well as individual needs, it is imperative that language teachers view their professional activities within a social framework broader than the immediate classroom situation. This framework should include an understanding of policy making at the community or national level, since in many cases, decisions taken at the course level have far-reaching social, cultural, economic, and political implications. This chapter will deal with some aspects of this policy-making hierarchy, and its relevance to the teaching of English as an additional language.[2]

THE FUNCTION OF LANGUAGE IN SOCIETY

Language policy is decided within a larger language setting which, according to Gumperz (1968, p. 102), refers to the "totality of communication roles" in a speech community. Language policy decisions are therefore af-fected and guided by the forces operating within the larger language setting. As teachers or policy makers, our first concern is to know the broader language setting within which we teach.

The broadest perspective of the language setting defines the community as basically monolingual, bilingual, or multi-lingual. In the monolingual community, the language that most members learn as their mother tongue is also the language used for all communal functions; therefore, overall policy concerning that language is not too complex. The situation becomes considerably more intricate when within the same speech community there are two major groups of speakers (equal in number or not); in this case the allocation of roles to each of the two languages may become an issue of ethnic or national identity and social or economic power. The situation may be further complicated by a multilingual situation where three or more groups share the same political, geographical, or cultural community, yet speak different languages. This type of situation may necessitate the establishment of one language as the accepted intergroup means of communication.

In the multilingual community, each language—depending on its status—may play different roles. The basic distinction between a standard language and a vernacular (Spolsky, 1978)[3] is significant in terms of the potential functions a language can fulfill. A standard language is a language which has four attributes: standardization, autonomy, historicity, and vitality. Standardization relates to a formal codification which allows for norms of "correctness" and usage, usually including a writing system. Accordingly, dictionaries and grammar books exist to describe a standard language. Autonomy refers to the fact that the speakers of the language perceive their language as unique and independent, and therefore have a name for it. Historicity refers to the fact that the present state of the language has grown as the result of normal, temporal development. Vitality refers to the fact that there is a community of native speakers who have acquired the language at home as a mother tongue, and whose children continue to acquire that language in the same way. By this definition of a standard language we imply that an official, or national, language must be a standard language; and, of course, if we look for examples among official European languages, we find that they all are standard languages with these four attributes.

A language which has three of the four attributes, but lacks standardization, is referred to as a vernacular. A vernacular is autonomous, historic, and has vitality, but it lacks formal norms. In a multilingual society, such languages have a lower status than a standard language and are, of course, very poor candidates for official functions. In such communities there are many children who reach school speaking only the vernacular and who have to learn the standard language as a school language. Sometimes, the school may decide to teach the vernacular and eventually help it become a standard language. The situation is somewhat more complex when one or more vernaculars lack autonomy and are therefore only dialects, which are even lower in status than vernaculars.

The official language of a speech community is the language used by law in political and cultural activities on a nationwide basis. An official language can also be the national language in a monolingual society, or in a situation where most of the members of the community speak that language; however, in multilingual societies, generally the official language is not also the national language—especially not in the early years of statehood.

In a multilingual society, where most of the speakers do not share the same language, it is necessary for the community to adopt a language of wider communication which will be acquired by most members as a second language, and which will serve as the means of communication between language groups.

The term LWC (language of wider communication) was coined by Ferguson in 1962 in his paper in Ferguson (1971). He suggests placing languages on a scale in terms of their actual use in the written medium in order to select the best candidates for the role of LWC. He presents the following scale:

W0 — a language which is not used for normal written purposes;
W1 — a language which is used for normal written purposes;
W2 — a language in which original research in the physical sciences is regularly published;
W3 — a language in which translations and résumés of scientific work in other languages are published regularly (pp. 52–53).

On the basis of the above scale it seems that a language which is used at the W3 level is a very suitable candidate for an LWC at the international level, in other words, for communication and contact with other speech communities which do not share the same language. Such an LWC is often referred to as an "international language", to distinguish it from an LWC used for communication within a multilingual speech community, such as the function of Amharic in Ethiopia, Swahili in East Africa, and English in India. In the latter case, the term "auxiliary language," which was suggested by Richards (1978), might also be useful.

The LWC as an international language can best be defined as a world language used to enable communities whose primary languages are not widely used outside their own area to communicate with members of other speech communities either for the promotion of foreign trade or in order to gain access to scientific, technical, and literary materials that do not exist in their own language. Sometimes such an LWC fulfills major functions within the community itself, e.g., when it has an official or semiofficial status. Even then, however, its main role is most probably to further the process of modernization by allowing for contact with the world outside the speech community.

There is little doubt that today English has gained the strongest and most widespread position as an LWC throughout the world. This spread of English, described and quantified in Fishman, Cooper, and Conrad (1977), has increased greatly in the last decade or two. English as the target language to be taught or learned in any community must therefore be viewed within the broader language setting, and the function that English plays in that particular setting must be defined most carefully (see Olshtain, 1979, 1980, for further elaboration of the following model).

ENGLISH AS THE TARGET LANGUAGE

In describing the complex factors that influence the role of English around the world, diverse elements have to be considered both independently and in the way in which they interact to affect language policy. In the previous section of this paper, we discussed the language setting within which the learning of the language is taking place; this is most certainly one of the important factors that affect policy making. Second, we need to evaluate the function of English in that particular environment and, accordingly, societal and individual needs that learners have in their acquisition of the language. In relation to the function of English in various speech communities, a number of terms have evolved: English as a second language (ESL), English as a foreign language (EFL), English as an international language, English as an auxiliary language, and English as an additional language. In order to define and evaluate the efficiency of each of these terms, we will set up a number of factors that will help place the terms on a continuum:

1. The setting within which the target language is learned in terms of language use
2. Societal needs for using the target language
3. The role of the target language within the educational system

4. Contact with the target speech community
5. National goals relating to the use of the target language

The Language Setting

English as a target language can be learned in one of four settings according to the above factors:

1. In a monolingual English-speaking community
2. In a multilingual society, where it functions as the intracommunity lingua franca
3. In a monolingual or multilingual society, where it functions only as an international lingua franca or LWC
4. In a school as a subject with no other special status

In spite of the fact that English is the most widely used LWC in the world today, it can function in any of the four settings described above. Thus setting 1 represents any of the English-speaking countries in the world: the United States, Australia, the United Kingdom, or New Zealand. In these countries, English can be considered the native language of the vast majority of the population. In setting 1, English is the only official language; all official activities are carried out in English and all facets of social life require the use of English. Immigrants to these countries, or people living in them for various periods of time, have to acquire English for basic survival needs and certainly for purposes of integration if they want to become part of the national and social environment. Furthermore, learners of English in an English-speaking country are in constant contact with the target language and the target culture (except for very special cases of "enclosure" where immigrants remain separated from the host environment). Learning English in setting 1 is referred to as ESL (English as a second language) since the learner—child or adult—may go on speaking the original language at home but use the second language in most situations outside the home.

Setting 2 is very different from setting 1, though learning English under these circumstances may also be referred to as ESL. In this setting we can include two types of countries or speech communities: countries in which English is the only official language but is not the native language of the majority of the community members, e.g., Botswana, Fiji, Gambia, Ghana, Liberia, and Nigeria. In most of these cases, English was the language of the former colonial power and thus remains the most important language in which all official activities are conducted. It is viewed by the members of the community as a vehicle for conducting legal, economic, and social transactions and, of course, it is used in the school system; while these are multilingual societies with a common official language, each language group views itself as distinct from all others with a different native language. Other cases that can be classified as belonging to setting 2 are countries in which English is one of two or more official languages. In most such countries, English is the language used for communication among nationalities or language groups that do not share the same language, e.g., India, Singapore, and South Africa. In most of the countries, English is gradually being adopted as the national unifying language, and speakers coming from these countries may feel that their particular kind of spoken English identifies them as belonging to their specific country (Richards, 1978). What is common to setting 2 is the fact that acquiring English as the target language is imperative for all members of the community, since the only way for them to function successfully in all facets of community life is to master English. On the other hand, while they are at home they may continue to speak their first language. Furthermore, English as it develops in these countries will soon be recognized as a dialect, since contact with a monolingual English-speaking community is limited. The function of English in such communities is often referred to as that of an auxiliary language (Richards, 1978); many sociolinguists have claimed that this type of English is a separate dialect that need not retain as its model English spoken in the United States or Britain since the major

objective of learners of English in this situation is to function within their own national entities and not to communicate with English speakers in other countries.

Setting 3 includes communities whose primary language is not one of wider communication, and therefore, as part of their contact with the international community, they must use an LWC which in most cases is English. Here again we might want to divide the countries into two groups: countries in which English has a special status, although it is not one of the official languages, e.g., Burma, Israel, Ethiopia, Kenya, Malaysia, and others[4] (Fishman et al., 1977, pp. 7–10); and countries where English is viewed as a crucial vehicle for international communication and is therefore given higher status in the school system than other foreign languages, e.g., the Scandinavian countries. In this setting we may refer to the study of English as either ESL or EFL, depending on its function as a language in education. For instance, in cases where English becomes the medium of instruction during at least part of the educational process, the use of English may be similar to that in an ESL situation; however, where English is only a preferred foreign language, the setting is EFL. In setting 3 it is possible to function without English, although knowledge of English can provide distinct advantages with regard to advancement in education, work, or social status. Furthermore, the support system in English is much more accessible than in setting 4, which is purely a foreign language situation. In setting 3, English is usually a compulsory school subject and one that is highly valued. It is usually the case that the main objective of learning English in setting 3 is to communicate with speakers of English from other countries, and therefore the target English model is very important. In such cases there is a need for an international LWC and contact with English-speaking communities is very important.

In setting 3, the learner has to be proficient in his/her first language or the local official language in order to function in society; English is an additional language.

Setting 4, which probably includes the rest of the world, refers to countries where English is only one foreign language among

TABLE 1 Settings in Which English is Learned

ESL		EFL	
1	2	3	4
Monolingual English-speaking community (most supportive environment)	English as an auxiliary language	English as an international language	English as a foreign language (least supportive environment)
Examples			
Australia	Fiji	Burma	France
United Kingdom	India	Israel	Germany
United States	Nigeria	Malaysia	Spain
New Zealand	Singapore	Scandinavia	(and most other countries)

other foreign languages. It may have more importance as a foreign language, in which case resource allocation is more generous for English than for the other languages; or it may just be one of two or three languages from which a high school student can choose, as is the case in most countries in the Council of Europe. In this setting, English is limited to the English classroom—the support system does not make use of English (even movies and television program are dubbed with the local language rather than using English subtitles) and English need only be learned for international communication. Because of the rapid spread of English as an LWC throughout the world, it is often the case that the majority of learners prefer English to other foreign languages, but this is not by official decision. Setting 4 is, of course, the typical situation in which English is learned as a foreign language. The four settings, placed on a continuum from the most supportive environment for the learning of the language to the least supportive, are shown in Table 1.

Societal needs

Societal needs with respect to the target language must be defined on the basis of the objective and the practical ways in which the members of the community need to use that language. The broadest and most global classification of such needs might simply view two perspectives as distinctive: a "utilitarian" versus a "nonutilitarian" approach. The utilitarian approach is compatible with communicative objectives which emphasize various purposes, such as reading for professional and academic purposes, speaking for very specific occupational purposes, or even overall communicative proficiency for higher-level jobs that set such requirements. On the other hand, a "nonutilitarian" approach might emphasize general educational objectives, such as developing the learner's intellectual power, increasing his or her personal knowledge and literary competence; or perhaps developing a better understanding of other cultures, or even focusing on personal goals where success in language learning is seen as a process of self-actualization.

If the national or official language of the community where the target language is learned is a world language (W3 in Ferguson's terms), it is very likely that the learning of another language will be mostly nonutilitarian. The exceptions arise in cases where there are specific reasons to focus on the utilitarian aspect, such as a large immigrant population which speaks the target language, or the need to travel to countries where the target language is spoken. This is often the case in English-speaking countries. If, however, as discussed in the previous section of this paper, the language setting is 2, 3 or 4, it is more likely that the objectives will be utilitarian in nature since English will have to fulfill functions that the local language cannot.

Whichever official objectives are stated formally, we cannot be sure that they actually reflect "true" societal needs. It is therefore necessary to survey and evaluate societal needs both qualitatively and quantitively. Perhaps the simplest way to evaluate the perceived needs as viewed by the members of the community itself is to collect data on the public's perception of the needs for the target language. (See Eastman, 1983, Chapter 7, for examples.) In order to obtain a useful sample of such perceived needs, we have to ensure a representative sample of different learner groups that make up the community: thus, the educated strata may need the target language for advancement in their professional positions; blue-collar workers may need it to use manuals accompanying technical equipment; and workers in the tourism industry may need it mainly to communicate in the spoken language. The language-policy process must be based on a detailed mapping of all such areas in which the need for the target language can be evaluated and defined.

Even when societal needs have been carefully investigated, further verification needs to be done to ensure that there is no conflict between individual attitudes toward the target language and the actual utilitarian needs for that language. Thus, in a previously colonized country, attitudes toward the language of the earlier colonizing power might be negative, although there may exist a real need for citizens to acquire the LWC for internal and external functions. Often such conflicts are covertly embedded in policy decisions, and when the question of allocation of resources arises, decisions may be based on attitudes rather than on real needs. Furthermore, national considerations[5] may require a fostering of the local language and thus indirectly restrict the use of the LWC.

In order to reach a feasible set of definitions of the community needs for the target language, we must obtain a thorough description of the role of English in three major areas: (1) in education, (2) in the labor market (for economic purposes), and (3) in furthering the process of modernization (i.e., providing access to science and technology). Ferguson and Heath (1981) provide information on these interrelated roles of English in the United States. Rubin and Jernudd (1971) offer

discussions of the types of language issues, often including uses of English and other languages of wider communication, that affect developing countries.

Language in education

In education, for any setting where English is not the native language of most of the members in the community (settings 2, 3, and 4), we need to consider two major issues: the role of English as a means for furthering one's education and the effectiveness of the existing curriculum and learning situation. The first and broadest question is whether English is the medium of instruction in the school system, in other words, whether the student studies geography, mathematics, and other general subjects in the native language or in English. Either of these two possibilities may exist in settings 2 or 3. However, if English is ever the medium of instruction, then in terms of the dichotomy between ESL and EFL, the situation more closely approximates an ESL context.

Situations where English is the medium of instruction can also differ. In some countries, the medium of instruction is the native language only during the early years of schooling with English being used elsewhere, while in other countries English is the medium of instruction only at university level. In other cases English as a medium of instruction may be limited to certain subjects for which no suitable teaching materials exist in the local language(s). In order to evaluate the true role of English in the school system, we need to have a full picture of all subjects taught at school, all available textbooks and other teaching materials, as well as some measure of the teachers' proficiency level in English, if most teachers are not native speakers. In a setting such as 2, there may be a local English dialect which is the target language, as in Singapore, for instance.

Another question arises in cases where English is not the medium of instruction: what is the role of English as a language of study? This question refers to the degree to which learners depend on their knowledge of English for access to the subject matter of their choice.

In other words, what level of English is actually necessary, for instance, for a person studying engineering at a university? Are there many textbooks, lectures, and other study materials in the native language, or are they available in English only? English as a language of study is sometimes referred to as EAP (English for academic purposes) but, in fact, the scope of a language for study is wider than that, and also includes scientific and technological subjects that may not exist at the university level, e.g., courses in vocational high schools or special professional courses.

We should also consider briefly the impact that a testing or examination system can have on the teaching of English. In countries as diverse as Japan, Egypt, and Brazil, for example, English is a test subject on university entrance examinations or on a national examination used to determine university eligibility. In such cases, almost all school-based teaching and learning of English is geared toward the impending examination. Since these examinations tend to focus only on grammar-translation skills and discrete points of grammar and vocabulary, this is what gets taught in English classes—not communicative competence. Thus the role of the examination system is also an important policy issue in that it may be necessary to change the type of English tests used if one wants to improve the way English is being taught.[6]

Once we have established the role of English in education, it is necessary to compare the outcomes of the existing English program and the actual need for English as a language of study. It is possible that a gap exists between the perceived need, as indicated in the public survey, and the stated educational goals. In such instances we might expect to find many private schools and courses offering special English programs, in response to the public's demand for "more English" than the system supplies. New policy making in this context will require decisions that can narrow the gap between outcome and need. In fact, if policy is to represent actual need, such evaluation will have to be conducted periodically (by experts in the field) so as not to allow the discrepancy between needs and stated goals to increase harmfully.

National goals

Political, national, and economic considerations are often closely interlaced and can therefore be viewed as an integrated factor. At the initial fact-finding stage, however, we need to devote some attention to each of these factors separately. Viewed at the highest level, political considerations have to do with the particular regime in power, and how it views the question of language in general and the LWC specifically.

National considerations are particularly relevant to nations which are still in the midst of the process of nationalizing, which is defined by Fishman (1968) as a sequence of stages moving from the ethnic group to the nationality. During this process, language comes to be viewed differently by the members of the group. Eastman (1983) and Judd (1978) discuss additional political considerations related to language.

Economic considerations relate to the particular community's or nationality's motivation to become an integral part of the worldwide community in terms of technological, economic, and scientific activities. For developing nations there are stages at which there is a conflict between the need to become part of the worldwide community, which requires a process of rapid modernization, and at the same time a need to develop a national self-identity. From the point of view of national identity, it is very important to establish the national language and direct all resources to bringing that about. Ferguson (1971) explains the significance of language in nationhood:

It is tacitly assumed by many that one of the features of the ideal nationhood is the possession of a standardized national language. The absolute ideal would apparently be a language which has a community of native speakers coterminous with the national boundaries and which has a single accepted norm of pronunciation, spelling, grammar, and vocabulary, used for all levels of speaking and writing, including both a unique national literature and work in modern science (p. 66).

This ideal situation that Ferguson is referring to does not usually exist; therefore, the combination of political, national, and economic considerations may also involve a choice between efficiency and instrumentality versus authenticity.

Fishman (1968) explains authenticity as related to questions of identity and sociocultural integration. Thus, it seems that authenticity involves the national or local language, while instrumentality and efficiency involve the LWC. The immediate needs of a developing nation might be to consider the language in terms of "efficiency" first, and to give it priority in the early stages of independence. Authenticity remains to be considered for long-range evaluation and need not necessarily be implemented immediately.

In a country which is at a developing stage in terms of modernization but has, on the other hand, a well-established, classical language, there might be a conflict between the process of modernization and the need to maintain the purity of the national language.

In many societies there has been strong resistance to the assimilation of borrowed terms from a world language. Instead, modern classical languages have tried to draw terms for new concepts from their ancient variants or mother languages: Romance languages from Latin, modern Greek from classical Greek, modern Arabic from classical Arabic, Hebrew from ancient Hebrew, Hindi from Sanskrit, and so on. The generation of new words from ancient resources is in many cases a way to combat the borrowing of foreign words. When an LWC is used widely in a society, however, there is a very good chance that a considerable amount of borrowing of words and concepts from the LWC will take place.

Economic considerations can be viewed as affecting two quite different spheres: on the one hand, there are economic developments in the country which provide incentives for the members of the society to learn English, because instrumentally it will help them progress in their fields of interest. On the other hand, there are economic limitations, mainly in terms of fund allocation, that need to be taken into account when policy is made. These two different types of economic considerations might be in conflict most of the time, and the making of certain choices will depend on national priorities. Economic considerations must therefore be viewed within the overall context of national, political, and economic factors.

THE DECISION-MAKING HIERARCHY

General policy making at the national level can be broadly defined as the formulation of certain governing principles which can guide a course of action. Once such policy is formulated and legislated, there is a national commitment to the goals and values defined in that policy.

In setting 1, where the target language is also the language of the community within which learning takes place, policy decisions will be influenced largely by the ideology affecting immigration and the assimilation that immigrants should undergo. Thus, the "melting pot" ideology led to policy decisions which brought about rapid and intensive assimilation (which was not always successful) to the complete disregard of the learner's first language. Recently, ideology in most countries of immigration has changed, and emphasis has been placed on bilingual programs in order to allow for a more gradual transition from the first language to the second. Most English-speaking countries have also come to recognize the need to design special programs for young immigrants joining the school system, and, as a part of such programs, ESL courses have been developed in many school systems.

The system is somewhat different where English is the LWC. The three branches of government—the executive, legislative, and judicial authorities—are involved in policy making. The initiation of policy making can come from any of these three authorities but is most likely to be promoted and directed by the executive branch. Thus the minister (or secretary) will set up an advisory committee which will be the actual policy-making authority, for the purposes of the present discussion.

All governmental decisions or decisions of the various advisory committees stem from three main sources: underlying ideology, various interest groups, and research related to national needs. These three factors bear upon the policy process, and the degree to which any of them may be influential at any particular time varies greatly according to circumstances. In particular, the mobility of interest groups may affect policy making considerably, and create conflicts in which each group may try to gain some advantage over the others.

The question therefore arises as to which of these groups in the community influences governmental policy. In the present paper, our concern is with policy making related to the teaching of the LWC (English) and, accordingly, the sphere of operation is the educational system. Policy making concerned with the LWC should be viewed as an integral part of the overall educational policy. Different societies may place different degrees of priority on the educational system, and during certain periods of time such priorities may change. It is therefore necessary for the language teacher to understand the principles guiding the overall educational policy in order to relate the language policy decisions to that framework.

The high-level formulated policy has to be translated into operational terms, so that it can eventually reach the classroom: to this end it is handed down to a series of lower-level agencies. One such lower-level agency could be a syllabus committee nominated to design an operational framework for language teaching within the whole school system (in a highly centralized system) or a suitable program for one school or course (in a decentralized system). Such a syllabus committee may require a relatively long period of time in order to complete its task and produce a comprehensive syllabus which incorporates the policy features established at the higher level. Furthermore, such a committee, which should consist of experts in language teaching, sociolinguistics, language teachers, and materials developers, will have to consider all the relevant language teaching theories and evaluate their compatibility with the specified needs and goals.

Once the syllabus is formulated, the next step in the policy hierarchy involves even lower-level agencies: a materials construction team or committee (sometimes a publisher is commissioned to carry out this job), a teacher training committee, an examination committee, and an evaluation committee. All of these agencies will need to further redefine the goals in practical terms suited to the process of selecting methods, procedures, and techniques of implementation. Such decisions will of course be governed by factors related to financial as well as human resources. As a result of the function of these committees or agencies, materials will be produced, examinations prepared, and evaluation systems developed. Is there any room for further policy making at the classroom level? Our belief is that even within the tightest and most controlled system there are very significant decisions the classroom teacher needs to make within the wider framework that has been described so far. Thus the teacher's role will be discussed in the final section of this chapter.

THE ENGLISH LANGUAGE TEACHER

The final and perhaps most important policy decisions are made in the classroom. These decisions need to fit the particular student population, their specific needs, and the learning environment within which the course is given. Although ideally it should be shared with the students, the responsibility for decision making lies mainly with the teacher. The teacher has the difficult task of translating the overall policy into the specific situation and of finding ways to involve the students in the actual implementation of this policy.

The decisions that need to be taken at the course or classroom level fall into several major categories:

1. Goals for the course: these should fit the overall goals for learning English, yet be suited to the particular group of learners at hand.

2. Goals for individual students: although the course goals are suited to the group as a whole, it is often necessary to adapt these goals to some of the students in order to allow for individual preferences or limitations.

3. Choice of language content and choice of general content: the language content needs to be suited to the students' level of knowledge at the beginning of the course, and to the goals specified for the course; however, this decision is affected by the particular approach to language learning favored by both teacher and students. Furthermore, the choice of general content is very important since it has to suit the students in terms of their age, experiential and cultural background, special interests, etc.

4. Choice of language activities: the activities in which students participate during the course of study have to be related to the general goals for the course and to the particular learning situation.

5. The role of the learner: the teacher and the students need to decide together what role the learners will play in the learning process. Modern methodology claims that the more involved student is likely to be the more successful student. The teacher needs to find out how students can become more involved in making their own choices and decisions in the learning process.

In order to cope with the decision-making process at the course level, modern language teachers have to develop a number of important attributes; they need to become flexible planners, keen observers, resource persons, positive counselors and constant evaluators. To this end, Yalden (1983) also provides several other useful guidelines for specifying learner goals and needs.

A flexible planner focuses on a variety of resource materials and on a variety of student activities, thus allowing for adaptations and changes to fit circumstances. Although the major elements of classroom management are still: (1) considerations of time, (2) specific daily goals, (3) selection of content, and (4) selection of learners' tasks, the plan must be flexible enough so as to allow students to make some of their own choices and contributions.

In order to be a flexible planner, the teacher has to rely considerably on observa-tion during the learning process. A keen observer develops genuine interest and friendly curiosity about the students, their interests, and their difficulties. Teacher decisions are thus based on close observation and on constant evaluation of these observations. As a result, the role of the teacher as a resource person can center around the following major tasks:

1. Provision of suitable language input via authentic, carefully chosen texts (both oral and written)

2. Provision of tasks and activities which will allow learners to experience natural use of the target language

3. Provision of learning aids which will enhance students' individual task completion

4. Provision of tools for individual student self-evaluation and feedback

5. Provision of suitable ways in which the learners can express their needs and wishes.

The actual implementation of the global language policy is therefore carried out at the classroom and course level. In order to do this, teachers must be well aware of all decisions made at the higher levels of the policy-making hierarchy because the teacher's job is to build a bridge between those broad decisions and the learning process that takes place in the classroom.

NOTES

1. The author wishes to thank Mary McGroarty for her insightful comments and suggestions on an earlier version of this chapter.

2. The term "additional language" has a wider scope than either "foreign" or "second" language and refers to any additional language beyond the first language which a person has acquired.

3. Spolsky (1978) defines a vernacular as being similar to a standard language in all respects except for standardization, which is something a vernacular lacks (p. 25).

4. Declared policy in such countries focuses on the "principal language," which is not English, yet it permits the use of English in internal affairs.

5. In a new state with a national language of a W-1 type (according to Ferguson's definition), language policy is likely to focus on promoting the use of the language toward a W-3 type. This may often require some declared restriction on the use of the LWC.

6. We have not explicitly dealt with another serious matter involving language teaching and language testing; namely, to what extent do language tests measure language proficiency rather than some other global attribute such as intelligence or IQ? See Oller and Perkins (1978) for good coverage of this issue.

DISCUSSION QUESTIONS

1. How important is it for the language teacher to have a clear picture of the language setting in which he or she teaches?

2. How would the teaching of English be different in settings 1, 2, 3, and 4 with respect to language exposure, contact with target language speakers, and anticipated outcomes of the course?

3. In what situations might societal needs be different from individual needs? How would this difference manifest itself?

4. Discuss "the classroom teacher as a policy maker" in a situation familiar to you.

SUGGESTED ACTIVITIES

1. Make a survey of the language situation in your community and try to describe the setting from the point of view of English as a target language.

2. Try to define all languages in your area in terms of Ferguson's scale: WO-W1-W2-W3. Is there a possible candidate for an LWC in addition to English?

3. If you are not living in a non-English speaking community, choose any such community and get as much information on it as you can in order to decide what needs for English that community might have.

4. Analyze the English language syllabus in the country in which you teach or the syllabus of a particular school or specific course of study and evaluate the information on societal and individual needs.

SUGGESTIONS FOR FURTHER READING

If classroom teachers want to be in a position to influence language policy at higher levels, they must, first of all, have good knowledge of current trends in language teaching theory, methodology, and syllabus design. The following references are useful in providing this needed background:

Communicative Competence: Theory and Classroom Practice.
1983. S. J. Savignon. Reading, Mass.: Addison-Wesley.

The Communicative Teaching of English—Principles and Exercise Typology.
1981. C. N. Candlin (ed.). Longman.

The Functional-Notional Approach—From Theory to Practice.
1983. M. Finocchiaro, and C. Brumfit. Oxford University Press.

Speaking in Many Tongues—Essays in Foreign Language Teaching.
1983. W. M. Rivers. Cambridge University Press.
Classroom teachers should also have some basic knowledge of language testing as part of their policy-implementing and policy-making responsibilities. The following two references are useful, and they are readable even if one has little or no background in language testing:

Testing Language Ability in the Classroom.
1980. A. D. Cohen. Rowley, Mass.: Newbury House.

Techniques in Testing.
1983. H. S. Madsen. New York: Oxford University Press.

REFERENCES

Eastman, C. M. 1983. *Language Planning.* San Francisco, Calif.: Chandler and Sharp.

Ferguson, C. A. 1971. *Language Structure and Language Use.* Essays by Ferguson, selected by A. S. Dil, Stanford University Press.

Ferguson, C. A., and S. B. Heath (eds.). 1981. *Language in the USA.* New York: Cambridge University Press.

Fishman, J. 1968. Nationality-nationalism and nation-nationalism. In Fishman, Ferguson, and Das Gupta (1968).

*Fishman, J., R. L. Cooper, and W. W. Conrad. 1977. *The Spread of English: The Sociology of Language as an Additional Language.* Rowley, Mass.: Newbury House.

Fishman, J., C. Ferguson, and J. Das Gupta. 1968. *Language Problems of Developing Nations.* New York: Wiley.

Gumperz, J. J. 1968. Types of linguistic communities. In Gumperz (1971), *Language and Social Groups.* Stanford University Press.

Judd, E. L. 1978. Language policy and TESOL: socio-political factors and their influence on the profession. In C. Blatchford and J. Schachter, *On TESOL '78.* Washington, D.C.: TESOL.

*Presently out of print.

Oller, J. W., and K. Perkins. 1978. *Language in Education: Testing the Tests*. Rowley, Mass.: Newbury House.

Olshtain, E. 1979. A theoretical model for developing the teaching of a language of wider communication (LWC) on a national scale. Ph.D. dissertation in Applied Linguistics, UCLA.

Olshtain, E. 1980. The fact-finding phase in the policy-making process: the case of an LWC (language of wider communication). In Povey (1980).

Povey, J. F. 1980. *Language Planning and Language Teaching: Essays in Honor of Clifford H. Prator*. Culver City, Calif.: English Language Services.

*Presently out of print.

Richards, J. C. 1978. The dynamics of English as an international, foreign, second, and auxiliary language. Paper presented at a conference on English as an international auxiliary language, East-West Culture Learning Institute, The East-West Center, Honolulu, April 1-15.

Rubin, J., and B. Jernudd. 1971. *Can Language Be Planned?* Honolulu, Hawaii: University Press of Hawaii.

*Spolsky, B. 1978. *Educational Linguistics*. Rowley, Mass.: Newbury House.

*Spolsky, B., and R. L. Cooper. 1977. *Frontiers of Bilingual Education*. Rowley, Mass.: Newbury House.

Yalden, J. 1983. *The Communicative Syllabus*. Oxford and New York: Pergamon Press.

BILINGUAL EDUCATION[1]

Andrew D. Cohen

Bilingual education has now enjoyed over two decades of implementation in the United States. In 1963, Dade County in Florida started a public school Spanish-English bilingual program for Cuban Americans and Anglos. In 1967, the Bilingual Education Act was added to the Elementary and Secondary Education Act of 1965. Federally funded Title VII bilingual education programs began in 1969. After that states passed legislation to fund bilingual programs (U.S. Commission on Civil Rights, 1975; Swanson, 1974; Bilingual Education Service Center, 1975). During the 1978–1979 school year, the federal government spent $150 million to fund 564 bilingual programs for 253,000 children, mostly Spanish-surnamed (*Los Angeles Times,* May 10, 1978, p. 17). Although the number of limited-English-speaking children in the United States has increased, federal support for bilingual education has declined. In fiscal year 1983 the Federal Title VII Program spent approximately $138 million and served an estimated 234,000 students in 555 projects. Rather than emphasizing only bilingual education, the Federal government has authorized a broadened range of instructional approaches that do not require instruction in the child's native language (U.S. Department of Education, 1984, pp. 1–2). During the same period of time, state funding levels for instructional services to limited-English-proficiency students have steadily increased, and in 1983 states spent approximately $224 million and served an estimated 925,000 students (U.S. Department of Education, 1984, p. 3).

Bilingual programs have been a reality in other parts of the world for many years (Andersson and Boyer, 1977; Mackey, 1972; Gudschinsky, 1977; Modiano, 1966, 1968; Davis, 1967; Lambert and Tucker, 1972; Macnamara, 1966; Malherbe, 1946, 1969; Engle, 1975; Cohen, 1975b; Bowen, 1977; Fishman, 1976; Spolsky and Cooper, 1978; Lewis, 1977). The basic difference between the foreign and the American experiences is that American bilingual education has been initiated primarily to correct an educational ill in the society: minority-group children were not experiencing regular progress through schools offering only the traditional brand of monolingual instruction. Although the learning of English was viewed as an economic and social necessity, it was felt that simultaneous or prior use of the children's native language would better combat minority students' low self-concept and sense of failure that often led to their being early school dropouts.

Abroad, the experience has largely been one of enhancing the linguistic repertoire of students. Prestige and learning have been linked to knowledge of other languages, particularly in the European experience.

Some American programs have had a few majority-group children participating, ostensibly to make them fluent speakers of a second language and to improve interethnic relations. These children have not generally been considered part of the so-called "target" population because they are not experiencing failure at school and are not frequent dropouts.

As the interest in bilingual education has increased in the United States, review articles and books on the subject have likewise become more prevalent (see, for example, Pacheco, 1973; Swanson, 1974; Spolsky, 1972; Andersson and Boyer, 1977; Blanco, 1977; Gaarder, 1977; Mackey and Beebe, 1977; Troike and Modiano, 1975; Stern and Weinrib, 1977; Alatis, 1980; Paulston, 1980; Trueba and Barnett-Mizrahi, 1979; Fishman and Keller, 1982). Clearly the English as a second language (ESL) teacher in the United States needs to know something about bilingual education because it has now become a reality of major proportions. Not only is ESL one component of a good bilingual education program, but teachers who began as ESL specialists are now often finding themselves involved with bilingual instruction. Available elementary and secondary school jobs are sometimes in bilingual education, as opposed to ESL alone. The phenomenon of bilingual education therefore warrants attention in an ESL text (see, for example, Alatis and Twaddell, 1976; Saville-Troike, 1976).

This chapter will (1) define bilingualism and bilingual education as practiced in the United States; (2) discuss models for bilingual programs, and the various educational settings for such programs; (3) note selected factors concerning the children and teachers involved, as well as problems in teaching bilingualism; (4) point out conflicts in initiating and researching such programs; and (5) indicate potential outcomes of bilingual education in the United States.

BILINGUALISM

Although the term "bilingualism" is frequently used, the users rarely define what they mean when they use the term (John and Horner, 1971). Jakobovits (1970) points out that both nonprofessional and professional judges have their own versions of "folk bilingualism." To the nonprofessional judge, things such as accent, pronunciation, and fluency may be given a disproportionate degree of importance. Thus, a speaker with a poor accent and less fluency but with greater knowledge of the language might not impress them as being bilingual. Some professionals require equal facility in two languages before they are willing to talk of bilingualism, while others are willing to speak of "incipient" bilinguals (Diebold, 1974).

Bilingualism actually refers to differential ability in the productive skills, speaking and writing, and in the receptive skills, listening and reading, associated with two languages. Macnamara terms bilinguals "persons who possess at least one of the language skills even to a minimal degree in their second language" (Macnamara, 1967, pp. 59–60). But

what constitutes a language? As Gumperz (1967, 1969) has documented with language groups in India, for example, peoples' perceptions of language may crosscut long-existing notions of what languages are, especially in places where languages are in contact (see Weinreich, 1968). It is possible, for instance, that one variety of a Chicano's speech may be viewed as English with Spanish "mixed in," Spanish with English "mixed in," or a variety combining both languages.[2]

Psychologists have referred to bilinguals as either "coordinate" or "compound" (Ervin and Osgood, 1954). Coordinate bilinguals are thought to have learned their two languages in separate functional contexts where direct translation from one language to the other was unlikely (e.g., English from playmates in the neighborhood and Spanish from the parents at home). Coordinate bilinguals are said to keep their two languages separate. They do not translate between their two languages when encoding and decoding information in one or the other. Compound bilinguals, on the other hand, are said to have learned their second language in a situation which encourages a translation approach, such as at school (Saville and Troike, 1971). When compound bilinguals speak or write in their second language, it is felt that they are not thinking in that language to the extent that there is grammatical, lexical, and phonological influence from the native language. Weinreich (1968) referred to this phenomenon of formulating second language thoughts in the native language as "interference." Selinker (1969) preferred the term "negative transfer," in contrast to "positive" transfer.

Fishman (1966) warns of labeling bilingual individuals as coordinate or compound, since many bilinguals show signs of both kinds of behavior, depending on the topic, the speakers, and other factors. Saville and Troike (1971) try to stress that coordinate and compound bilingualism are extremes and that few bilinguals would be purely one or the other type. Segalowitz (1977) offers a brief but thorough review of the empirical attempts to demonstrate that compound or coordinate language acquisition background really does have different behavioral consequences for the bilingual. He reports that the evidence is ambiguous at best.

This distinction between "compound" and "coordinate" appeared to have a certain degree of validity with reference to linguistic outcomes in a bilingual program that I evaluated (Cohen, 1975b). Two groups of Spanish-speaking Mexican-American students were studied longitudinally. One group was schooled bilingually, through a simultaneous-translation approach. Hence, they received input promoting compound bilingualism. The other group was schooled monolingually in English, an approach supportive of coordinate bilingualism (in that Spanish was acquired only at home). The results showed that the Mexican-Americans schooled in *English only* over time were less likely to experience interference from *English* in their *Spanish* than those students schooled bilingually through simultaneous translation from English to Spanish. In other words, the teachers' constant translating from Spanish to English produced some "compounding" in the development of the native language among Mexican-American children schooled bilingually. (For more on the simultaneous translation or concurrent method, see "Techniques for bilingual instruction in the classroom" below.) It would be expected that both groups of students would experience interference from Spanish in their English, as was the case, but it would be conjectured that their Spanish might be reasonably free from interference. This was true only for those taught monolingually in English at school.

Another way of looking at bilingualism is by domain. Fishman (1971b; 1977) coined the term "bilingual dominance configuration" to refer to a bilingual in terms of language use and proficiency for each of the four language skills, across language varieties and across societal domains. Domains are clusters of social situations typically constrained by a common set of behavioral rules. The domains relevant for a bilingual community may include family, neighborhood, religion, education, and occupation. A domain is more than a place or context. It also comprises roles of interlocutors within particular settings and the topics these interlocutors are likely to discuss.

For example, within the educational domain, a teacher and a student are two interlocutors in a socially prescribed relationship, talking, say, about a math problem (the topic) in the classroom (the setting). Hymes (1974) notes that there may be interference "not only between phonologies and grammars, but also between norms of interaction and interpretation of speech" (pp. 123–124).

Although the term "balanced" bilingual has received some currency, Fishman (1971a) points out that the notion of balance is unrealistic because "societally patterned bilingualism can exist as a stabilized phenomenon *only* if there is functional *differentiation* between the two languages rather than merely global domain or balance" (p. 560). In other words, bilinguals who use both their languages equally in all contexts cease to be bilingual because no society needs two languages to fulfill the same function. For example, once English is spoken extensively in the Mexican-American home, Spanish ceases to function as the household language. Spanish will give way to English— the societally dominant, more prestigious language—unless conscious efforts are made to preserve special functions for Spanish use.

There has been an extensive literature on bilingualism and intelligence, with the bulk of the early literature documenting that monolinguals were more intelligent than bilinguals (see Darcy, 1953, 1973; Diebold, 1968; Cohen, 1975b). More frequently than not those studies were done in communities where members of the monolingual group were speakers of the societally dominant language, where the bilinguals were subject to racist attitudes and often were from a lower socioeconomic level than the monolinguals. Furthermore, the extent of bilingualism of the so-called bilinguals was not established, suggesting the possibility of improper testing techniques. For example, an inappropriate language may have been used for testing, as well as a biased test, improperly normed and interpreted (see De Avila, 1972).

Peal and Lambert (1962) controlled for the factors cited above, and French-English bilinguals in Montreal emerged superior to monolinguals in verbal and nonverbal intelligence. In Ireland, Macnamara (1966) found that bilinguals were less intelligent than monolinguals, and asserted that the balanced bilinguals Lambert and Peal selected were more intelligent to begin with "because they had been able to make themselves bilingual." Lambert and Peal-Anisfeld (1969) replied that the implication of Macnamara's comment was that only the more intelligent children became balanced bilinguals. "It is difficult to understand," commented Lambert and Peal-Anisfeld, "how studies purported showing that bilinguals are inferior can be used to support the interpretation that the more intelligent become bilingual rather than vice versa" (p. 127). MacNab (1979) has also challenged the studies linking bilingualism with intelligence.

Perhaps there is some truth to the notion that more intelligent children are *quicker* at learning a second language and at using this language as a vehicle for learning the subject matter in school. But there is no strong evidence that the process of becoming bilingual in turn adversely affects intelligence, or that less intelligent children never become bilingual if their situation expects it of them. There is some evidence from several longitudinal studies that children can add a second language through bilingual schooling without suffering a cognitive deficit (see Lambert and Tucker, 1972; Cohen, 1975b).

DEFINITION OF BILINGUAL EDUCATION

There has been confusion as to what constitutes bilingual education. There are many ways to produce bilinguals. Monolingual instruction in a second language is one way, but technically this is not bilingual education. The process of bilingual education, at least in the United States, implies the use of two languages as vehicles of instruction for students in part or all of the content subjects of the curriculum (see U.S. Office of Education, 1971). Bilingual education is not merely instruction in a second language (e.g., ESL) or in a foreign language (e.g., foreign language in the elementary school, FLES). In ESL and FLES programs, learning the language is often an

end in itself. U.S. bilingual programs have an ESL component for nonnative speakers of English and a FLES component for nonnative speakers of the foreign language (if there are any), but the intent is to make both languages vehicles for learning the content subjects (at least in theory). Using both languages for instruction is intended to give greater legitimacy to both languages and to enhance language learning, since a good way to learn a language is to use it as a vehicle for learning something else.

As stated earlier, bilingual education programs in the United States have generally been directed at children who do not speak English natively. The programs allow these children to continue their cognitive and linguistic growth in their native language while acquiring English as a second language (Saville and Troike, 1971). All the same, these programs are mostly two-way in that at least some native English speakers participate. Out of 72 Title VII programs started in 1969, an average of 27 percent of the participants were English-dominant. Of 55 programs started in 1970, an average of 34 percent of the children were English-dominant (BEST, 1971). A later report found that from a sampling of 38 Spanish/English bilingual projects, less than one-third of the students enrolled in grades 2 through 6 were of limited English-speaking ability (American Institutes for Research, 1977). This may mean that the bulk of the students were, in fact, English-dominant. But language is clearly not the only factor. Ethnic group and socioeconomic level of the family are other key variables determining participation in such state and federally funded programs. From the outset, there was some effort made to play down the participation of "Anglos" in such programs in that these were considered the "privileged" children. In reality, many of these Anglo children also have come from socioeconomically depressed homes.

MODELS FOR BILINGUAL SCHOOLING

Models for bilingual schooling have been carefully delineated elsewhere (Andersson and Boyer, 1977; Ulibarri, 1970; John and Horner, 1971; Mackey, 1970; Valencia, 1969;

Fishman and Lovas, 1970); so the intent here is not to describe all possible types. Instead, five major dimensions will be identified and issues related to each will be discussed. The dimensions are: (1) the age at which to commence bilingual schooling, (2) the breadth of bilingual schooling at a given site, (3) the language characteristics of the groups involved, (4) the manner in which the two languages are utilized, and (5) techniques for bilingual instruction in the classroom.

The age at which to commence bilingual schooling

Experts in the field of language teaching vary in their recommendations about program implementation. Andersson (1974) recommends that bilingual education start several years before school entry. He bases his conclusions on an extensive review of research relating to early childhood development. He notes an agreement among early childhood specialists that children between birth and age 5 have an extraordinary learning potential. Ervin-Tripp (1974), however, concluded from research on 4- to 9-year-olds learning French as a second language that the older learners learned faster because they had "more efficient memory heuristics" (p. 122). Concurrently, Saville-Troike (1973) suggests "there is some reason to believe that a child will experience more interference between language systems if the second is added before the first is completely developed (at about age ten)" (pp. 29–30). On the basis of preliminary findings from research on 3-year-old through adult nonnative learners of Dutch, Snow (1975) went even further. She concluded that "youth gives no special advantage in language learning. Older children and adults do better at all aspects of language acquisition than the younger children ..." (pp. 14–15). She also concluded that the strategies and stages of acquisition seemed very similar for all age groups.

Thus, evidence appears to suggest that younger learners are not as efficient at second language learning as are teen-agers and adults. However, there are other considerations that could, in fact, weigh more heavily in the long run and that have implications for school programs.[3] First, Snow (1975) points out that there is more free choice in learning a second language than in learning the first language. Therefore, second language learning is more affected by motivation, desire to be able to communicate with native speakers, interest in and admiration of the culture to which the language gives access, and willingness to endanger one's own personality by using a different, less effective idiom. Intuition and observation have repeatedly confirmed that the younger the learners, the less they are likely to question their own motives for learning a second language, the more uninhibited they are in their willingness to communicate, the more open they are to other cultures (the negative stereotypes are not as ingrained), and the more willing they are to make mistakes. At the teen-age and adult levels, individual differences become so overriding that researchers currently are trying to sort out just what learner characteristics make for good language learning (see Rubin, 1975; Naiman, Fröhlich, Stern, and Todesco, 1978; Politzer and McGroarty, 1985; O'Malley, Chamot, Stewner-Manzañares, Kupper, and Russo, 1983).

Thus, younger learners may not be as efficient at learning; they may in fact be less resistant to the learning process. Furthermore, as Krashen and Seliger (1975) point out, they may be more receptive to the most natural or "quasinatural" approach to language learning that can be implemented in a classroom. Such an approach would, by implication, avoid tedious drilling. Angel (1975) goes so far as to suggest that gross damage can be done to children in the early grades of the elementary school by the imposition of adult language structures on them, especially if the approach is formal rather than experiential. And without careful study of how children learn first and second languages, structured curriculum merely reflects adult intuitions about the language a child "should" learn. A formal curriculum is arduous to prepare and possibly even of dubious validity in terms of the selection and sequencing of structures, given what is beginning to be learned about first language acquisition patterns in totally natural environments (exposure to second language through nonclassroom experiences exclusively). In fact, Krashen (1981), Terrell (1981) and Krashen and Terrell (1983) have incorporated notions of natural language learning into second language pedagogy.

Stern (1976), however, suggests that a false dichotomy has been established between early and late learning. He would emphasize that there are advantages and disadvantages to starting at any age. Stern suggests that the important issues include: (1) the ultimate proficiency levels desired and (2) the amount of time necessary to produce those levels of proficiency, given the methodologies and expertise available.

The breadth of bilingual schooling at a given site

It is necessary to determine whether the program will start at a broad or narrow level. Some projects initiate bilingual education at the kindergarten level and add a grade each year. Others provide bilingual schooling for all 13 grades (K to 12) at once. Actually, 12 of the 72 Title VII projects started in 1969 began with coverage of all or many of the grades. However, only two of the 55 projects started in 1970 did so (BEST, 1971). Perhaps the results of the projects which attempted it in 1969 discouraged many 1970 projects from doing so.

Another decision is whether to make an entire school or group of schools bilingual. One major problem with having one out of, say, three or four classrooms at a given grade level the "bilingual" class is that friction invariably arises between the bilingual teacher and the other teachers not participating in the program, usually out of a jealousy associated with not benefiting from extra funds, teacher aides, etc. (see Fier, 1974). An all-bilingual program at a specified grade level allows for teacher sharing and harmony. However, such an approach puts pressure on the administration to replace monolingual teachers with bilingual ones. The administration must determine its priorities, and the status of tenured teachers may well take precedence over the best way to meet the educational needs of the students.

The language characteristics of the groups involved

Title VII programs started in 1969 and 1970 show the target population to be about 70 percent non-English-dominant (BEST, 1971). Actually there was a range, with 8 of the 127 programs being exclusively for non-English-dominant students. These would be referred to as one-way bilingual programs. The vast majority of programs are designed to be two-way, with teaching in English and in the minority language to both English-dominant and non-English-dominant students.

Because of the stigma placed on segregation, Title VII programs have discouraged efforts to separate the two "language" groups for a significant period of time for most academic subjects. According to Shore (1974),[4] actually only 24 percent of a sampling of Title VII projects reported having the students segregated by language group for most academic subjects. The locally funded Coral Way Elementary School bilingual program in Dade County, Florida, has practiced segregation in most subject matter until about the fifth grade. The program staff contended that segregation allowed children to develop bilingual skills without fear of comparison and perhaps teasing from native speakers of their second language. More importantly, the levels of vocabulary difficulty for the content areas have been adjusted according to the group. The research results speak well for the method (De Inclán, 1977).

Segregated or integrated, there is the issue of whether both groups of children in a bilingual program receive all subjects in both languages or just certain subjects. Also, one could ask what "receiving all subjects in both languages" really means. The section entitled "Techniques for bilingual instruction in the classroom" below addresses itself to this concern.

The manner in which the two languages are utilized

Fishman and Lovas (1970) identified four

basic models for bilingual schooling: (1) the *full bilingualism* model, by which all subjects are taught bilingually, (2) the *partial bilingualism* model where only certain subjects are taught in certain languages, (3) *transitional bilingualism,* where instruction commences in the native language and then at some point (e.g., second grade), all instruction is switched to a second language, and (4) *monoliterate bilingualism,* where both languages are used as media of instruction but literacy is taught only in the second language.

Early statistics from Title VII projects showed that 69 percent of the 1969 and 1970 projects chose the full bilingualism model for the nonnative English speakers; 21 percent preferred the partial bilingualism model and 10 percent used the transitional bilingualism model (Shore, 1974). The statistics for English-dominant students were similar, with slightly more projects espousing the transitional model. The moniliterate approach is not considered applicable, since the U.S. approach generally implies a desire to produce biliterate individuals. In other parts of the world, the moniliterate approach is more common.

With respect to how long the full bilingualism or partial bilingualism model is projected, most projects (37 percent) indicated that it would be continued to the fifth or sixth grade. However, the next largest group (23 percent) indicated through the tenth to twelfth grade (Shore, 1974). Thus, there is some interest in preserving bilingual schooling through to college.

There are modifications of the Fishman and Lovas model. Saville and Troike (1971), for example, proposed a model which calls for monolingual instruction in the vernacular from kindergarten to second grade, and then reflects the partial bilingualism approach from grades 3 through 8. They suggested that mathematical or computational skills be developed in the dominant language of the society, i.e., English in the United States, "since advanced work in mathematics will probably be done in this language and later switching of these skills is difficult. The other language can and should be used for non-computational purposes..." (p. 26).

Engle (1975) referred to the "native language approach" and the "direct method approach" as two methods of teaching a nondominant language group. The native language approach implies transitional bilingualism. The direct method approach has been referred to as the "immersion" approach. Although Engle's reference group for the direct method were the nondominant-language students, the approach of immersion, or initial monolingual instruction in the second language, eventually becoming bilingual instruction, has been tried out extensively on the dominant-language group in Canada (Lambert and Tucker, 1972; Bruck, Lambert, and Tucker, 1974, 1975; Swain and Barik, 1976) and in the United States (Cohen, 1974a, 1975a; Lebach, 1974; California State Department of Education, 1984). This immersion approach is not to be confused with the traditional brand of "submersion," whereby minority groups were "absorbed" without any special provisions to ensure their success in school. Such provisions would include bilingual teachers (who use only English in class), teachers with high expectations for student success, homogeneous grouping of students by level of English skills, no formal ESL materials, and a number of contextual factors— including ways of dealing with racism (see Cohen and Swain, 1976, for discussion of successful immersion education projects in North America). Immersion education in the United States has been found to motivate the majority student to make the effort to speak the foreign language. It is not considered "showing off," as is the case in some bilingual education programs (see Cohen and Lebach, 1974).

The language chosen for initial reading is a subject which has engendered considerable controversy. It has been stated that initial reading in the mother tongue or native language is essential (UNESCO, 1953). Some research findings have supported this view (Gudschinsky, 1977). Gudschinsky presents pedagogical, social, and psychological reasons for teaching a student in his vernacular first. The main pedagogical reason is to exploit the student's fluency in his own language in learning how to read and write, expecting him to be able to transfer the reading skill gained in the first language to reading in the second language. The social and psychological reasons for learning in the vernacular (whether first, or concurrently with learning in the second language) are that it minimizes culture shock for the child (the traumatic experience of facing a strange school environment with a foreign language and foreign cultural values), it augments his sense of personal worth (since language is an exteriorization of self), and it helps him establish a habit of academic success.

The opposing approach, of literacy in the second language first, has been tried successfully in Canada and the United States, as noted above. In the United States, there has been a history of educational difficulty in attempting to make nonnative speakers of English literate in the language right from the start of their schooling. If *success* is assured through initial second-language literacy, the contention is that this approach can work most effectively. The notion is that students can learn through a language that is new to them and can feel secure doing so (Wilson, 1973, p. 173). Wilson contends that the lessons must be carefully written, using small, systematic steps. Use of small segments at a time helps the children think directly in their new language. The teachers, however, must be sufficiently trained in the use of the materials to make this curriculum effective. The use of small segments also helps the teacher verify whether the children have grasped them.

Although it is initially easier to teach children literacy in their own language rather than in a second language, total or extensive instruction through the native language delays the transition to the second language, and ultimately may make this transition more difficult. The argument for literacy in a second language first is based on a different position with respect to *transfer* from that alluded to by Gudschinsky above. The argument is that it is easier to transfer from a second language back to the native language than to do the reverse. Recent reviews of language education in the vernacular worldwide show some support for this view (see Engle, 1975; Bowen, 1977). The extra time required to teach learners in the new language may well be compensated for by the ease of transfer. Conversely, the time that might be saved by teaching the children first in their native language may be lost in the effort to overcome the difficulties of transferring from the native to the second language later. Learning something in the native language does not ensure that the concept or process will be transferred to the second language.

Gudschinsky underscores the learner's capacity for transferring to reading in the second language. However, when the learners have to switch to reading in the second language, the syntactic and semantic systems of the other language may give them trouble. When reading in the first language, the learners do not have to learn the unfamiliar syntax and semantics. So, while learning to read first in the *second* language may be more difficult initially, the eventual payoffs may be greater. By the time the children begin classroom reading in the first language, they will not have to learn reading strategies because they will have already mastered these (see Valdés-Fallis, 1972, for support of this argument in the bilingual schooling of Spanish-speaking children). They will simply need to learn the alphabet and how meanings correspond with sounds and symbols in their own language. Also, although it may be easier to motivate children to read in their native language, it may then be particularly difficult to motivate them to read in *another* language that they are *unfamiliar* with. They may then feel that knowing how to read in one language is sufficient. However, motivation is not a problem when the second language in which reading is to be learned is the *native* language.

It is believed by some educators that there are risks in introducing reading in two languages simultaneously or in close succession. Such introduction is seen to produce interference between the native language and English. As noted above, interference occurs when two languages come into contact such that they are used alternately by the same person (Weinreich, 1968). An example of phonological interference from English while reading in Spanish would be reading the silent *h* in *hay libros* as the aspirated English *h*. In silent reading, such an error would not be so serious unless the reader misconstrued the meaning of *hay* by aspirating the initial *h* (e.g., by thinking it meant the greeting "Hi" in English with phonological interference, thus sometimes leading to semantic interference).

Interference also takes place at the syntactic and semantic levels, where such interference may be more troublesome. An example of syntactic interference could involve word-order confusion. For example, the student fails to understand *vestido rojo* or *el libro de Juan* because of expecting the English order *red dress* (the adjective preceding the noun it modifies) and *John's book* (the possessor preceding the thing possessed). An example of semantic interference could involve the difference in Spanish and English expressions. The child might read *voy a dar un examen* as "I'm going to give an exam." (*Dar* usually does mean "give," but not in this context.)

After observing data of both minority learners and majority learners engaged in simultaneous acquisition of reading in two languages, my own opinion is that students with reasonable listening and speaking skills in each of two languages and with some depth of vocabulary acquire both native and second language reading at about the same rate. And this rate does *not* seem to be depressed *because* the children are learning to read bilingually. If children are "good" readers, they read well in both languages, and if they are poor readers, they read poorly in both languages. The real issue may be whether those children diagnosed as poor readers or slow learners should learn to read simultaneously in two languages.

Statistics on the 1969 and 1970 Title VII programs show that 52 percent of the projects introduce reading in the two languages simultaneously, while 43 percent introduce first language reading initially, and 4 percent introduce second language reading first (Shore,

1974). Twenty-three projects failed to indicate the language sequence for reading. None of the *verified* projects indicated that they taught reading in the second language before reading in the dominant language. Four out of the 67 projects that declined to verify the BEST project descriptions supposedly used the second-language-first approach to reading. Perhaps even more than four of them used this approach but felt it was somehow unwise to let this fact be known.

It has been pointed out that in the United States, bilingual schooling implies the teaching of at least one content subject in two languages, aside from language arts in both languages. However, it may be difficult to distinguish language arts activities from content subjects. For example, if science is taught to Chicanos only in Spanish, Saville and Troike (1971) suggest that the science terms be built into the ESL lessons—not so much to repeat the concepts themselves as to provide the English terms for the concepts.

As Engle (1975), Cohen and Laosa (1976), and Bowen (1977) point out, the research results do not by any means support one utilization of two languages in bilingual schooling over another. It depends very much on the circumstances of the particular community. Engle, for example, suggests a number of variables that will affect the performance of a group of children enrolled in one or another bilingual program: the manner of second language learning; the child's prior knowledge of the first and second languages; the exposure of the child to the second language; the child's age, cognitive level, maturity, experience, and motivation; the child's facility at language learning; the child's experience at success in school; the linguistic relationship between the first and the second language; the status and function of the first and the second language in the community; and the emphasis placed on the two languages at the child's school. To Engle's variables we should add the variable of parental language competency, since in homes where both parents are bilingual or multilingual, children appear to become bilingual with greater ease than in homes where only one parent is bilingual (Padilla and Lindholm, 1983).

Techniques for bilingual instruction in the classroom

The basic question in determining classroom techniques is that of whether the two languages of instruction are to be mixed or used simultaneously in the classroom. There is controversy over this point. Mackey (1971, 1972) points out that languages can be alternated freely in a two-way bilingual program without any detrimental effect on language learning. Mackey (1977) offers five approaches to language alternation as practiced at the Berlin bilingual school in Germany: part of a lesson in the first language and the other part in the second language; all material in the first language with repetition of some of it in the second language; all material in the first language with a summary in the second language; continuous alternation of the first and second language; speaking to some students in the first language and to others in the second language—"sensing the child's dominant language and comprehension at the moment." More recently, Jacobson (1982) has spelled out with greater precision just what a successful concurrent approach would consist of—i.e., such that the switching from one language to the other is properly strategized by the teacher and implemented in accordance with certain learning objectives that are linguistically and culturally relevant. Milk (1984) provides evidence showing that the concurrent approach, when properly implemented, creates language-use patterns similar to the language-separation approach.

As noted above, some longitudinal data collected on a Title VII project in northern California (Cohen, 1975b) suggest that simultaneous use of two languages did tend to stimulate "compounding" or interference—notably interference from the second language in speaking the first language. These results would seem to vindicate those educators that have tried so diligently to keep the languages separate in a bilingual program, through methods that will be described

below. But it may well be that the *nature* of concurrent instruction is the overriding factor, as Jacobson (1982) suggests and Milk's study (1984) confirms.

In the early 1970s, the Title VII bilingual programs in East Los Angeles embraced the concurrent approach to bilingual schooling, in what was actually a form of simultaneous translation. The teacher explained each concept in one language and then immediately thereafter in the other language, taking care not to resort to *literal* translation, but rather to explain each concept only in terms which are idiomatic to the language being used. This approach was intended to maximize communication, facilitate concept acquisition, maximize exposure to the second language, economize on the use of teaching time, promote student participation, and foster intercultural appreciation.

Andersson and Boyer (1977) and others argue against switching freely between two languages throughout the day. It has been noted that the concurrent approach puts demands on the teacher to be efficient at switching back and forth from one language to another. It is possible to make translation errors even in back translation from the teacher's second language to his native one. Also, students could tune out the language they do not want to listen to (as happened in some of the classrooms Fillmore, 1982 observed), so that true *bilingual* learning may not take place. Jacobson's approach (1982) supposedly avoids such problems.

Another model calls for alternating the language by day and eventually by week. Perhaps the prototype for alternate day/week bilingual schooling has been the Nestor Elementary School in Chula Vista, California. In grades 1 to 3, the math, science, and social studies lessons have been taught to Chicanos and Anglos in Spanish or English depending on the day. The teacher aide has *previewed* the lesson in the native language of the students when the lesson is to be in their second language. Next, the lesson has been given to a mixed group of non-English-dominant and English-dominant students. Then the lesson has been *reviewed* in the format of a second language lesson, again for the group who were nonnative speakers of the language of instruction.

In grades 4 and 5, math, science, and social studies have alternately been taught in English or Spanish, depending on the week. This Title VII program shifts from 80 percent use of the dominant language in kindergarten to 50 percent use in grade 5.

The alternate-days model was also tried out in the Philippines (Tucker, Otanes, and Sibayan, 1970) and in Redwood City, California (Cohen, 1975b). In both cases, it met with mixed success and was discontinued. In Redwood City and in the Philippines as well, the same teacher taught alternately in one language or the other, depending on the day. This pattern demands much preparation time and careful linguistic execution on the part of the teacher. The Chula Vista program uses team teaching, such that a teacher prepares the lesson in only one language.

Another approach is that of repeated teaching of the same subject matter in both languages—e.g., a math lesson in English in the morning and in Spanish in the afternoon. This approach is flourishing in Dade County, Florida, and was tried in Las Cruces, New Mexico (John and Horner, 1971). The biggest potential pitfall is that repetition of the same content can become monotonous (Valencia, 1972). In Dade County, however, daily one-hour planning sessions have helped the Spanish and English language teachers to determine jointly the objectives that will be covered in math, science, etc., and just how they will be handled in each language. An attempt has been made to have the "repeat" lesson act as review and reinforcement. The teachers have been able to meet for an hour a day because the teacher aides have taken the classes for physical education and music during that time.

Another approach to bilingual schooling is through immersion education (California State Department of Education, 1984). In this approach, all instruction is through the child's second language until reading is introduced in the native language, usually in grade 2 but sometimes later (see Cohen and Swain, 1976).

Transitional use of a language usually manifests itself as conventional schooling in the vernacular in the early years, with the second language introduced as a subject. Then the program switches abruptly to immersion education or a gradual phasing in of the second language and phasing out of the first language.

Given the various models of bilingual schooling, *which* ones are being used in the Title VII programs in the United States? Of the 58 programs which verified their models, only 9 percent said that neither the teachers nor the aides switched languages in the classroom. Nineteen percent reported that there was concurrent use of both languages during the same class period, but on a team-teaching basis, with the teacher using one language and the aide using the other. Thirty-three percent said that the teacher switched constantly from one language to another. Thirty-one percent said the teacher reinforced any conversation initiated by the child through whatever language the child had used. The picture is thus one of concurrent education generally.

This concurrent model may work reasonably well for the non-English-dominant child (except for possibilities of language interference, as mentioned above). Its effectiveness in teaching the second language to the English-dominant child is questionable. Of course, as stated above, Title VII programs never had as their prime target the English-dominant student. The target population was not only the socioeconomically disadvantaged minority students but also the non-English dominant ones. Few programs were aimed at English-dominant minority children. Even the idea of a language restoration program for English-speaking minority children was not considered a priority except in rare cases (e.g., the education of English-speaking Pomo Indians from Ukiah in the Pomo language). The *Anglo* children who comprise a minority of the student group in the federal programs were more or less considered tagalongs (Cohen, 1974a). The results of this policy have shown in that some bilingual programs have taught Anglos the second language for five or more years without producing fluent second language speakers.[5] Classroom observations (Edelsky and Hudelson, 1982) also explain why Anglos may learn very little Spanish in bilingual classrooms. It may be of no surprise that evaluation of Anglos' performance in bilingual programs is generally overlooked altogether. Anglos might benefit more from an immersion or AM-PM approach to bilingual schooling than from the concurrent one, if there is a serious desire to make this group fluent in a second language.

Closely related to techniques for bilingual instruction in the classroom is the issue of classroom language itself. Language use in the classroom differs from language use outside the classroom. While the language the child acquires at home is informal and is used to communicate in face-to-face situations, the language of the school becomes increasingly formal and academic. Even monolingual majority children experience a mismatch between their home language and the spoken and written varieties of language they encounter in school. The mismatch is often particularly severe when one is dealing with children whose first language is different from the school language. Such children are learning academic formal language at the same time that they must learn a second language that differs in significant ways from their home language. Research indicates that children who successfully make this transition from home language to school language realize early that written language is different from spoken language. They are also able to understand language even when it is decontextualized (see Olson, 1977; Cummins, 1979).

EDUCATIONAL SETTING FOR BILINGUAL SCHOOLING

Frequently the bilingual schooling part of a bilingual program is only *one* innovation of several. According to the project BEST statistics (Shore, 1974) only 11 of 58 programs (i.e., 19 percent) stated that their curriculum was typical or regular for the state—apart from the inclusion of the non-English-mother-tongue instruction. The remaining 47 had one or more *other* innovations as well.

Seventy-one percent had small-group instruction, 65 percent had individualized instruction, and 24 percent had flexible or modular scheduling, 21 percent had nongraded classrooms (heterogeneous age groupings), and 19 percent used the open-classroom approach (providing a free environment in which students make decisions about the arrangement of space, time utilization, sequencing of activities, and choice of reading materials).

There usually are also some innovative curriculum materials in use. The need for non-English materials sparked extensive activity by a number of publishing companies. When the Title VII programs began in the fall of 1969, there were few appropriate non-English materials to choose from. Now there are many—often displayed at, or even disseminated through, regional bilingual education centers.

Finally, the bilingual classroom usually has at least two adults in it, the teacher and a paid aide, who often work together as a team. There are also teachers in training and volunteer helpers, not to mention the project coordinator, curriculum writer, evaluator, and other staff who may take part in class activities. Innovative language programs have tended to attract helpers. Lowering the teacher-pupil ratio is an innovation which also provides more individualized instruction.

Thus, to assume that the only thing innovative going on in a bilingual education classroom is bilingual schooling would be incorrect. The existence of other innovations has implications for evaluation of the success of bilingual schooling. It means that there are a number of other factors which would possibly intervene in the analysis.

THE CHILD

U.S. bilingual programs have had as their primary target population children who were not only non-English-speaking but also from impoverished homes. This implied in many cases that aside from not knowing English, the students had problems of undernourishment, inadequate clothing, and lack of parental attention (in cases where parents were working long hours and/or had many children).

The lack of English has been a genuine problem, but helping these children succeed at school has been seen to go far beyond making them bilinguals (comfortable in English, and literate in their native language). In fact, second- or third-generation children from these families might speak fluent English and still fail at school. Often the learning styles within the home differ sharply from those expected of children at school (Kagan, 1980). For these children, the school program must provide enhancement of self-esteem through teachers who care about whether the children succeed, peers who are supportive, and a curriculum which motivates the children to want to learn.

Some problems cannot be solved immediately by even the most enlightened program. These problems include the majority society's attitudes toward the minority group. Instilling pride in a low-prestige language and culture is a difficult task. Societal attitudes have to be modified, such as through greater majority-society participation in bilingual education.

Also, minority children must see that they are capable of "getting ahead" in the society—that with proper education, they are able to become anything they want to be. It is important to provide a model—for bilingual children and for their parents—of teachers and administrators functioning professionally as *bilinguals* within bilingual programs. It is also important for minority children to see bilingual professionals, such as doctors, lawyers, and other public servants. Some bilingual programs invite such people to school to talk with the children as a part of certain lessons (e.g., social studies) or informally.

The participation of majority-group children in bilingual programs was intended to help promote interethnic understanding, not only among children but also among their parents. This phase of bilingual schooling has

perhaps met with mixed success. As noted above in discussing immersion vs. concurrent instruction, as long as the Anglo students are not *really* taxed to express themselves in the second language, they always have the upper hand psychologically and culturally. When they *must* speak in the second language for a considerable part of the school day, their admiration for the minority child appears to increase noticeably (Cohen and Lebach, 1974). But unquestionably this is still a matter of speculation and calls for further research and observation (see "Research and Evaluation" below).

THE TEACHER

The ethnicity and background experience of the teacher in the bilingual classroom has been a controversial issue. Some feel that a teacher who is a member of the ethnic group of the child is needed to provide an appropriate model for the minority child. When practiced to its extreme, however, this approach might result in hiring teachers with the "right ethnicity" who either do not know the minority language very well and/or do not know how to teach the content subjects in the minority language (see Shanker, 1972a, 1972b). There is also the possibility of an "ethnically appropriate" teacher with unrealistically high expectations for the performance of, say, Mexican-American children (Carter, 1970). In fact, research by the U.S. Commission on Civil Rights (1973) found that in classes with Mexican-American and Anglo students, Mexican-American teachers called on Anglo children more frequently than Anglo teachers did. The investigators explained this behavior as resulting from the fact that Mexican-American teachers had lower expectations for the academic success of Mexican-American pupils than for that of Anglos.

An argument can also be made for having some fluently bilingual Anglo teachers from a bicultural community to provide models. There are Anglo teachers in many bilingual programs who in fact are monolingual English speakers. Sometimes they team with bilingual teachers of minority background. In other cases, the teacher aide provides all the minority-language instruction.

It may reflect use of a double standard to insist on bilingualism on the part of the minority teachers and aides who teach in a bilingual program but to permit monolingual Anglo teachers to participate. In many cases, administrators have to succumb to matters of tenure, job priority, etc., regardless of the best means of providing for the children's needs. Ideally, all Anglo teachers working in bilingual programs should achieve fluency in the minority language. In one bilingual program that I evaluated in Rosemead, California, the kindergarten teacher, an Anglo, actually used *only* Spanish for the entire year while the aide, a male Chicano, used only English.

Perhaps more important than ethnicity is the teacher's set of expectations about the children's performance in the program. They should have no preconceived stereotypic notions about how well or poorly the students are going to perform. They should have an open-mindedness with regard to innovative practices in education, particularly with respect to bilingual education. Project BEST (Shore, 1974) reports that only 4 out of 58 verified projects said that part of their teacher training explicitly included the fostering of this kind of open-mindedness. But there is little doubt that the teacher's belief in the success of the method is important. If the teacher does not give the approach a fair chance, it is doomed to failure. One such example concerning the alternate-days model of bilingual education can be cited in the Title VII program I was directly involved with in Redwood City: several of the teachers gave up on the method almost immediately; they started switching back and forth from one language to the other. They did not give the method a fair chance.

Much has been written on teacher training elsewhere. Providing a long list of bilingual education training courses to take would be superfluous here, except to note that a teacher involved in bilingual education should have training in applied linguistics (Politzer, 1978)—particularly in those areas related to first and second language teaching and acquisition, bilingualism, language varieties

(regional and social dialects and registers), and language testing (see Corder, 1973; Wardhaugh and Brown, 1976). In particular, the teacher should have more than a superficial understanding of the field of English as a second language, since bilingual education does not mean only the development and maintenance of the minority child's language and culture. It also involves the acquisition of English and the mainstream culture.

The teacher should have enough understanding of curriculum planning to be able to adapt existing curriculum to individual student needs. Although less so than at the outset of federal programs, U.S. bilingual programs demand teacher initiative to fill in gaps where bilingual materials are not available and to correct deficiencies in existing materials.

Finally, if the program provides for a paid aide and/or volunteer teachers, the teacher should know how to maximize the contribution of these people. For instance, the teacher may receive more motivated service from an aide who is treated as a colleague than from one who is treated as a subservient clerical person. Some curriculum materials are more prescriptive than others and so provide greater guidance for an aide. One such curriculum was developed by a company in operation for about five years, Consultants in Total Education (CITE). This curriculum has been used extensively on the Navajo Reservation and in Mexican-American bilingual programs (Cohen, 1974b). In fact, the aide, while using the CITE curriculum, is trained to do all the tasks that the teacher does.

Some excellent minority teachers in bilingual programs in fact began as aides and were motivated to continue their studies in order to obtain a teaching credential.

CULTURE IN THE CLASSROOM

Biculturalism has been defined as "the ability of a person to shift and operate with relative ease and comfort into two . . . given cultures" (Valencia, 1972, p. 30). The "ease" with which the minority child operates in the mainstream culture is largely dependent on the attitudes of the majority society. As Swanson (1974) points out, "the only way to dispel ethno-centric notions is not to let them form from the beginning. The majority of Anglo-American children ... need to learn about other cultures; they need to be brought out of their isolation" (p. 85). Swanson's point emphasizes the need for truly two-way bilingual programs, with the Anglos broadening their bicultural awareness.

Perhaps the Anglos are not going to become truly bicultural and internalize the beliefs, values, and customs of the minority culture, but proper preservice and in-service training of teachers (Baty, 1972) and sensitive schooling of Anglo children can make both groups appreciate the minority culture more. The teacher can become more biculturally sensitive in learning the language and/or dialect of the minority children, reading about the culture, visiting in the minority community, and the like. Anglo children can learn much at school, depending on their degree of positive interaction with minority children. Interactions in school must be orchestrated by the teachers so that they lend prestige, importance, and appeal to the minority culture. Here, an enthusiastic, involved Anglo teacher might be as effective at bicultural lessons as a minority teacher.

It has been pointed out that schools have for the past 100 years been devoted to the task of eliminating cultural differences, despite politico-philosophic statements about the beauty of diversity and the contributions of all Americans (Ether, 1969). The recent wave of bilingualism brings with it problems of how biculturalism should be treated. The facts of culture, such as history (holidays, etc.), literature, fine arts (songs, dances, etc.), and geography, can be taught to minority children in an effort to help them preserve their heritage. But the values of culture need not and perhaps *cannot* really be "taught" to these children. They know them. Beliefs, values, and customs concerning ways of establishing friendships, the relationships between the sexes, family, work ethics, orientation toward time, etc., are transmitted in the home and the community.

Biculturalism is relevant to Anglo teach-ers in helping them understand that minority children may have different learning styles from majority children. The teachers must be aware that their teaching patterns may conflict with learning styles characteristic of the minority cultures in areas such as the following: the meaning of "order," acceptable dimensions of action and noise, perspectives on time and space, what constitutes "work" and "play," "coping" in class, negative sanctions (discipline) and how they are perceived (see Saville-Troike, 1973).

It is also important to note cultural differences between, say, the third-generation Chicano and the recent immigrant from Mexico, the Mexican national. The cultural patterns of these two groups could be different enough (clothing, grooming, etc.) to cause intraethnic rivalries.

CONFLICTS IN THE INITIATION OF A BILINGUAL PROGRAM

The Bilingual Education Act of 1967 was a response to political pressures from minority spokespersons, who pointed out that the children of the ethnic minority taxpayers were getting a second-class education because of language barriers, racist attitudes, etc. The Supreme Court ruling in the Lau vs. Nichols case (see *The Linguistic Reporter*, March, 1974) emphasized that public school systems are required by federal law to take positive action to help children who do not speak English. The crux of the plaintiffs' case was that some pupils were "effectively foreclosed from any meaningful education" by a language barrier.

The Bilingual Education Act had more or less stated that the way to solve the minority child's problems at school was through use of the child's native language in classroom instruction. The Supreme Court ruling did not make that assumption. The High Court left it up to the local school district to determine how best to meet the child's schooling needs, conceivably through exclusive use of the second language in an enlightened way. (See Teitelbaum and Hiller, 1977, for more on legal aspects of bilingual education.)

Project BEST statistics (Shore, 1974) show that of 58 verified Title VII programs, only 31 percent asked minority parents whether they wanted their children taught in their native language. It is not just idle banter to speak of community needs assessment. For instance, Fishman and Lovas (1970) stress the importance of determining (1) what languages and varieties people are using in the community by domain, (2) their performance levels in each language and variety, (3) their attitudes toward these, and (4) their attitudes toward changing the existing pattern.

It is probably true that many minority parents would argue against teaching their children though their native language. My own experience in Redwood City (Cohen, 1975b) was that Mexican-American mothers in particular wanted their children schooled almost exclusively in English.[6] It was the fathers who were more concerned about preserving Spanish skills. Arguments given for teaching English fast and effectively were that English was needed to get ahead economically and for purposes of social interaction (see Cohen, 1974c, for more on language orientation among Redwood City parents). The fathers who were concerned about Spanish maintenance were in some cases thinking of returning with their families to Mexico, but others just seemed better informed than their wives about the potentially beneficial effects of bilingual schooling.

The Project BEST statistics (Shore, 1974) show that only half of the verified projects made any effort to survey the sociolinguistic situation in the community. In some cases, Spanish surnames or lack of such surnames have deceived administrators into drawing false conclusions about the language dominance in the community. In some cases, supposed Spanish-native-language components of programs have really been Spanish-as-a-second-language—or Spanish restoration—components, calling for radical changes in curriculum. The possibility that a program might involve mostly English speakers brings up the question of who the bilingual program is for and why. Does one have to be poor and non-English-speaking to get a bilingual education in the United States? Research generally shows that poverty and lack of English skills go together for Spanish speakers in the Southwest (Grebler, Moore, and Guzman, 1970, Ch. 18), suggesting that the acquisition of better-paying jobs still depends largely on knowing English.

Educators involved with bilingual schooling have learned that such a program involves an enormous amount of time in educating the community before and during the program. The Redwood City program demonstrated that parental attitudes toward the benefits of bilingual schooling change over time (Cohen, 1975b). Parents see that their children can learn through two languages without loss in content areas, in reading, or in cognitive development. It is probably unrealistic to assume that parents with little formal schooling are going to be instantly knowledgeable about the intricacies of programs that call for some educational sophistication to understand. Even so-called experts are constantly learning new things about bilingual education.

One positive move is the involvement of minority parents as paid aides, volunteers, and frequent spectators in the project classes and special events. Through such contacts, community members become more aware of what bilingual schooling is about. There is no doubt that parents' attitudes about a program can change through participation in it and through the participation of their children. One anecdote dealing with an Anglo parent in Redwood City perhaps typifies the kind of change that can occur. A particular Anglo father had grown up in Los Angeles among Mexican-Americans and had considered them his adversaries. He recounted to the author stories about the many fist fights he had had with Mexican-Americans. After his little blond-haired, blue-eyed daughter had spent two happy years in the bilingual program and had acquired some good Mexican-American friends, the father admitted that his attitudes had changed. He had gained a new respect for Mexican-Americans through the positive experiences of his daughter.

RESEARCH AND EVALUATION

At a time when the implementation of bilingual programs reached such a peak, the evaluation of programs lagged far behind. Despite millions spent on the development of programs, the United States experience yielded few meaningful insights into various aspects of program design (U.S. Commission on Civil Rights, 1975; Ramirez et al., 1977). Reasons for this lack of hard data include the following:

1. It is difficult, if not impossible, to obtain meaningful research results from pilot programs that are constantly undergoing modification, presumably for the better. Even if summative results are obtained, the researcher is hard put to give a label to a particular treatment, since it is in such a state of flux.

2. There has been such a pressing need for formative evaluation of project-oriented goals, i.e., behavioral objectives contained in the curriculum, that no time has remained for evaluating other things.

3. Until recently it has not been easy to find assessment instruments that could be considered for use with bilingual populations, and even now further test development and norming are called for.

4. Political threats to bilingual schooling have virtually forced evaluation reports to be public relations documents.

5. Evaluators have tended to be persons unfamiliar with the particular needs and characteristics of bilingual education, often because of the transience of potentially appropriate evaluators.

The "fledgling program" reason for a dearth of usable results should no longer apply, since bilingual projects nationwide now have more stability, as a result of a gradually growing accumulation of experience, methods, and materials (Blanco, 1977). But if bilingual education is to continue to advance, better and more meaningful evaluation is necessary.

With respect to project-centered instructional objectives, more than ever before there is a need to entertain the larger questions as well. Tucker and d'Anglejan (1971) question whether "self-centered" project goals such as meeting specific teaching objectives are valid criteria for evaluating the success or failure of a program (e.g., 75 percent of the children can answer 90 percent of the questions in a certain section of a book). Whether or not such criteria are valid, there is more to formative evaluation, such as investigation of the following areas (adapted from Saville and Troike, 1971):

1. The teaching techniques that prove most successful in different situations (grouping, sequencing and pacing of materials, and correction procedures).

2. The effect of program design (e.g., partial or full bilingual schooling using a concurrent, dual language, or alternate-days approach to instruction).[7]

3. The effect of teacher training and patterns of staff utilization.

4. The selection of materials best suited for certain children—depending on the achievement pattern of a child in the given area (reading, math, science, etc.), the child's aptitude for the subject, the child's attitude toward each language, etc. Politzer and Hoover (1974) suggest that there may be attitude-treatment interaction in bilingual programs, i.e., that minority children who have more favorable attitudes toward their native language will succeed better in a program that emphasizes more or exclusive use of their native language, and that minority children who have less favorable attitudes toward their native language may prefer programs with more or exclusive use of English.

It is encouraging to see that bilingual education evaluations have begun to take into consideration the *bilingual schooling model*. The Chicago Board of Education (1977), for example, compared five models: team teaching/same room, team teaching/separate room, integrated (modified pull out), self-contained, and departmentalized. Tentative findings were that team teaching in separate rooms produced the highest gains among students, while team teaching in the same room produced the lowest gains.

The lack of adequate assessment instruments is still a problem, although not as severe as in the mid-sixties when federally funded program evaluations were initiated (see, for example, Dissemination Center for Bilingual-Bicultural Education, 1975). Progress in this area can be seen in the work of Silverman (1976), Burt and Dulay (1978), and Dietrich and Freeman (1979). However, some widely used standardized instruments, such as the Peabody Picture Vocabulary Test and the Cooperative Primary Test of Reading, have been subject to criticism (Cicourel et al., 1974). We seem to be entering an era in which ethnomethodological scrutiny of tests and even of individual test items are common practice.

Regardless of whether it is still necessary to prove that bilingual schooling works, evaluation reports would serve us better if they reflected more than a morass of tabular data and a scattering of carefully selected and tentatively or even ambiguously worded findings. Instead, it is time that findings reflected specific weaknesses as well as strengths so as to provide feedback that could help in improving ongoing programs in the weakest area. It is regrettable that at least in former years, the tendency to avoid measures which might have produced negative results all but precluded the possibility of learning from project deficiencies (Berman and McLaughlin, 1974).

In later work, there began to appear reports such as that by the American Institutes for Research (1977), which gained considerable attention expressly because of its negative findings. In this case, the major finding was that a sampling of 286 classrooms from 38 Title VII Spanish/English bilingual programs showed no apparent gains in English language development. Subsequently, a series of flaws in the research design were identified (*The Linguistic Reporter*, 1978). For example, although the report noted that some Title VII classrooms were more successful than others in producing gains in English reading, no attempt was made to describe the features that characterized the more successful classrooms (such as by model of instruction, as in the Chicago Board of Education, 1977, report). Sumner and Zellman (1977), in a Rand Corporation study, note that it may, in fact, be the less successful programs or classrooms which discredit the bilingual approach to schooling:

Projects that suffer from inadequate design, poor assessment instruments, poorly trained and largely monolingual staff and the dilution of resources because of a need for rapid expansion of the program, may be pointed to as evidence of failure of the idea of bilingual education itself (p. 36).

Given the current developments in the field of bilingual education, the moment may now be propitious for conducting the types of evaluations that readers have been awaiting. Such evaluations would reflect the following elements:

1. Careful collection of meaningful baseline data from selected subjects.
2. The identification and development of instruments to measure key variables.
3. The identification of treatment characteristics.
4. The establishment of longitudinality and comparability of data across programs.
5. The interpretation of results in implementable terms that are meaningful to teachers, policy makers, and researchers.

OUTCOMES OF BILINGUAL EDUCATION

By way of conclusion, it may be useful to discuss what the ideal outcomes of bilingual education should be. Perhaps the prime concern is that the minority children involved make normal progress through the grades, i.e., without being retained indefinitely in a particular grade. It is also hoped that the children will maintain better attendance records at school (success at school depends, at least to some extent, on attendance) and that they will be motivated not to drop out along the way.

It is hoped that all participants will develop strong language skills in two languages, both in the oral skills (speaking, listening) and in the literacy skills (reading, writing). For the minority child, this means professional-caliber literacy skills in both the native language and English. For the majority child, this means not just literacy skills in the second language, but comfortable fluency as well. An ideal program would also have its students advancing normally in all content subjects, regardless of the language of instruction.

Such a program should foster and enhance the self-esteem of all participants, as well as promoting esteem for the minority and majority languages and cultures. All the children should feel important and should *want* to succeed in their studies. The children from different language and cultural backgrounds should have positive patterns of social and academic interaction—built on mutual respect and understanding. The children should be equally motivated to use both languages, in and also out of school, depending on the sociolinguistic context of speech encountered. The children should also experience a sense of bicultural mobility—a feeling that they can partake of activities in either culture without feeling out of place.

The program should bridge the gap between community and school. The greater community should be directly involved in school activities. Majority and minority parents should interact with one another, take pride in the bilingual program, and participate in its activities. Likewise, these parents should feel more motivated to learn each other's language.

There should be generated a clear notion that professional-level jobs are available in the community for minority-language speakers. The bilingual program can serve as a model for the kinds of jobs open to minority-language speakers—e.g., teachers, administrators, researchers, curriculum developers—who use the minority language professionally in their work.

It is not too early to study the long-term outcomes of bilingual programs initiated in the mid to late sixties; the concerned teacher, administrator, researcher, and other observers should be asking questions about possible outcomes such as those enumerated above. Developments in these areas might well determine the future of bilingual education in American schools. In fact in 1982, System Development Corporation in Santa Monica, California, received funding to pursue a national longitudinal evaluation of the effectiveness of educational services for limited-English-proficiency students. Findings from this study should begin coming out as this anthology goes to press.

NOTES

1.   An initial version of this chapter was written in the early 1970s during the heyday of the first wave of bilingual education in the United States. It has subsequently been revised and updated three times. The author would like to thank Mary McGroarty and Margarita Vincent for their useful suggestions on this final version.

2.   For more on Chicano speech, see Hernández-Chavez et al., 1975; Bowen and Ornstein, 1976; and Amastae and Elías-Olivares, 1982.

3.   McLaughlin (1978) provides a clear and thorough consideration of additional aspects of second language learning in childhood.

4.   The Bilingual Education Applied Research Unit of Project BEST, N.Y.C. Bilingual Consortium, Hunter College Division, devised a content analysis schedule for the 125 bilingual education programs funded by Title VII in 1969 and 1970. Project BEST initially filled out the questionnaire from secondary data taken from proposals and evaluation reports during the 1971–1972 school year. Then these questionnaires were sent to the projects for verification; 51 percent of the 1969 projects and 41 percent of the 1970 projects verified the content analysis (58 in all). Reference made to "verified projects" refers to those that confirmed they were actually doing what they were purported to be doing on the basis of their proposals, etc.

5.   I am personally aware of bilingual programs which fall into this category, but they will remain nameless for reasons of confidentiality.

6.   Samuel Manna found similar results in a study of attitudes toward bilingual education in the Pico-Union community in Los Angeles (Manna, 1975).

7.   In the United States little research is available comparing the effectiveness of different models of bilingual education. In Canada there has been some research on the effectiveness of various immersion education models (Cummins and Swain, 1978).

DISCUSSION QUESTIONS

1. What do you mean when you use the term "bilingual"? Does it have a pejorative, complimentary, or neutral connotation for you? Why?

2. Do you think that by becoming bilingual, a child can enhance his intelligence? If so, in what ways? Do you feel that bilingual schooling might be detrimental to cognitive development? If so, why?

3. Do you think it matters whether a child learns to read in his native language first? If there is a wait time between the introduction of reading in one language and the introduction of reading in the other language, how long should this wait time be?

4. Is being of a lower socioeconomic status (SES) an obstacle to learning a second language effectively in a school program? If so, in what ways might low SES have adverse effects?

5. Do you think there might be attitude-treatment interaction in a bilingual program; i.e., the minority children who have more negative attitudes toward their native language benefit *less* from a bilingual program than from a monolingual English program? Do you think that a bilingual education program could make these pupils' attitudes toward their native language more positive? If so, how?

6. Do you think that bilingual schooling can improve interethnic relations among children and their parents out of school?

7. In what ways do you think that the ethnicity of the teacher is a factor in bilingual schooling?

SUGGESTED ACTIVITIES

1. Suppose you had been called upon to set up (and perhaps coordinate) a bilingual program somewhere, what steps would you take? What would you do first, second, third,

etc.? Where would you place your priorities? How would you decide what models for bilingual schooling to endorse? Draft a statement of the action you would take with respect to organizing a bilingual program.

2. Design a teacher training program for teachers who are to participate in bilingual schooling programs.

3. Visit one or more bilingual education programs in your vicinity, using the checklist below (or one you devise) to observe the key elements. After careful observation, draft a statement of how the ideal bilingual program you have read about compares with the actual programs you have seen. In what ways have the actual programs lived up to your notions of an ideal model? What is the *reality* of bilingual education, at least in the federal or state projects you have seen?

CHECKLIST FOR OBSERVATION OF BILINGUAL CLASSES

The learners

1. What language do they use in class, for what purpose, to whom?

2. What kinds of groups are they in and how did they get there? For example, are they grouped by ability, by language dominance? How were these assignments made (teacher assessment, formal testing, etc.)?

3. Are the children learning to read concurrently in two languages? If not, what pattern is being followed?

4. Levels of differentiation: none (all children doing exactly the same thing), pacing (all on the same materials but at different speed), materials (different materials for different children, e.g., according to personal preference of child), materials and pacing (different materials and at a different pace)?

5. Nature of the children's activity in class: are the children seemingly engaged—actively or productively involved in learning? What kind of learning (social learning, academic

learning)? Is there aimless behavior, detachment? Are the children in discussion groups? If so, who is doing the talking—the children or an adult? If there is an adult presentation, are the students involved?

The adults (teachers, aides, volunteers, etc.)

1. What language do the adults use when, to whom, and why?

2. What appear to be the attitudes and manifested behaviors of adults toward certain or all students?

3. How adequate is adult command of the language of instruction? Are adult explanations on teaching points clear?

4. How consistent with the interests and intellectual behaviors of the pupils are the activities selected by adults?

5. What percent of time do adults spend supervising, lecturing or presenting, discussing, etc.?

6. How are nonteacher adults utilized in the classroom?

Classroom

1. What is the setup? Traditional classrooms with desks in rows or innovative arrangements of class space? Use of audio-visual and other media?

2. How are the two or more cultures represented ostensibly in the classroom and how are they manifested behaviorally (if you are able to observe any social studies, etc.)?

3. Does the classroom seem to be a learning environment—i.e., a place where children become independent, self-starting thinkers and learners? Or is the only added extra the "bilingual language frill"?

SUGGESTIONS FOR FURTHER READING

The literature on bilingual education has been growing to such an extent that there are now a number of books and monographs dealing with the subject. The following is a list of some of the more important ones.

Bilingual Schooling in the United States, 2d edition.
1977. Theodore Andersson, and Mildred Boyer, Austin,, Tex.: National Educational Laboratory Publishers, P.O. Box 10003, Austin, Tex. 78767.

This book, when it originally appeared in a two-volume set, had an enormous impact on the then fledgling field of bilingual education. It still remains an important resource book for those interested in better understanding the princples and practices of bilingual schooling.

Bilingual Education: Current Perspectives.
1977. Center for Applied Linguistics. Vol. 1: Social Science, Vol. 2: Linguistics, Vol. 3: Law, Vol. 4: Education. Arlington, Va.: Center for Applied Linguistics.

This series of publications presents a keynote paper in each given area of interest, followed by a series of "viewpoint" papers. The issues are addressed by experts in an interesting, scholarly fashion.

Bilingualism and Special Education: Issues in Assessment and Pedagogy.
1984. J. Cummins. Clevedon, Avon, England: Multilingual Matters Ltd.

This excellent new book looks at alternatives to traditional assessment and pedagogical practices for bilingual children. It examines the assumptions underlying special education, especially in the handling of linguistically- and culturally-different students. The book critically analyzes constructs such as "learning disability," "language proficiency," and "bilingual proficiency," as well as the causes of minority students' underachievement.

Bilingual Education for Hispanic Students in the United States.
1982. Joshua A. Fishman, and Gary D. Keller. New York: Teachers College, Columbia University.

This is a fine volume of important reprints dealing with goals of bilingual education, language problems, attitudes, research findings, and the process of becoming bilingual.

Bilingual Education and Public Policy in the United States.
1979. Raymond V. Padilla (ed.). Ypsilanti, Mich.: Eastern Michigan University.

This volume marks an important trend in the bilingual education literature toward greater representation of the viewpoints of minority-group educators and researchers. Papers relate to law, politics, community, and models of bilingual schooling.

Bilingualism or Not: The Education of Minorities.
1981. Tove Skutnabb-Kangas. Clevedon, Avon, England: Multilingual Matters Ltd.

This is a fine new volume by one of the foremost researchers and thinkers on the topic of bilingualism and bilingual schooling. A good portion of the book is devoted to defining terms such as "bilingualism," "semilingualism," and "mother tongue." One of the real strengths of the book is that it places the issues in a truly international context.

*Case Studies in Bilingual Schooling.
1978. Bernard Spolsky, and Robert L. Cooper (eds.).
Rowley, Mass.: Newbury House.

This volume serves to remind Americans that while innovative in the United States, bilingual education has been practiced in other parts of the world for many years. The volume also considers social perspectives regarding bilingual schooling.

Bilingual Multicultural Education and the Professional: From Theory to Practice.
1979. Henry T. Trueba, and Carol Barnett-Mizrahi (eds.).
Rowley, Mass.: Newbury House.

This volume was prepared to assist the school administrator, supervisor, board member, and teacher in coming to grips with key issues in bilingual education, and includes sections not only on bilingual models, language, and culture but also on the teaching of specific content areas in a bilingual program.

REFERENCES

Alatis, James E. (ed.). 1980. *Current Issues in Bilingual Education.* Georgetown University Round Table on Languages and Linguistics 1980. Washington, D.C.: Georgetown University Press.

Alatis, James E., and Kristie Twaddell (eds.). 1976. *English as a Second Language In Bilingual Education.* Washington, D.C.: Teachers of English to Speakers of Other Languages.

Amastae, Jon, and Lucía Elías-Olivares (eds.). 1982. *Spanish in the United States: Sociolinguistic Aspects.* Cambridge: Cambridge University Press.

American Institutes for Research. 1977. *Evaluation of the Impact of ESEA Title VII Spanish/English Education Program, Volume I: Study Design and Interim Findings.* Palo Alto, Calif.: ERIC ED 138 090.

Andersson, Theodore. 1973. Children's learning of a second language: another view. *The Modern Language Journal, 57,* 5–6, 254–259.

Andersson, Theodore. 1974. Bilingual education and early childhood. *Hispania, 57,* 1, 77–78.

Andersson, Theodore, and Mildred Boyer. 1977. *Bilingual Schooling in the United States.* 2nd edition. Austin, Tex.: National Educational Laboratory Publishers.

Angel, F. 1975. Three different conceptualizations of bilingual education, their implications and consequences: An exploration and a critique. Los Angeles: National Dissemination and Assessment Center, California State University, Los Angeles.

Baty, Roger M., and Stanford International Development Education Center. 1972. *Re-educating Teachers for Cultural Awareness: Preparation for Educating Mexican-American Children in Northern California.* New York: Praeger.

Berman, Paul, and Milbrey McLaughlin. 1974. *Federal Programs Supporting Educational Change, Vol. 1: A Model of Educational Change.* Santa Monica, Calif.: The Rand Corporation, R-1589/1-HEW.

BEST. 1971. 1969, 1970 Title VII Projects grouped by language, culture, and grade level. New York: Bilingual Education Applied Research Unit, Project BEST, Hunter College.

Bilingual Education Service Center. 1975. *Guide to State-Funded Bilingual Education Programs. Downstate Illinois 1975–76.* 500 S. Dwyer Avenue, Arlington Heights, Ill. 60005.

Blanco, George. 1977. The educational perspective. In *Bilingual Education: Current Perspectives/Education.* Arlington, Va.: Center for Applied Linguistics, 1–66.

Bowen, J. Donald. 1977. Linguistic perspectives on bilingual education. In *B. Spolsky and R. L. Cooper (eds.), Frontiers of Bilingual Education.* Rowley, Mass.: Newbury House, 106–118.

Bowen, J. Donald, and Jacob Ornstein (eds.). 1976. *Studies in Southwest Spanish.* Rowley, Mass.: Newbury House.

Bruck, Margaret, Wallace E. Lambert, and G. Richard Tucker. 1974. Bilingual schooling through the elementary grades: The St. Lambert project at grade seven. *Language Learning, 24* (2), 183–204.

Bruck, Margaret, Wallace E. Lambert, and G. Richard Tucker. 1975. Assessing functional bilingualism within a bilingual program: The St. Lambert project at grade eight. Montreal: Department of Psychology, McGill University.

Burt, M., and H. Dulay. 1978. Some guidelines for the assessment of oral language proficiency and dominance. *TESOL Quarterly, 12.*

California State Department of Education, Office of Bilingual/Bicultural Education. 1981. *Schooling and Language Minority Students: A Theoretical Framework.* Los Angeles, Calif.: Evaluation, Dissemination and Assessment Center, California State University, Los Angeles.

California State Department of Education, Office of Bilingual/Bicultural Education. 1984. *Studies on Immersion Education.* Sacramento, Calif.: California State Department of Education.

Carter, Thomas P. 1970. *Mexican Americans in School: A History of Educational Neglect.* New York: College Entrance Examination Board.

Chicago Board of Education. 1977. *Chicago's Bilingual Programs Evaluation Report 1975–76.* Department of Research and Evaluation.

Cicourel, A. B., K. H. Jennings, S. H. M. Jennings, K. C. W. Leiter, R. MacKay, H. Mehan, and D. R. Roth. 1974. *Language Use and School Performance.* New York: Academic Press.

Cohen, Andrew D. 1974a. The Culver City Spanish Immersion Program: The first two years. *The Modern Language Journal, 58,* 3, 95–103.

Cohen, Andrew D. 1974b. Formulation of a curriculum. Los Angeles: Consultants in Total Education.

Cohen, Andrew D. (1974c). Mexican American evaluational judgments about language varieties. *International Journal of the Sociology of Language, 3,* 33–51.

Cohen, Andrew D. 1975a. Progress report on the Culver City Spanish immersion program: the third and fourth years.

*Presently out of print.

Workpapers in Teaching English as a Second Language, 9, University of California, Los Angeles, 47–65, ERIC ED 121 093.

Cohen, Andrew D. 1975b. *A Sociolinguistic Approach to Bilingual Education: Experiments in the American Southwest.* Rowley, Mass.: Newbury House.

Cohen, Andrew D., and Luis M. Laosa. 1976. Second language instruction: Some research considerations. *Journal of Curriculum Studies, 8* (2), 149–165.

Cohen, Andrew D., and Susan M. Lebach. 1974. A language experiment in California: Student, teacher, parent, and community reactions after three years. *Workpapers in Teaching English as a Second Language, 8* University of California, Los Angeles, 33–46.

Cohen, Andrew D., and Merrill Swain. 1976. Bilingual education: The "immersion" model in the North American context. *TESOL Quarterly, 10,* 45–53.

Corder, S. Pit. 1973. *Introducing Applied Linguistics.* Harmondsworth, Middlesex: Penguin.

Cummins, J. 1979. Linguistic interdependence and the educational development of bilingual children. *Review of Educational Research, 49.*

Cummins, J., and M. Swain. 1978. French immersion: Early, late, or partial? *The Canadian Modern Language Review.*

Darcy, Natalie T. 1953. A review of the literature on the effects of bilingualism upon the measurement of intelligence. *Journal of Genetic Psychology, 82,* 21–57.

Darcy, Natalie T. 1973. Bilingualism and intelligence: Review of a decade of research. *Journal of Genetic Psychology, 103,* 259–282.

Davis, Frederick B. 1967. *Philippine Language-Teaching Experiments.* Quezon City, Philippines: Alemar-Phoenix .

DeAvila, Edward A. 1972. Some cautionary notes on attempting to adapt IQ tests for use with minority children and a neo-Piagetian approach to intellectual assessment. In *Bilingual Testing and Assessment: Proceedings of BABEL Workshop and Preliminary Findings.* Multilingual Assessment Project, Bay Area Bilingual Education League, 1414 Walnut Street, Berkeley, Calif. 94709, 65–105.

DeInclán, Rosa G. 1977. Bilingual schooling in Dade County. In *W. F. Mackey and T. Andersson (eds.). Bilingualism in Early Childhood.* Rowley, Mass.: Newbury House, 367–379.

Diebold, A. Richard. 1968. The consequences of early bilingualism in cognitive development and personality formation. In E. Norbeck et al. (eds.), *The study of Personality: An Inter-disciplinary Approach.* New York: Holt, Rinehart, and Winston, Inc., 218–245.

Diebold, A. Richard. 1974. Incipient bilingualism. In Dell Hymes (ed.), *Language in Culture and Society: A Reader in Linguistic and Anthropology.* New York: Harper and Row, 495–508.

Dietrich, T. G., and C. Freeman. 1979. *Language in Education: Theory and Practice: A Linguistic Guide to English Proficiency Testing in Schools.* Arlington, Va.: Center for Applied Linguistics.

Dissemination Center for Bilingual-Bicultural Education. 1975. *Evaluation Instruments for Bilingual Education: A Revision of Tests in Use in Title VII Bilingual Education Projects.* 6504 Tracor Lane, Austin, Tex. 78721.

Edelsky, Carole, and Sarah Hudelson. 1982. Reversing the roles of Chicano and Anglo children in a bilingual classroom: On the communicative competence of the helper. In J. A. Fishman and G. A. Keller (eds.), *Bilingual Education for Hispanic Students in the United States.* New York and London: Teachers College Press, 303–325.

Engle, Patricia L. 1975. The use of vernacular language in education. Arlington, Va.: Center for Applied Linguistics.

Ervin-Tripp, Susan. 1974. Is second language learning like the first? *TESOL Quarterly, 8,* 111–127.

Ervin, Susan, M., and Charles E. Osgood. 1954. Second language learning and bilingualism. *Journal of Abnormal and Social Psychology, 49,* 139–146.

Ether, John. 1969. Cultural pluralism and self-identity. *Educational Leadership, 27,* 232–234.

Fier, Violet. 1974. The Culver City Spanish immersion program: An overview. M.A. Thesis, Occidental College.

Fillmore, Lily Wong. 1982. Instructional language as linguistic input: Second-language learning in classrooms. In L. C. Wilkinson (ed.), *Communicating in the Classroom.* New York and London: Academic Press, 283–296.

Fishman, Joshua A. 1966. *Language Loyalty in the United States.* The Hague, Netherlands: Mouton and Co. ERIC ED 036 217.

Fishman, Joshua A. 1971a. Sociolinguistic perspective on the study of bilingualism. In J. A. Fishman, R. L. Cooper, and R. Ma et al. *Bilingualism in the Barrio.* Bloomington, Ind.: Language Science Monographs, Indiana University, 556–582.

Fishman, Joshua A. 1971b. *Sociolinguistics: A Brief Introduction.* Rowley, Mass.: Newbury House.

*Fishman, Joshua A. 1976. *Bilingual Education: An International Sociological Perspective.* Rowley, Mass.: Newbury House.

Fishman, Joshua A. 1977. The spread of English as a new perspective for the study of "language maintenance and language shift." In J. A. Fishman, R. L. Cooper, and A. W. Conrad (eds.), *The Spread of English.* Rowley, Mass.: Newbury House, 108–133.

Fishman, Joshua A., and Gary D. Keller. 1982. *Bilingual Education for Hispanic Students in the United States.* New York and London: Teachers College Press.

Fishman, Joshua A., and John Lovas. 1970. Bilingual education in sociolinguistic perspective. *TESOL Quarterly, 4,* 3, 215–222.

*Gaarder, A. Bruce. 1977. *Bilingual Schooling and the Survival of Spanish in the United States.* Rowley, Mass.: Newbury House.

Grebler, Leo, Joan W. Moore, and Ralph C. Guzman. 1970. *The Mexican-American People: The Nation's Second Largest Minority.* New York: The Free Press.

Gudschinsky, Sarah C. 1977. Mother tongue literacy and second language learning. In *W. F. Mackey and T. Andersson (eds.), *Bilingualism in Early Childhood.* Rowley, Mass.: Newbury House, 250–258.

*Presently out of print.

Gumperz, John J. 1967. On the linguistic markers of bilingual communication. *Journal of Social Issues, 23*, 2, 48–57.

Gumperz, John J. 1969. How can we describe and measure the behavior of bilingual groups? In L. G. Kelly (ed.), *Description and Measurement of Bilingualism*. Toronto, Canada: University of Toronto Press, 242–249.

Hernández Chavez, Eduardo, Andrew D. Cohen, and Anthony F. Beltramo. 1975. *El lenguaje de los chicanos: Regional and Social Characteristics of Language Used by Mexican Americans*. Arlington, Va.: Center for Applied Linguistics.

Hymes, Dell. 1974. *Foundations in Sociolinguistics: An Ethnographic Approach*. Philadelphia: University of Pennsylvania Press.

Jacobson, Rodolfo. 1982. The implementation of a bilingual instruction model THE NEW CONCURRENT APPROACH. In R. Padilla (ed.), *Bilingual Education Technology*. Ypsilanti, Mich.: Eastern Michigan University.

Jakobovits, Leon A. 1970. *Foreign Language Learning*. Rowley, Mass.: Newbury House.

John, Vera P., and Vivian M. Horner. 1971. *Early Childhood Bilingual Education*. New York: Modern Language Association Materials Center, 62 Fifth Avenue.

Kagan, Spencer. 1980. Cooperation-competition, culture, and structual bias in classrooms. In S. Sharan, P. Hare, C. D. Webb, and R. Herz-Lazarowitz (eds.), *Cooperation in Education*. Provo, Utah: Brigham Young University Press, 197–211.

Krashen, Stephen D. 1981. *Second Language Acquisition and Second Language Learning*. Oxford and New York: Pergamon Press.

Krashen, Stephen D., and Herb W. Seliger. 1975. The essential contributions of formal instruction in adult second language learning. *TESOL Quarterly, 9*, 172–183.

Krashen, Stephen D., and Tracy Terrell. 1983. *The Natural Approach: Language Acquisition in the Classroom*. Hayward, Calif.: The Alemany Press.

Lambert, Wallace E., and Elizabeth Peal-Anisfeld. 1969. A note on the relationship of bilingualism and intelligence. *Canadian Journal of Behavioral Science, 1*, 123–128.

*Lambert, Wallace E., and G. Richard Tucker. 1972. *Bilingual Education of Children: The St. Lambert Experiment*. Rowley, Mass.: Newbury House.

Lebach, Susan M. 1974. A report on the Culver City Spanish immersion program in its third year: Its implications for language and subject matter acquisition, language use and attitudes. Unpublished M.A. Thesis in TESL, University of California at Los Angeles.

Lewis, E. Glyn (ed.). 1977. Bilingual education. *International Journal of the Sociology of Language, 14*.

Mackey, William F. 1970. A typology of bilingual education. *Foreign Language Annals, 3*, 4, 569–608.

Mackey, William F. 1972. *Bilingual Education in a Binational School*. Rowley, Mass.: Newbury House.

Mackey, William F. 1977. Free language alternation in school. In *W. F. Mackey and T. Andersson (eds.), *Bilingualism in Early Childhood*. Rowley, Mass.: Newbury House, 333–348.

*Mackey, William F., and Von Nieda Beebe. 1977. *Bilingual Schools for a Bicultural Community: Miami's Adaptation to the Cuban Refugees*. Rowley, Mass.: Newbury House.

MacNab, G. L. 1979. Cognition and bilingualism: a reanalysis of studies. *Linguistics, 17*, 231–255.

Macnamara, John. 1966. *Bilingualism and Primary Education*. Edinburgh: Edinburgh University Press.

Macnamara, John. 1967. The bilingual's linguistic performance—a psychological overview. *Journal of Social Issues, 23*, 2, 58–77.

Malherbe, E. G. 1946. *The Bilingual School*. London: Longmans, Green and Co., Ltd.

Malherbe, E. G. 1969. Commentary to R. M. Jones, "How and when do persons become bilingual?" In L. G. Kelly (ed.), *Description and Measurement of Bilingualism*. Toronto, Canada: University of Toronto Press, 41–51.

Manna, Samuel. 1975. An inquiry into community attitudes toward bilingual-bicultural education. M.A. Thesis in TESL, University of California at Los Angeles.

McLaughlin, Barry. 1978. *Second-Language Acquisition in Childhood*. Hillsdale, N.J.: Lawrence Erlbaum Associates. (A second edition (1984) is now available.)

Milk, Robert D. 1984. The issue of language separation in bilingual methodology. Paper presented at the American Educational Research Association meeting, New Orleans, La., April 25.

Modiano, Nancy. 1966. Reading comprehension in the national language: Comparative study of bilingual and all Spanish. Ph.D. Dissertation, New York University.

Modiano, Nancy. 1968. National or mother language in beginning reading? *Research in the Teaching of English, 2*, 32–43.

Naiman, N., M. Fröhlich, H. H. Stern, and A. Todesco. 1978. *The Good Language Learner*. Toronto: Ontario Institute for Studies in Education.

Olson, D. R. 1977. From utterance to text: the bias of language in speech and writing. *Harvard Educational Review, 47*.

O'Malley, Michael, Anna Uhl Chamot, Gloria Stewner-Manzañares, Lisa Kupper, and Rocco P. Russo. 1983. Learning strategies utilized in developing listening and speaking skills in English as a second language. Unpublished manuscript. Inter-America Research Associates.

Pacheco, Manuel T. 1973. Approaches to bilingualism: Recognition of a multilingual society. In D. L. Lange (ed.), *Pluralism in Foreign Language Education*. Skokie, Ill.: National Textbook Company, 97–124.

Padilla, A. M., and K. L. Lindholm. 1983. Child Bilingualism: The same old issues revisited. Publication 19 of the National Center for Bilingual Research. Los Alamitos, California.

Paulston, Christina Bratt. 1980. *Bilingual Education: Theories and Issues*. Rowley, Mass.: Newbury House.

Peal, Elizabeth, and Wallace E. Lambert. 1962. The relation of bilingualism to intelligence. *Psychological Monographs, 76*, 27.

Politzer, Robert L. 1978. Some reflections on the role of linguistics in the preparation of bilingual/cross-cultural

*Presently out of print.

teachers. Paper presented at American Council of Teachers of Foreign Languages meeting, San Francisco, Calif., May.

Politzer, Robert L., and Mary R. Hoover. 1974. On the use of attitude variables in research in the teaching of a second dialect. *International Review of Applied Linguistics in Language Teaching*, 12, 1, 43–51.

Politzer, Robert L., and Mary McGroarty. 1985. An exploratory study of learning behaviors and their relation to gains in linguistic and communicative competence. *TESOL Quarterly*, 19 (1).

Ramírez, M., R. K. S. Macaulay, A. González, B. Cox, and M. Pérez. 1977. *Spanish-English Bilingual Education in the U.S.: Current Issues, Resources, and Research Priorities.* Bilingual Education Series: 5. Arlington, Va.: Center for Applied Linguistics.

Rubin, Joan. 1975. What the "good language learner" can teach us. *TESOL Quarterly*, 9, 41–51.

Saville-Troike, Muriel R. 1973. *Bilingual Children: A Resource Document.* Bilingual Education Series: 2. Arlington, Va.: Center for Applied Linguistics.

Saville-Troike, Muriel R. 1976. *Foundations for Teaching English as a Second Language.* Englewood Cliffs, N.J.: Prentice-Hall.

Saville, Muriel R., and Rudolph C. Troike. 1971. *A Handbook of Bilingual Education.* Revised Edition. Washington, D.C.: Teachers of English to Speakers of Other Languages.

Segalowitz, Norman. 1977. Psychological perspectives on bilingual education. In *B. Spolsky and R. L. Cooper (eds.), Frontiers of Bilingual Education.* Rowley, Mass.: Newbury House, 119–158.

Selinker, Larry. 1969. Language transfer. *General Linguistics*, 9 (2), 67–92.

Shanker, Albert. 1972a. The shift to ethnicity: A new form of discrimination. *New York Times*, Sunday, March 5 (weekly column: Where We Stand).

Shanker, Albert. 1972b. Urgent need for bilingual education. *New York Times*, Sunday, June 18 (copies from United Federation of Teachers, Local 2, 260 Park Avenue South, New York, N.Y. 10010).

Shore, Marietta Saravia. 1974. *Final Report on the Content Analysis of 125 Bilingual Programs Funded by Title VII.* New York: Bilingual Education Applied Research Unit, Project BEST, New York City Bilingual Consortium, Hunter College Division.

Silverman, N. R. 1976. *Issues in Language Testing: Oral Language Tests for Bilingual Students.* Northeast Educational Laboratory.

Snow, Catherine E. 1975. *Semantic Primacy in First and Second Language Acquisition.* Amsterdam: Institute for General Linguistics, University of Amsterdam.

Spolsky, Bernard (ed.). 1972. *The Language Education of Minority Children: Selected Readings.* Rowley, Mass.: Newbury House.

*Spolsky, Bernard, and Robert L. Cooper (eds.). 1978. *Case Studies in Bilingual Education.* Rowley, Mass.: Newbury House.

*Presently out of print.

Stern, H. H. 1976. Optimal age: Myth or reality? *Canadian Modern Language Review*, 32 (3), 283–294.

Stern, H. H., and Alice Weinrib. 1977. Foreign languages for younger children: Trends and assessment. *Language Teaching and Linguistics: Abstracts*, 10 (1), 5–25.

Sumner, Gerald, and Gail Zellman. 1977. *Federal Programs Supporting Educational Change, Vol. VI: Implementing and Sustaining Title VII Bilingual Projects.* Santa Monica, Calif.: The Rand Corporation, R-1589/6-HEW.

Swain, Merrill, and Henri C. Barik. 1976. Bilingual education for the English Canadian: Recent developments. In A. Simões, Jr. (ed.), *The Bilingual Child.* New York: Academic Press, 91–111.

Swanson, María Medina. 1974. Bilingual education: The national perspective. In Gilbert A. Jarvis (ed.), *Responding to New Realities.* Skokie, Ill.: National Textbook Company, 75–127.

Teitelbaum, Herbert, and Richard J. Hiller. 1977. The legal perspective. In *Bilingual Education: Current Perspectives/Law.* Arlington, Va.: Center for Applied Linguistics, 1–64.

Terrell, Tracy D. 1981. The natural approach in bilingual education. In California State Department of Education, *Schooling and Language Minority Students.* Sacramento, Calif.: California State Department of Education, 117–146.

Troike, Rudolph C., and Nancy Modiano (eds.). 1975. *Proceedings of the First Inter-American Conference on Bilingual Education.* Arlington, Va.: Center for Applied Linguistics.

Trueba, Henry T., and Carol Barnett-Mizrahi (eds.). 1979. *Bilingual Multicultural Education and the Professional.* Rowley, Mass.: Newbury House.

Tucker, G. Richard, Fe T. Otanes, and Bonifacio P. Sibayan. 1970. An alternate days approach to bilingual education. In James E. Alatis (ed.), *Report of the 21st Annual Round Table Meeting on Linguistics and Language Studies.* Washington, D.C.: Georgetown University Press, 281–299.

Tucker, G. Richard, and Alison d'Anglejan. 1971. Some thoughts concerning bilingual education programs. *Modern Language Journal*, 55, 8, 491–493.

Ulibarri, Horacio. 1970. *Bilingual Education: A Handbook for Educators.* Dallas, Tex.: Southern Methodist University Press.

UNESCO. 1953. *The Use of Vernacular Languages in Education. Monographs on Fundamental Education VIII.* Paris: UNESCO, 17–44.

U.S. Commission on Civil Rights. 1973. *Teachers and Students: Differences in Teacher Interaction with Mexican American and Anglo Students.* Mexican American Education Study, Report V. Washington, D.C.: Government Printing Office.

U.S. Commission on Civil Rights. 1975. *A Better Chance to Learn: Bilingual Bicultural Education.* U.S. Commission on Civil Rights Clearinghouse Publication 51, May.

U.S. Department of Education. 1984. *The Condition of Bilingual Education in the Nation.* A report from the Secretary of Education to the President and the Congress. T. H. Bell, Secretary.

U.S. Office of Education. 1971. *Programs under Bilingual Education Act (Title VII. ESEA). Manual for Project Applicants and Grantees.* Washington, D.C.: Bureau of Elementary and Secondary Education, Health, Education, and Welfare. OMB-51-R0838.

Valdés-Fallis, Guadalupe. 1972. Bilingual education: Early efforts supply cues to meeting current needs. *Accent on ACTFL,* November, 28–30.

Valencia, Atilano A. 1969. *Bilingual/Bicultural Education: A Perspective Model in Multicultural America.* Southwest Cooperative Educational Laboratory, Inc., Albuquerque, N.M.

Valencia, Atilano A. 1972. *Bilingual-Bicultural Education for the Spanish-English Bilingual.* Las Vegas, N.M.: New Mexico Highlands University Press.

Wardhaugh, Ronald, and H. Douglas Brown. 1976. *A Survey of Applied Linguistics.* Ann Arbor: University of Michigan Press.

Weinreich, Uriel. 1968. *Languages in Contact: Findings and Problems.* New York: Linguistic Circle of New York. Sixth Printing, The Hague: Mouton and Co.

Wilson, Robert D. 1973. Assumptions for bilingual instruction in the primary grades of Navajo schools. In Paul R. Turner (ed.), *Bilingualism in the Southwest.* Tucson, Ariz.: The University of Arizona Press, 143–175.

INDEX

cultural background 82, 86, 164
    in biculturalism 181
    in determining behavior 83
    in test content 140
    in test format considerations 142, 147
    influences of on perceptual processes 85
cultural conventions 85
cultural diversity 6
    in ESL classroom 82
cultural predilections
    in teaching 83, 85
cultural relativity 81
culture 81–91
    approaches to teaching See also approaches to teaching culture 29, 86–89, 93
    definition of 81
    effect of, on cognitive style 16, 20, 21
    effect on immersion programs 4–13
    in attitudinal research 6–8
    in instrumental motivation 4
    in integrative motivation 4
    in test content 140
    in the bilingual classroom 171, 179, 180–181
    influence of, in children's second language learning 84, 179, 180
culture affects expectations 82, 84
culture asides See also approaches to teaching culture 89
culture assimilators See also approaches to teaching culture 88
culture capsules See also approaches to teaching culture 88
culture clusters See also approaches to teaching culture 88
culture-specific expectations
    in the role and training of teachers 84
cultures
    caution when discussing descriptions of 86
    information about 86, 87, 89, 93–94
culturgrams See also approaches to teaching culture 88
Culver City Spanish Immersion Program See also immersion programs 7, 10, 12, 50
Cummins, J. 178, 185, 187, 189
cut-score 139
Cziko, G. A. 8, 14, 139, 151

d'Anglejan, A. 183, 191
Darcy, N. T. 169, 189
Das, J. P. 20, 21, 31
Das Gupta, J. 165
data collection in classroom research See non-coding human recording, observational coding systems, and mechanized data collection
data-gatherers 44, 50
Dato, D. 31
Davidson, F. 127, 148, 151
Davis, F. B. 167, 189
Davis, G. A. 28, 31
Day, M. E. 18, 31
Day, R. R. 8, 14, 73, 75
De Avila, E. A. 169, 189

decision-making 144, 162–163
    contexts for, in operationalization 144–147; classroom assessment 145–146; competency testing 146; hypothesis testing 146; program evaluation 145; research questions 146; student advancement 145–146
decision validity 143
deductive method of second language learning 16, 17, 23, 25, 26, 27, 28, 30, 125
De Inclán, R. G. 172, 189
Dellacio, C. 24, 31
DeRenzi, E. 18, 31
descriptive analysis See also analysis 109
Deutsch, G. 30
developmental errors 41
    as a reflection of learner strategies 62
    in error analysis See also systematicity in learner errors 61
developmental influences
    interaction with language transfer at linguistic level 68
de Villiers, J. 126, 130, 135
de Villiers, P. 126, 135
Dezure, R. 17, 31
diagnostic testing 145
dialects See also transitional dialects 64, 73, 74, 156, 158, 160, 180, 181
diary study See non-coding human recording 115, 116, 117
dictation test 30
Diebold, A. R. 168, 169, 189
Dietrich, T. G. 184, 189
Dil, A. S. 165
Di Pietro, R. J. 61, 75
Direct Method See approaches to language teaching
direct translations
    as a form of interference 51
discourse See also potential discourse, social discourse, and corrective discourse 51, 54, 71, 73
    patterns in 53, 84
discourse analysis See also analysis 71–72, 99, 100, 114, 133
discourse features
    in linguistic performance analysis 126
    studying in research design task 127
discourse maintenance 99
discrete point test 30, 161
    in research design considerations 127
    in test operationalization 141
    in testing field independence 98
distance
    psychological 11, 116
    social 8, 11, 116
    typological 67
Dodd, C. H. 92, 93
domain
    in bilingual communities 169, 182
domain-referenced measurement See criterion-referenced measurement
dominance 11

interlanguage analysis 60
    in applied linguistics research *See also* applied linguistics research 64–73
    major approaches 65–72; input 69–72; language transfer 67–69; language universals approach 65–66; linguistic markedness theory 66–67
    significance of error evaluation in 64, 73
interlanguage development 108
interlanguage interference 62
interlingual errors *See also* error analysis *and* intralingual errors 61, 63, 73
international language *See also* auxiliary language *and* Language of Wider Communication 156
intonation 56, 107
    cultural connotations of 90
    in question formation 42, 44, 49
intralingual errors *See also* error analysis *and* interlingual errors 61, 62, 63
introspective studies *See also* second language acquisition research 125, 126
inversion
    in AUX system sequencing *See also* sequences in language learning 40, 43, 44, 46
inversion rule
    in learner strategies *See also* learner strategies 41, 43, 44, 46
item analysis 133
item refinement
    in test development; achievement of reliability in 143, 144; achievement of validity in 143, 144
item statistics
    use of in NRM and CRM test development 143, 144
Itoh, H. 38, 50, 58

Jacobson, R. 176, 190
Jacoby, K. 119
Jakobovits, L. A. 168, 190
Jakobson, R. 66, 76
James, C. 61, 76
Jarvis, G. A. 191
Jaspars, J. 83, 92
Jeffrey, W. E. 19, 20, 21, 33
Jennings, K. H. 188
Jennings, S. H. M. 188
Jerison, H. J. 30
Jernudd, B. 160, 166
John, V. P. 84, 92, 168, 170, 177, 190
Johnson, P. 140, 151
Johnston, P. H. 141, 142, 151
Jones, R. A. 116, 120, 190
Jordens, P. 67, 76
Judd, E. L. 161, 165
judgmental analysis
    in CRM for judging content validity 144
Jupp, T. C. 91

Kachru, B. 151
Kagan, J. 19, 31
Kagan, S. 179, 190
Kearny, E. N. 94

Kearny, M. A. 94
Keenan, E. 66, 76
Keller, F. 150, 151
Keller, G. 167, 187, 189
Kellerman, E. 67, 76
Kelly, L. G. 190
Kempler, D. 59
Kenyeres, A. 58
Kenyeres, E. 58
Kerlinger, F. N. 138, 143, 151
Kessel, F. 130, 134, 135
Khampang, P. 73, 76
Kim, Y. Y. 91
Kimura, D. 17, 20, 31
King, J. K. 109, 110, 120
Kinsbourne, M. 18, 31
Kinsella, V. 76
Klapper, Z. 128, 135
Klassen, B. R. 84, 92
Kleinmann, H. 63, 73, 74, 76
Kliebard, H. 101, 120
Klima, E. S. 49, 58
Kocel, K. 18, 31
Krashen, S. 11, 15, 17, 21, 22, 23, 30, 32, 52, 58, 70, 75, 108, 119, 120, 121, 128, 135, 171, 172, 190
Kumpf, L. 65, 73, 76
Kupper, L. 171, 190

L2 research *See* second language acquisition research
Lado, R. 60, 76
La Madrid, E. 24, 31
Lambert, R. D. 11, 14, 15
Lambert, W. E. 3, 4, 5, 6, 7, 8, 14, 15, 167, 169, 170, 173, 188, 190
Landes, R. 83, 92
Lange, D. L. 190
language *See also* Language of Wider Communication
    function of, in society 155–164
    in education 158, 160–161
    in nationhood 161–162
    official 156, 158
    setting 155–157, 157–159
    standard 155–156, 164
    vernacular 127, 155–156
    what constitutes a language 168
language acquirers
    differences among language learners and 22
language acquisition *See also* first language acquisition *and* second language acquisition 4, 11, 37
    behaviorist model of 23, 60, 61
    difference between first and second 37, 49, 61
    difference between language learning and 22
language classroom anxiety *See also* anxiety 117
Language Contact Profile 98
    use of, in determining motivation 97
language cues 52
language learners *See also* aptitude, immersion programs, learner errors, learner orientation, learner strategies, classroom research, attitudinal research, *and* second language acquisition research

Shanker, A. 179, 191
Shapira, R. 38, 58
Shapiro, H. 88, 92
Sharan, S. 190
Shavelson, R. J. 138, 152
Sherman, J. G. 151
Sherman, O. 94
Sherman, T. G. 151
Sherzer, J. 84, 91
Shintani, M. 73, 77
Shirts, R. G. 88, 92
Shohamy, E. 148, 152
Shore, M. S. 172, 173, 175, 178, 180, 182, 191
Sibayan, B. P. 177, 191
Sigel, I. E. 19, 31
Silent Way See approaches to language teaching
Silverman, A. J. 19, 31
Silverman, A. M. 88, 92, 94
Silverman, N. R. 184, 191
Simoes, A., Jr. 121, 191
simplification
    in explaining copula deletion 46
    in explaining WH-fronting 46
    in language learner strategy See also learner strate-
        gies 45–46, 49, 55, 56
simulation games See also approaches to teaching cul-
    ture 88
simultaneous synthesis cognitive style
    as a cognitive style model See also cognitive style 20
simultaneous-translation approach See also concurrent
    method 169, 176
Sinclair, J. M. 101, 114, 121
Skutnabb-Kangas, T. 187
Slobin, C. 58
Slobin, D. I. 46, 48, 58, 59, 68, 69, 77, 87, 92
Smart, J. C. 32
Smith, E. C. 92
Smith, F. L. 101, 120
Smythe, P. C. 11, 12, 14, 15, 117, 120
Snow, C. 52, 59, 171, 191
Snow, M. A. 10, 12, 15
Snow, R. E. 16, 31
Snyder, W. A. 91
social context 9
social discourse See also discourse 53, 54
social distance See also distance 8, 11, 116
social orientation
    influence on childrens' second language learning 84
social-psychological model 11
social-psychological research See also research and social-
    psychological variables 3–13
social-psychological variables See also social-psychologi-
    cal research
    developments in research on 3, 11, 12
    incorporation into second language acquisition theories
        3, 11
    influence of on second language acquisition 3, 5, 8, 10,
        11, 12, 13
    relationship to language use 9
social rituals, in an English-speaking culture 90

social skills See Embryonic Category System
socio-affective filter 11
socio-cultural factors
    influence on attitudinal research 6
socio-linguistic factors
    in language use 10
source language See also native language 60, 66, 67, 72,
    73, 74
specification
    of test content 140–141
speech
    data of, in morpheme studies 70
    function of, in learning rules of social discourse 54
    in communities See also speech communities 155–
        162
    in second language learners 37, 44, 45, 49, 54, 56, 57,
        63, 107, 127, 128, 133
    in teacher trainees 107–108
    in teachers 97, 99, 107, 108
    study of, in longitudinal approach 126
speech communities 155–162
    bilingual 155
    monolingual 155, 156, 157, 158
    multilingual 155–156, 157
Sperry, R. 17, 20, 32
Spindler, G. D. 91, 92
Spinnler, H. 18, 31
Spiro, R. J. 151
Spolsky, B. 155, 164, 166, 167, 188, 191
Spradley, J. P. 87, 92, 93
Springer, S. 30
Spurling, S. 128, 135
St. Clair, R. 120
St. Lambert Program See also immersion programs 5, 7
standard 145
    operationalization of for evaluating a language skill or
        trait 139
standard language See language
statistical analysis See also analysis 24, 100, 101, 137
statistics
    appropriate use of as research design criteria 132–133
Stauble, A. 64, 72, 77, 129, 135
stay-ins 12
Stenson, N. 108, 120, 121
Stern, H. H. 21, 32, 167, 171, 172, 190, 191
Stewner-Manzañares, G. 171, 190
Stockwell, R. P. 61, 74, 77
strategies, of second language learning 37, 46, 55, 57, 107,
    116, 171
    as a process of interlanguage See also interlanguage
        62, 64
    use of linguistic markedness theory in 67
Straw, S. B. 92
Strayer, F. F. 18, 30
Street, R. F. 18, 32
Street test
    in hemisphericity 18, 29, 30
structural format
    in test operationalization 141, 143

Turner, P. R.   192
turn-taking analysis   *See also* analysis   99
turn-taking process   99
Twaddell, K.   168, 188
Twitchin, J.   91, 95
typological distance   *See also* distance   67
typological survey   62, 63

Ulibarri, H.   170, 191
universal accessibility hierarchy   66
universals of language acquisition   44, 62, 65–66, 72
Upshur, J. A.   32, 133

Valdés-Fallis, G.   174, 192
Valencia, A. A.   170, 177, 180, 192
Valette, R. M.   22, 32
validation   *See also* construct validation   143, 147
validity   144, 147
    achievement of, in test item refinement   143
    as research design criteria   130
    categorization of   143
Vander Werf, W.   73, 77
variables   *See* affective variables *and* social-psychological variables
verbal coding approach
    as a cognitive style model   *See also* cognitive style   19
vernacular   *See also* language   127, 164
    in bilingual education   173, 174, 177
video recordings   *See* mechanized data collection   96
videotapes   *See also* approaches to teaching culture   23, 87, 93, 95, 103, 109, 110, 111
    in research design considerations   127, 128, 133
Vigil, N. A.   64, 77, 117, 121
Vincent, M.   185
vocabulary   21, 23, 24, 29, 50, 52, 53, 54, 89, 112, 128, 144, 161, 175
    difficulty of, in bilingual programs   172
    impoverishment: as an explanation for language mixing   52; as form of interference   52
    in foreigner talk study   71
    items   50, 51

WH-fronting
    in first language acquisition   49
    in language learning sequencing   42
    in second language acquisition studies   39, 40

    in simplification   46
    systematicity of, in language learner errors   39

Wagner-Gough, J.   *See also* Gough, J. W.   38, 58, 129, 132, 135, 136
"wait-time"   109
Waldman, E.   7, 8, 15
Wales, R.   58
Walmsley, J. B.   83, 93
Wang, W.   59
Wardhaugh, R.   23, 32, 61, 77, 180, 192
Warner, E. G.   88, 91, 92
Webb, C. D.   190
Webb, N.   138, 152
Wechsler, D.   18, 32
Wechsler Similarities test
    in hemisphericity   18, 29, 30
Wei, H.   82, 93
Weinreich, U.   37, 59, 68, 73, 74, 77, 168, 175, 192
Weinrib, A.   167, 191
Weitan, W.   20, 32
Weksel, W.   49, 58
Welty, P. T.   93
Widger, R. C.   93
Wilkinson, L. C.   82, 92, 93, 189
Williamsen, V.   32
Wilson, R. D.   174, 192
Witkin, H. A.   16, 18, 19, 20, 21, 27, 28, 30, 33
Wittrock, M. C.   18, 28, 30, 33
Woerdhoff, F. J.   22, 31
Wong-Fillmore, L.   *See also* Fillmore, L. W.   55, 59
word order   112
    in adding to difficulty of acquisition   47, 48
    in second language acquisition research   47, 48, 51
Wright, J. C.   31
Wu, Z.   73, 77

Yalden, J.   164, 166
Yorio, C. A.   120, 121, 135
Yoshida, M.   73, 77
Young, D. I.   38, 50, 59
Yousef, F.   85, 92, 93

Zamora, G. L.   106, 107, 121
Zellman, G.   184, 191
Zelniker, T.   19, 20, 21, 33
Zobl, H.   68, 69, 73, 77

WITHDRAWN

DAT[E]

J